Practice Speaking, Listening, Reading and Writing

Contemporary Japanese WORKBOOK

VOLUME 1

SECOND EDITION

ERIKO SATO

TUTTLE Publishing

Tokyo | Rutland, Vermont | Singapore

ABOUT TUTTLE
"Books to Span the East and West"

Our core mission at Tuttle Publishing is to create books which bring people together one page at a time. Tuttle was founded in 1832 in the small New England town of Rutland, Vermont (USA). Our fundamental values remain as strong today as they were then—to publish best-in-class books informing the English-speaking world about the countries and peoples of Asia. The world has become a smaller place today and Asia's economic, cultural and political influence has expanded, yet the need for meaningful dialogue and information about this diverse region has never been greater. Since 1948, Tuttle has been a leader in publishing books on the cultures, arts, cuisines, languages and literatures of Asia. Our authors and photographers have won numerous awards and Tuttle has published thousands of books on subjects ranging from martial arts to paper crafts. We welcome you to explore the wealth of information available on Asia at **www.tuttlepublishing.com**.

Published by Tuttle Publishing, an imprint of Periplus Editions (HK) Ltd.

www.tuttlepublishing.com

ISBN-13: 978-0-8048-4714-8

Distributed by:

North America, Latin America & Europe
Tuttle Publishing
364 Innovation Drive
North Clarendon, VT 05759-9436
Tel: (802) 773 8930; Fax (802) 773 6993
info@tuttlepublishing.com
www.tuttlepublishing.com

Japan
Tuttle Publishing
Yaekari Building, 3rd Floor
5-4-12 Osaki, Shinagawa-ku Tokyo 141-0032
Tel: (81) 3 5437 0171; Fax: (81) 3 5437 0755
sales@tuttle.co.jp
www.tuttle.co.jp

Asia Pacific
Berkeley Books Pte. Ltd.
61 Tai Seng Road, #02-12
Singapore 534167
Tel: (65) 6280 1330; Fax: (65) 6280 6290
inquiries@periplus.com.sg
www.periplus.com

22 21 20 19 18   10 9 8 7 6 5 4 3   1808RR
Printed in China

TUTTLE PUBLISHING® is a registered trademark of Tuttle Publishing, a division of Periplus Editions (HK) Ltd.

Preface

Contemporary Japanese Workbook was created as a supplementary material for *Contemporary Japanese*: *An Introductory Language Course*. A workbook which is best used for reviewing and reinforcing the concepts and learning materials introduced in the textbook, it is also designed to function as a standalone comprehensive workbook. Some of the features included for this purpose are (a) presentation of a brief note on the concept tested before every question, (b) providing of vocabulary and kanji glossaries on unfamiliar words, and (c) an audio input by native speakers ⊙. This workbook also offers materials in the business, traveling and daily life contexts, in addition to the college life context featured greatly in the textbook.

Structure

Contemporary Japanese Workbook series comes in two volumes, consisting of 26 chapters (Chapter One to Fourteen in Volume One and Chapter Fifteen to Twenty-Six in Volume Two) in all. It integrates all the information provided in the textbook. Each chapter in the workbook has specific objectives and includes the following six sections.

- **Kanji and Vocabulary**
- **Grammar**
- **Conversation and Usage**
- **Listening Comprehension**
- **Reading Comprehension**
- **Writing**
- **New Vocabulary Reference List**

Exceptions to this format are limited to Chapter One, which also includes the hiragana section, and Chapter Four, which includes the katakana section, in the first volume.

Orthography

In *Contemporary Japanese Workbook Volume One*, hiragana characters are introduced in Chapter One in the form of questions along with audio recordings, and are used in subsequent chapters without ruby, in this case in romaji. Katakana characters are introduced in Chapter Four, also in the form of questions, and are used in subsequent chapters without ruby. Kanji characters are introduced in the form of questions, accompanied by detailed information such as meanings, component equations, remembering guides 📖, stroke order, and usage examples. The required kanji characters in every chapter are introduced without ruby. When they appear again in the following chapters, ruby is sparingly provided, wherever it is thought to be helpful, and the use of this pronunciation guide is gradually reduced. Non-required kanji characters occasionally appear with ruby to help learners get accustomed to kanji and thus, able to see the phrase boundaries in a sentence easily.

Reference:
Henshall, Kenneth G. (1988) *A Guide To Remembering Japanese Characters*, Charles E. Tuttle Publishing Co.

Contents

How to Download the Online Audio of this Book.

1. Make sure you have an Internet connection.

2. Type the URL below into your web browser.

http://www.tuttlepublishing.com/contemporary-japanese-workbook-volume-1-downloadable-content

For support, you can email us at info@tuttlepublishing.com.

CHAPTER ONE

Basic Sounds, Words, Phrases and Kana

Objectives:
- to recognize, pronounce and write basic hiragana
- to learn short Japanese phrases for greeting, thanking and apologizing

Hiragana and Vocabulary

1. Recognizing Basic Hiragana

Hiragana is one of the two phonetic writing systems in Japanese language. It consists of 46 characters; each representing one syllable sound that forms the basis of Japanese pronunciation. It is therefore important for one to master the sounds of these characters in order to read Japanese words fluently.

 Let's read the characters in the following table aloud, from top to bottom, and right to left, along with the CD.

ん	わ	ら	や	ま	は	な	た	さ	か	あ
n	wa	ra	ya	ma	ha	na	ta	sa	ka	a
/	/	り	/	み	ひ	に	ち	し	き	い
		ri		mi	hi	ni	chi	shi	ki	i
/	/	る	ゆ	む	ふ	ぬ	つ	す	く	う
		ru	yu	mu	fu	nu	tsu	su	ku	u
/	/	れ	/	め	へ	ね	て	せ	け	え
		re		me	he	ne	te	se	ke	e
/	を	ろ	よ	も	ほ	の	と	そ	こ	お
	o	ro	yo	mo	ho	no	to	so	ko	o

2. Reading and Writing Basic Hiragana I

Even though one can theoretically write the whole Japanese text in hiragana, it is mainly used to write grammatical items such as verb endings and particles. It is also widely used in materials for children's books, comic books and textbooks; sometimes written above or alongside kanji to indicate pronunciation (known as furigana).

A) In the boxes provided, write each hiragana character following the correct stroke order.

a	あ	一ナあ	あ	あ				
i	い	いい	い	い				
u	う	、う	う	う				
e	え	、え	え	え				
o	お	一おお	お	お				
ka	か	うカが	か	か				
ki	き	一二ギき	き	き				
ku	く	く	く	く				
ke	け	ノー｜ーけ	け	け				
ko	こ	一こ	こ	こ				

B) Let's read each of the following aloud several times, then check how well you've mastered the hiragana characters you've just learned.

1. あいあいう　　　うえうえおあお　　　あいうえお
2. かきくきか　　　くけこけきけこ　　　かきくけこ
3. あかいこう　　　えうえおああお　　　えけうくこ

 C) Listen to each Japanese word carefully, then say it aloud on your own and write it down in hiragana.

1. _____　2. _____　3. _____　4. _____　5. _____

　　house　　　　　*mosquito*　　　*train station*　　　　*carp*　　　*chrysanthemum*

3. Reading and Writing Basic Hiragana II

A) In the boxes provided, write each hiragana character following the correct stroke order.

sa	さ	⌐ぎさ	さ	さ			
shi	し	し	し	し			
su	す	一ず	す	す			
se	せ	一ザせ	せ	せ			
so	そ	そ	そ	そ			

ta	た	゛ナだた	た	た				
chi	ち	こ ち	ち	ち				
tsu	つ	っ	つ	つ				
te	て	て	て	て				
to	と	ゝど	と	と				

B) Let's read each of the following aloud several times, then check how well you've mastered the hiragana characters you've just learned.

1. さしさすし	せすそせそすし	さしすせそ
2. たちつたち	ってとてとつち	たちつてと
3. たちさちつ	せそせすつすつ	ってたそち

 C) Listen to each Japanese word carefully, then say it aloud on your own and write it down in hiragana.

1. _____	2. _____	3. _____	4. _____	5. _____
sake	*umbrella*	*sushi*	*octopus*	*desk*

4. Reading and Writing Basic Hiragana III

A) In the boxes provided, write each hiragana character following the correct stroke order.

na	な	ニナだな	な	な				
ni	に	じにに	に	に				
nu	ぬ	゛ぬ	ぬ	ぬ				
ne	ね	ｱｲね	ね	ね				
no	の	の	の	の				
ha	は	じにば	は	は				
hi	ひ	ひ	ひ	ひ				
fu	ふ	゛ふふふ	ふ	ふ				
he	へ	へ	へ	へ				
ho	ほ	じにぼ	ほ	ほ				

B) Let's read each of the following aloud several times, then check how well you've mastered the hiragana characters you've just learned.

1. なになにぬ　　　にぬねのねのに　　　なにぬねの
2. はひふひは　　　へほははほひふへ　　　はひふへほ
3. なははほはほ　　ぬねぬねのひふ　　　へになぬね

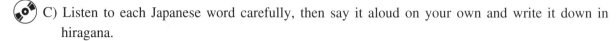 C) Listen to each Japanese word carefully, then say it aloud on your own and write it down in hiragana.

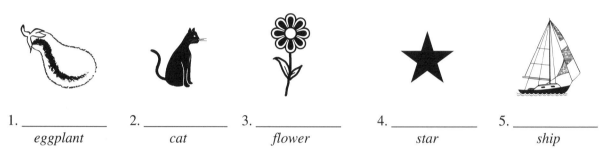

1. _____   2. _____   3. _____   4. _____   5. _____
   eggplant   *cat*   *flower*   *star*   *ship*

5. Reading and Writing Basic Hiragana IV

A) In the boxes provided, write each hiragana character following the correct stroke order.

ma	ま	一 = ま	ま	ま				
mi	み	ス み	み	み				
mu	む	ー も む	む	む				
me	め	ゝ め	め	め				
mo	も	も も も	も	も				

ya	や	つづや	や	や				
yu	ゆ	わ ゆ	ゆ	ゆ				
yo	よ	：よ	よ	よ				

B) Let's read each of the following aloud several times, then check how well you've mastered the hiragana characters you've just learned.

1. まみむみむ   めもまもまみむ   まみむめも
2. やゆよゆよ   やまゆきよやゆ   まよねゆや

C) Fill in the parts of the face in hiragana using the words provided.

1: _____

2: _____

3: _____

4: _____

みみ
め
くち
はな

6. Reading and Writing Basic Hiragana V

A) In the boxes provided, write each hiragana character following the correct stroke order.

ya	ら	゙ ら	ら	ら				
yu	り	゙ り	り	り				
yo	る	る	る	る				

re	れ	れ	れ	れ				
ro	ろ	ろ	ろ	ろ				
wa	わ	わ	わ	わ				
o	を	を	を	を				
n	ん	ん	ん	ん				

B) Let's read each of the following aloud several times, then check how well you've mastered the hiragana characters you've just learned.

1. らりらるり　　　　るれろるろるら　　　　らりるれろ
2. わんわゆを　　　　わねまもよゆむ　　　　やわるろり

 C) Listen to each Japanese word carefully, then say it aloud on your own and write it down in hiragana.

1. _____　　2. _____　　3. _____　　4. _____　　5. _____
　　crocodile　　　　　*squirrel*　　　　　　*tiger*　　　　　　*cotton candy*　　　　　*lotus root*

7. Recognizing Voiced and Plosive Sounds

In the hiragana system, you will notice that some characters may be marked with a diacritic and pronounced in more than one sound. Each of these characters is marked with ゛ for its voiced sound and ゜ for its plosive sound.

A) Listen to the voiced sounds and plosive sounds of these characters. Learn to read them on your own.

ぱ pa	ば ba	だ da	ざ za	が ga
ぴ pi	び bi	ぢ ji	じ ji	ぎ gi
ぷ pu	ぶ bu	づ zu	ず zu	ぐ gu
ぺ pe	べ be	で de	ぜ ze	げ ge
ぽ po	ぼ bo	ど do	ぞ zo	ご go

B) For each question, listen to the item pronounced and circle the correct answer.

1. (a) だいがく   (b) たいがく   (c) たいかく
2. (a) だいがく   (b) たいがく   (c) たいかく
3. (a) ぎり   (b) きり
4. (a) ががく   (b) かがく
5. (a) ががく   (b) かがく
6. (a) はんば   (b) はんぱ
7. (a) はんば   (b) はんば

8. Recognizing Double Consonants and Long Vowels

In Japanese text, several characters are often written in smaller size; for example つ in ざっし (zasshi, *magazine*). This particular character, つ in small size, represents the "sudden silence" which realizes the first consonant of a double-consonant. In writing, it is necessary to use about one full-character space for each of these smaller characters. On traditional composition paper, a small character may take different quadrants depending on whether the text is written horizontally or vertically as shown here.

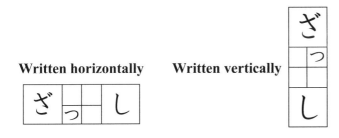

Written horizontally   **Written vertically**

Long vowels are represented by adding the hiragana character あ, い, う, え or お to another hiragana character, for example おかあさん (okāsan, *mother*). But long vowel ē is represented by adding い, as in せんせい (sensē, *teacher*) and long vowel ō is represented by adding う, as in おとうさん (otōsan, *father*). However, there are some exceptions.

Listen carefully as each of the following is read out to you, then write it down in hiragana.

1. _____ *ticket*   4. _____ *sound*

2. _____ *air*   5. _____ *husband*

3. _____ *stem (of a plant)*

9. Recognizing Palatalized Sounds

Palatalized sounds are represented by adding smaller-sized や, ゆ or よ to a hiragana character.

A) Listen to how each of the syllables in the table below (from top to bottom, right to left) is pronounced, then practice along with the CD.

りゃ	みゃ	ぴゃ	びゃ	ひゃ	にゃ	ちゃ	じゃ / ぢゃ	しゃ	ぎょ	きゃ
rya	**mya**	**pya**	**bya**	**hya**	**nya**	**cha**	**ja**	**sha**	**gya**	**kya**
りゅ	みゅ	ぴゅ	びゅ	ひゅ	にゅ	ちゅ	じゅ / ぢゅ	しゅ	ぎゅ	きゅ
ryu	**myu**	**pyu**	**byu**	**hyu**	**nyu**	**chu**	**ju**	**shu**	**gyu**	**kyu**
りょ	みょ	ぴょ	びょ	ひょ	にょ	ちょ	じょ / ぢょ	しょ	ぎょ	きょ
ryo	**myo**	**pyo**	**byo**	**hyo**	**nyo**	**cho**	**jo**	**sho**	**gyo**	**kyo**

B) For each question, listen to the item pronounced and circle the correct answer.

1. (a) ひゅく   (b) ひょく   (c) ひゃく
2. (a) じょう   (b) りょう   (c) びょう
3. (a) かいぎょう   (b) かいきょう   (c) かいじょう
4. (a) こんにゃく   (b) こんじゃく   (c) こんみゃく

C) Fill in the cities of Japan in the map below using the words provided.

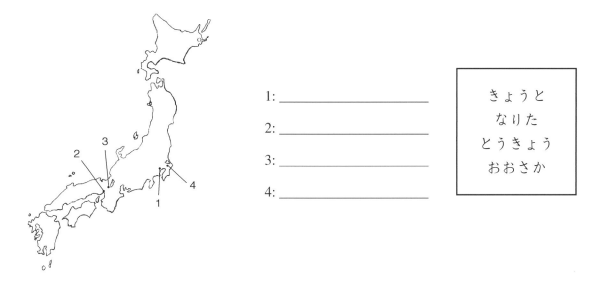

1: _____

2: _____

3: _____

4: _____

きょうと
なりた
とうきょう
おおさか

10. Counting One to Ten

A) Let's count one to ten in Japanese along with the CD, then repeat on your own until you are able to say them fluently by heart.

B) Write one to ten in hiragana. Use the words provided in the box.

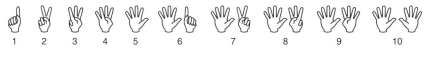

さん	きゅう
に	ろく
ご	よん
いち	はち
じゅう	なな

1: _____   2: _____   3: _____   4: _____

5: _____   6: _____   7: _____   8: _____

9: _____   10: _____

11. Naming Japanese Dishes

Can you find 5 Japanese dishes (including うなぎ) that are hidden in the puzzle?

う	な	ぎ	く	す
ま	す	は	に	き
さ	し	み	な	や
あ	る	れ	か	き
ら	て	ん	ぷ	ら

Conversation and Usage

1. Introducing Yourself

When you meet someone for the very first time, you say はじめまして (literally *This is the first time to see you*) which is often translated as *How do you do?* Then you introduce yourself and say よろしく (literally *favorably*) which means *Pleased to meet you* in this context. The typical reply to よろしく is こちらこそよろしく. In this case, こちらこそ (literally *That is I*) means *Pleased to meet you*, too.

 John Smith is introducing himself to Yoko Yamada. Listen carefully and then complete the dialog in hiragana.

ジョン　　： はじめまして。スミスです。よろしく。

ようこ　　： はじめまして。＿＿＿＿＿＿＿ です。＿＿＿＿＿＿＿ よろしく。

Note:

- です is a copula and it means *am*, *is*, or *are*. Unlike in English, it is placed right after a noun rather than right before a noun. For example, スミスです means *(I) am Smith*. The subject is often unsaid in Japanese.
- The marker 。 is placed at the end of each sentence, just like a period in English.

2. Greeting

You greet in Japanese by saying おはようございます (*Good morning!*), こんにちは (*Good afternoon!*), or こんばんは (*Good evening!*) depending on the time of the day. If you are greeting your subordinate, you say おはよう instead of おはようございます.

 Yoko Yamada bumped into her professor at a bookstore. Listen to their conversation carefully and then complete the following dialog in hiragana.

ようこ　　： ああ、せんせい。おはよう ＿＿＿＿＿＿＿＿。

せんせい： ああ、やまださん。おはよう。

ようこ　　： (Smiles) じゃあ、＿＿＿＿＿＿＿＿ します。さようなら。

せんせい： はい。さようなら。

Note:

- The marker 、 is placed at the end of a phrase, just like a comma in English.
- Add the respectful title 〜さん at the end of a person's first name or family name, as in やまださん or ようこさん. Don't ever add さん to your own name.
- When you are departing from someone, say さようなら. If you are departing from your superior, say しつれいします, first. If you may be seeing the person later on the same day, say じゃあ、また (*See you later!*) instead of さようなら.
- はい means *Yes*.

3. Small Talk

おげんきですか literally means *Are you well?*, but it is similar to *How are you?* in English, except that it is used only for those you haven't seen for a while. お in おげんきですか is the polite prefix, and か at the end of it is the question particle. The typical reply to おげんきですか is はい、げんき です (*I'm fine*). Don't ever reply with はい、おげんきです. It sounds silly to use the polite prefix お to describe yourself. A more sophisticated reply to おげんきですか is はい、おかげさまで (*I'm fine thanks to you and others*).

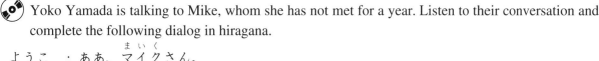 Yoko Yamada is talking to Mike, whom she has not met for a year. Listen to their conversation and complete the following dialog in hiragana.

ようこ　：ああ、マイク（まいく）さん。

マイク（まいく）：ああ、ようこさん。

ようこ　：おげんきですか。

マイク（まいく）：ええ、＿＿＿＿＿＿＿＿＿＿ です。ようこさんは？

ようこ　：ええ、＿＿＿＿＿＿＿＿＿＿＿＿＿。

Note: ええ is an informal version of はい.

4. Getting Attention

To get someone's attention, say すみません (*Excuse me*), or ちょっとすみません. ちょっと literally means *a little bit*, but it is used to make the expression soft and nice.

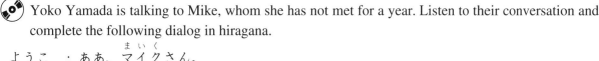 Takeshi is talking to a woman who has left her purse at the table in a cafeteria. Listen to their conversation carefully and then complete the following dialog in hiragana.

たけし　：あのう、＿＿＿＿＿＿＿＿＿＿ すみません。

Woman　：はい。

たけし　：(Shows the purse to her.)

Woman　：あ、わたしのです。

たけし　：＿＿＿＿＿＿＿＿＿＿＿＿＿＿＿＿。

Woman　：どうもありがとうございます。

たけし　：いいえ。

Note:

- The Japanese tend to say あのう before they start talking.
- When surprised, the Japanese say あ or あっ (*Oh!*).
- For offering someone with something or encouraging him/her to do something, say どうぞ (*Please ...*, or *Go ahead and do/take ...*).
- To thank someone, ありがとうございます (*Thank you*) or どうもありがとうございます (*Thank you very much*). The shorter version ありがとう (*Thanks*) can only be used by children, or by superiors on their subordinates. In general, it is safer to say ありがとうございます. You can just say どうも very safely in any context, too. The typical and sophisticated reply to it is いいえ (*Not (at all)*). どういたしまして (*You're welcome.*) is another common reply to ありがとうございます, but it is used less frequently than いいえ by the native speakers of Japanese.

Listening Comprehension

1. Naming Some Places of Japan

Listen carefully as the names of some places in Japan are read out to you. Write them down in hiragana.

1. _____   4. _____

2. _____   5. _____

3. _____

2. Making Daily Conversation

You will carry out a simple conversation with Ms. Tanaka. Listen to what she is saying to you, then write down your replies in hiragana.

1. _____

2. _____

3. _____

4. _____

5. _____

New Vocabulary Reference List

FAMILIAR JAPANESE WORD

おりがみ（折り紙）*origami*
からて（空手）*karate*
きもの（着物）*kimono*
けんどう（剣道）*kendo (Japanese fencing)*
じゅうどう（柔道）*judo (Japanese wrestling)*
にほん / にっぽん（日本）*Japan*
にほんご（日本語）*Japanese language*

FAMILIAR JAPANESE FOOD

うなぎ（鰻）*eel*
さしみ（刺身）*sliced raw fish*
すきやき（鋤焼き）*sukiyaki*
すし（寿司・鮨）*sushi*
てんぷら（天麩羅）*tempura*

NUMBER

いち（一）*one*
に（二）*two*
さん（三）*three*
よん / し（四）*four*
ご（五）*five*
ろく（六）*six*
なな / しち（七）*seven*
はち（八）*eight*
きゅう / く（九）*nine*
じゅう（十）*ten*

CLASSROOM

がくせい（学生）*student*
がっこう（学校）*school*
しつもん（質問）*question*
しゅくだい（宿題）*homework*
せんせい（先生）*teacher*
なまえ（名前）*name*

CLASSROOM INSTRUCTION

もういちど（もう一度）*once more*
ゆっくり *slowly*
いっしょに（一緒に）*together*
いってください（言ってください）*Please say (it).*

BODY PART

あし（足 / 脚）*foot, leg*
くち（口）*mouth*
て（手）*hand, arm*
はな（鼻）*nose*
みみ（耳）*ear*
め（目）*eye*

FAMILY

おとうさん（お父さん）*father*
おかあさん（お母さん）*mother*
おにいさん（お兄さん）*older brother*
おねえさん（お姉さん）*older sister*

JAPANESE CITY

とうきょう（東京）*Tokyo*
おおさか（大阪）*Osaka*
きょうと（京都）*Kyoto*
なりた（成田）*Narita*

CHAPTER TWO

Identifying Things and People

Objectives:
- to learn how to read and write kanji
- to name the things and people around you
- to learn short Japanese phrases for conversing with new acquaintances
- to learn and use the grammar items XはYです, demonstrative pronouns, and question words

Kanji

1. Basic Kanji Strokes

All kanji characters are written with some combination of various basic strokes. To learn how to write these basic strokes will help you greatly in your kanji writing. In general, the horizontal stroke is written from left to right, vertical stroke from top to bottom, and angled stroke from left to right, and then go down, or go down, and then left to right. Each basic stroke ends in a hook, stop, flow or stop-flow.

Horizontal Stroke	Vertical Stroke	Angled Stroke		
—	l	7	∟	⎿

Hook	Stop	Flow		Stop-flow
J	l	l	ノ	＼

In the boxes provided, write each basic stroke following the correct direction.

—	—	—					
l	l	l					
J	J	J					

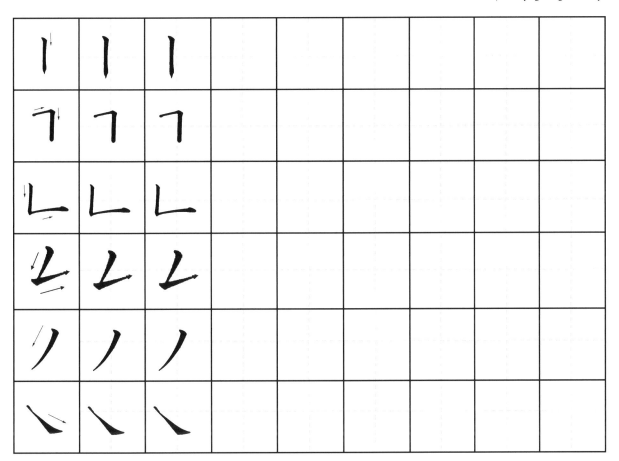

2. Basic Rules of Kanji Stroke Order

A kanji character must be written according to a fixed stroke order so it will look neat, well-balanced and therefore easier to read. By knowing the stroke order, it will also help you to remember the kanji character more easily. Although there are many exceptions, one general rule is to write from top to bottom, and from left to right.

Top to bottom

三 (さん *three*) 　一 二 三

会 (あ - う *to meet*) 　丿 人 𠆢 会 会 会

Left to right

川 (かわ *river*) 　丿 川 川

休 (やす - む *to rest*) 　丿 亻 仁 什 休 休

In the boxes provided, write the kanji characters following the correct stroke order.

川	川	川					
三	三	三					
会	会	会					
休	休	休					

Kanji and Vocabulary

Most kanji characters have at least two ways of reading. One is おんよみ, a Japanese approximation of the Chinese pronunciation of the character at the time it was introduced. The other reading is くんよみ, a reading based on the pronunciation of the corresponding native Japanese word. Which reading should be used depends on the context. For example, 人 is read as ひと by its くんよみ, when used independently to mean *person* or used in a phrase such as あの人 (*that person*), or read as じん by its おんよみ, when used in a kanji compound such as 日本人 (*Japanese person*).

A) Let's read the following words, phrases, or sentences on your own. The ふりがな (small pronunciation-aid hiragana characters) is provided to guide you.

わた(くし)し
私　*I, me*
ひと
人　*person*
ひと
あの人　*that person*
ほん
本　*book*
いぬ
犬　*dog*

にほんじん
日本人　*Japanese person*
じん
ちゅうごく人　*Chinese person*
なに
何　*what*
なん
何ですか。　*What is (it)?*

B) In the boxes, write each kanji character following the correct stroke order, paying attention to its stroke count, pronunciation and usage examples.

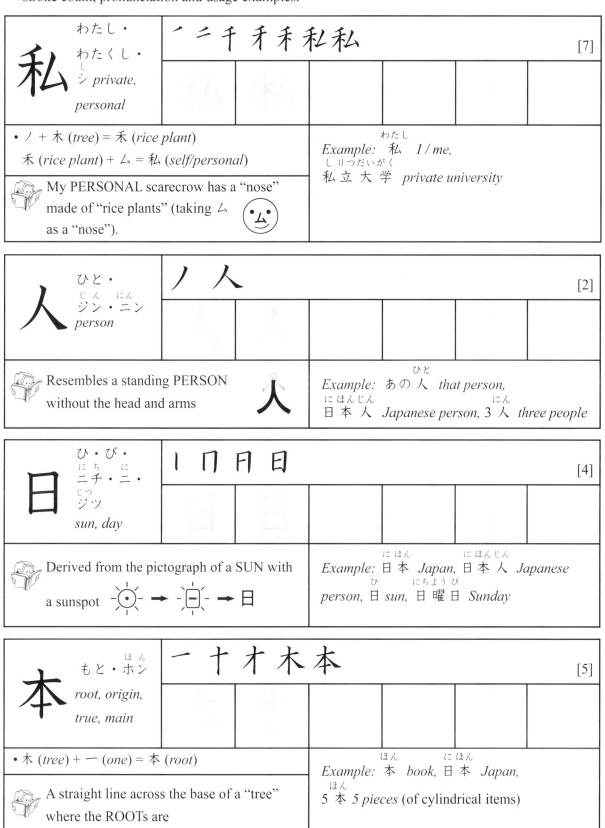

私　わたし・わたくし・シ　private, personal

ノ 二 千 禾 禾 私 私　[7]

• ノ ＋ 木 (tree) = 禾 (rice plant)
禾 (rice plant) ＋ ム = 私 (self/personal)

My PERSONAL scarecrow has a "nose" made of "rice plants" (taking ム as a "nose").

Example: 私　I / me,
私立大学　private university

人　ひと・ジン・ニン　person

ノ 人　[2]

Resembles a standing PERSON without the head and arms

Example: あの人　that person,
日本人　Japanese person, 3人　three people

日　ひ・び・ニチ・ニ・ジツ　sun, day

１ 冂 日 日　[4]

Derived from the pictograph of a SUN with a sunspot

Example: 日本　Japan, 日本人　Japanese person, 日　sun, 日曜日　Sunday

本　もと・ホン　root, origin, true, main

一 十 才 木 本　[5]

• 木 (tree) ＋ 一 (one) = 本 (root)

A straight line across the base of a "tree" where the ROOTs are

Example: 本　book, 日本　Japan,
5本　5 pieces (of cylindrical items)

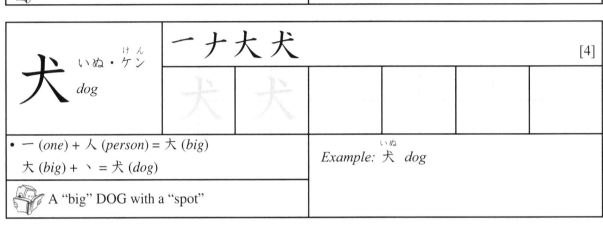

C) Let's read each sentence aloud. Do you know what it means? You will soon find reading sentences with kanji words easier because they clarify the word boundaries.

1. 私は日本人です。
2. あの人も日本人です。

3. A: あれは何ですか。
   B: 犬です。

4. A: それは何ですか。
   B: これは本です。

2. Reading and Writing Kanji Characters II

A) Let's read each of the following kanji words or phrases aloud several times.

ぶん学 *literature*
山田 *Yamada* (family name)
学生 *student*
車 *car*

すう学 *mathematics*
川口 *Kawaguchi* (family name)
先生 *teacher*

B) In the boxes provided, write each kanji character following the correct stroke order.

山 やま・サン mountain	丨 凵 山 [3]				

Resembles a range of three MOUNTAINS

Example: 山田 Yamada (family name), 山 *mountain*, 富士山 *Mount Fuji*, 火山 *volcano*

田 た・だ・デン field, rice paddy	丨 冂 冊 用 田 [5]				

Resembles a RICE PADDY

Example: 山田 Yamada (family name), 田 *rice paddy*, 田舎 *countryside*, 油田 *oil field*

川 かわ・がわ・セン river	丿 丿丿 川 [3]				

Resembles the flowing water of a RIVER

Example: 川口 Kawaguchi (family name), 川 *river*

口 くち・ぐち・コウ mouth	丨 冂 口 [3]				

Resembles a MOUTH that's wide opened

Example: 川口 Kawaguchi (family name), 口 *mouth*, 人口 *population*

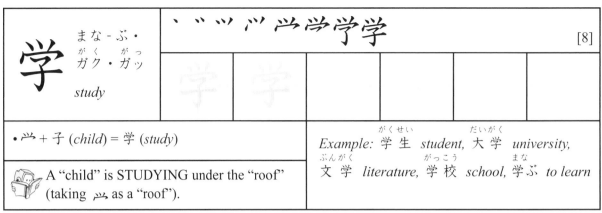

学 まな-ぶ・ガク・ガッ *study*

` 丶 丶ツ ツ 丷 学 学 学` [8]

学 学

• 丷 ＋ 子 (*child*) = 学 (*study*)

A "child" is STUDYING under the "roof" (taking 丷 as a "roof").

Example: 学生 *student,* 大学 *university,*
文学 *literature,* 学校 *school,* 学ぶ *to learn*

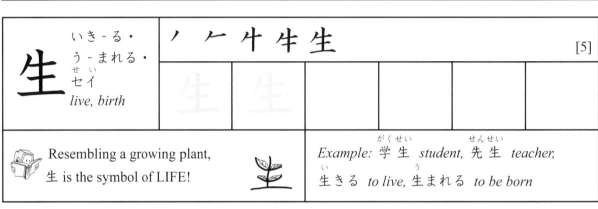

生 いき-る・う-まれる・セイ *live, birth*

`ノ ー 牛 牛 生` [5]

生 生

Resembling a growing plant, 生 is the symbol of LIFE!

Example: 学生 *student,* 先生 *teacher,*
生きる *to live,* 生まれる *to be born*

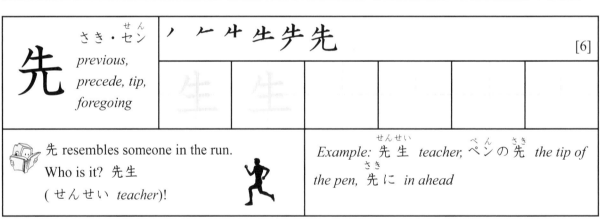

先 さき・セン *previous, precede, tip, foregoing*

`ノ ー 牛 生 牛 先` [6]

生 生

先 resembles someone in the run. Who is it? 先生 (せんせい *teacher*)!

Example: 先生 *teacher,* ペンの先 *the tip of the pen,* 先に *in ahead*

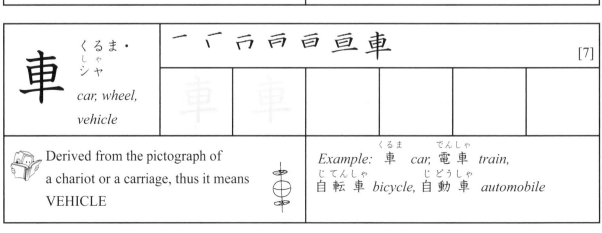

車 くるま・シャ *car, wheel, vehicle*

`一 厂 厅 旨 百 亘 車` [7]

車 車

Derived from the pictograph of a chariot or a carriage, thus it means VEHICLE

Example: 車 *car;* 電車 *train,*
自転車 *bicycle,* 自動車 *automobile*

C) Fill in the correct kanji characters in the boxes provided.

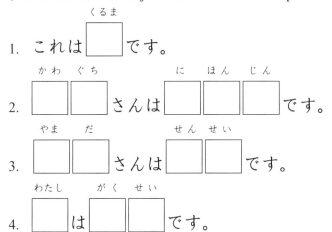

1. これは〔くるま〕です。

2. 〔かわ ぐ ち〕さんは〔に ほん じん〕です。

3. 〔やま だ〕さんは〔せん せい〕です。

4. 〔わたし〕は〔がく せい〕です。

D) From the list of kanji characters provided below, pair up any two to form three compound words.

| 生 ・ 学 ・ 先 ・ 日 ・ 本 |

1. ☐☐   2. ☐☐   3. ☐☐

3. Naming the Things Around You

Do you know what these things are called in Japanese? Write them down in hiragana.

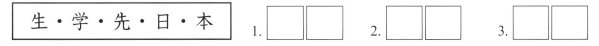

1. _____   2. _____   3. _____   4. _____

5. _____   6. _____   7. _____

4. Naming Some Buildings Around You

Draw lines to match.

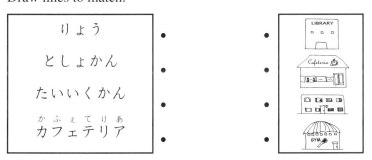

りょう
としょかん
たいいくかん
カフェテリア〔か ふ ぇ て り あ〕

Grammar

1. XはYです

In Japanese, we say X は Y です to mean *X is Y*, and X は Y じゃありません or X は Y じゃないです to mean *X is not Y*. はい means *yes*, and いいえ means *no*.

Complete the following short dialogs by filling in the blanks appropriately.

1. 山田さんは日本人ですか。— はい、私は _____ 。
2. スミスさんはアメリカ人 _____ 。— はい、私はアメリカ人です。
3. チェンさんはかんこく人ですか。— いいえ、私はかんこく人 _____

Note:

- は is a topic marker. It is pronounced as WA, not "ha". It usually marks a subject noun, even though it can also mark a direct object or other nouns. For example, 私はこの本をよみました literally means *As for myself, I read this book*, and この本は私がよみました literally means *As for this book, I read it*. Both sentences, however, simply mean *I read this book*.
- じゃ in Y じゃありません or Y じゃないです is actually a variation of では. Y では is pronounced as Y de wa. The former is more frequently used in conversation, but they mean the same.
- Most of the time はい means *yes*, and いいえ means *no*. But please note that in a negative question, their meanings are reversed — はい signals agreement, and いいえ signals disagreement.

2. Demonstrative Pronouns

Use これ (*this one*), それ (*that one near you*), or あれ (*that one over there*) to refer to something that both you and the person you're talking to can see. However, when using along with a common noun, their adjective counterparts この (*this ...*), その (*that ... near you*), and あの (*that ... over there*) respectively should be used instead, as in この本 (*this book*), その本 (*that book near you*), and あの本 (*that book over there*).

Underline the suitable option in the parentheses.

1. (あの・あれ) は犬です。
2. (あの・あれ) 犬はポチです。(ポチ a dog's name)
3. BMW は (あの・あれ) です。
4. それはわえいじてんですか。— はい、(これ・それ) はわえいじてんです。
5. あれはとしょかんですか。— はい、(あれ・これ) はとしょかんです。

3. Question Words

In Japanese, *what* is 何 (pronounced as なに , but becomes なん when followed by some items such as です), *which one* is どれ , *who* is だれ or its polite counterpart どなた , and *where* is どこ or its polite counterpart どちら . In a question, these words appear where the answers would be placed, and they must be used with the sentence final question particle か , as in これは何ですか (*What is this?*). Never use a question word with the topic particle は . So, to mean *Which one is the library?*, you should say としょかんはどれですか , and not どれはとしょかんですか . The latter is ungrammatical.

A) Fill in the blanks in the following short dialogs with appropriate question words.

1. しゅみは ＿＿＿＿＿＿ ですか。— からてです。
   What is your hobby? — (It's) karate.

2. これは ＿＿＿＿＿＿ ですか。— えいわじてんです。
   What is this? — (It's) an English-Japanese dictionary.

3. あの人は ＿＿＿＿＿＿ ですか。— 川口さんです。
   Who is that person (over there)? — (That's) Mr. Kawaguchi.

4. あの先生は ＿＿＿＿＿＿ ですか。— 山田先生です。
   Who is that professor (over there)? — (That's) Prof. Yamada.

5. 川口さんは ＿＿＿＿＿＿ からですか。— とうきょうからです。
   Where Is Mr. Kawaguchi from? — (He) is from Tokyo.

Note: から means *from*. 日本からです means *I'm from Japan*.

B) Order the items in each set to form a grammatical sentence.

1. {何・あれ・は・です・か} ＿＿＿＿＿＿＿＿＿＿＿＿＿＿＿ 。
2. {あの・だれ・人・か・です・は} ＿＿＿＿＿＿＿＿＿＿＿＿＿＿＿ 。
3. {あの先生・です・か・どなた・は} ＿＿＿＿＿＿＿＿＿＿＿＿＿＿＿ 。
4. {どれ・としょかん・か・は・です} ＿＿＿＿＿＿＿＿＿＿＿＿＿＿＿ 。
5. {は・から・どちら・山田さん・か・です} ＿＿＿＿＿＿＿＿＿＿＿＿＿＿＿ 。

Conversation and Usage

1. Meeting Someone for the First Time

Never use a demonstrative pronoun such as これ, それ, and あれ to refer to a person. You must use their adjective counterparts along with a common noun such as 人 or 学生, as in この人 (*this person*) or あの学生 (*that student*). In a polite context, この人 is replaced by この方 or こちら, as in この方はスミスさんです.

 Ms. Yamada has just been introduced to Mr. Chen at a party. Listen to their conversation carefully and then answer the questions that follow.

山田 　　：スミスさん、この方はどなたですか？

スミス　：こちらはチェンさんです。

チェン　：はじめまして。チェンです。よろしく。

山田 　　：はじめまして。山田です。こちらこそよろしく。チェンさんはどちらからですか。

チェン　：私はシャンハイからです。

山田 　　：ああ、そうですか。じゃあ、リーさんをしっていますか。

チェン　：いいえ。

山田 　　：そうですか。リーさんもシャンハイからですよ。

チェン　：ああ、そうですか。

[***Unfamiliar words:*** しっていますか *Do you know ...?*]

1.　Where is Mr. Chen from? _____

2.　Where is Mr. Lee from? _____

Note:

- Japanese has personal pronouns such as **I**, **you**, and **he**, but in actual conversational contexts, only the first person pronoun is used, and the second and third person pronouns are usually avoided.
- じゃあ is an interjection for marking the transition from one stage to another during a conversation.
- The particle も is added right after the item that is additional to what was previously introduced in the context to mean *too* or *also*.
  Example: 私はとうきょうからです。山田さんもとうきょうからです。
  　　　　I'm from Tokyo. Ms. Yamada is from Tokyo, too.
- Every time when you get some information from the person you are talking to, acknowledge it by nodding and saying ああ or ああ、そうですか. Depending on the interpretation, this means *Oh, I see,* or *Oh, really.*
- The particle よ can be placed at the end of the sentence for emphasis.

2. Asking about Hobby (しゅみ)

 You will continue to hear the conversation between Ms. Yamada and Mr. Chen. They are now talking about their hobbies. Listen carefully and answer the questions.

山田　　　：チェンさん、趣味は何ですか。

チェン　　：茶道です。

山田　　　：え？本当ですか。

チェン　　：はい。

山田　　　：むずかしいですか。

チェン　　：いいえ、まあまあかんたんです。

山田　　　：そうですか？

チェン　　：はい。山田さんの趣味は何ですか。

山田　　　：テニスです。

チェン　　：ああ、そうですか。

[***Unfamiliar words:*** 趣味 *hobby,* 茶道 *the art of tea ceremony, chanoyu,* 本当 *true*]

1. What is Mr. Chen's hobby?　_____

2. What is Ms. Yamada's hobby?　_____

Note:　To show the degree of some property, use adverbs such as ちょっと (*a little, a bit, or slightly*), とても (*very much*), and まあまあ (*more or less, relatively, or so so*). Use ちょっと for unfavorable properties. For example, ちょっと むずかしいです (*It is a little bit difficult.*) or ちょっときたないです (*It is a little dirty*). Use まあまあ for favorable properties. For example, まあまあおいしいです (*It is relatively delicious.*) or まあまあやさしいです (*It is pretty easy*). とても can be used for both favorable and unfavorable properties.

3. Situational Response

In the following situations, what would you say in Japanese?

1. You are meeting 川口さん for the very first time at a party and

    (a) you would like to ask him where he is from.　_____

    (b) you would like to ask him what his hobby is.　_____

    (c) you found out that he is a student of Tokyo University and you would like to ask him what his major is.　_____

2. When you are taking a sightseeing bus in Tokyo, you see a big building in the distance and you want to ask the guide what it is. _____

Listening Comprehension

1. Learning Some Japanese names

You will hear some Japanese family names read out to you. Pay attention to the length of the vowel, and whether there is a small つ or a voiced sound, as you hear them. Write the names down in hiragana.

1. _____ 2. _____ 3. _____ 4. _____

2. Learning about People

You will hear some sentences in Japanese. Write them down using a mixture of hiragana and the kanji you learned.

1. _____

2. _____

3. _____

3. Talking about Yourself

You will be asked some questions about yourself. Reply in Japanese and write down your answers in hiragana.

1. _____

2. _____

3. _____

Reading Comprehension

Reading a Train Route Map

This is the Yamanote-sen (Yamanote Line) route map in Tokyo. Study it carefully and find the stations listed below. Circle the station if you can manage to find it. You will have to look at the unfamiliar kanji very carefully.

とうきょう
1. 東京
しながわ
2. 品川
しんじゅく
3. 新宿
はらじゅく
4. 原宿
あきはばら
5. 秋葉原

New Vocabulary Reference List

NOUN

アメリカ the United States of America
いす（椅子）chair
いぬ（犬）dog
えいご（英語）English language
えいわじてん（英和辞典）English–Japanese
 dictionary
えんぴつ（鉛筆）pencil
かばん（鞄）bag
カフェテリア cafeteria
かんこく（韓国）South Korea
くつ（靴）shoes
くるま（車）car
すうがく（数学）mathematics
せんこう（専攻）(academic) major
せんもん（専門）specialty
たいいくかん（体育館）gymnasium
たてもの（建物）building
ちゅうごく（中国）China
つくえ（机）desk
どうぶつ（動物）animal
とけい（時計）watch, clock
としょかん（図書館）library
にほんじん（日本人）Japanese person
ねこ（猫）cat
ひと（人）person. (cf. ～かた）
ぶんがく（文学）literature
ぼうし（帽子）cap, hat
ほん（本）book
まど（窓）window
りょう（寮）dormitory
わえいじてん（和英辞典）Japanese–English
 dictionary

PRONOUN

あなた（貴方）you (2nd person pronoun)
あれ that one (over there)
こちら this way, this side, this person
これ this one
それ that one (near you)
わたし（私）I, me (1st person pronoun)

QUESTION WORD

だれ（誰）who
どちら which way, which direction
どなた who (polite) (cf. だれ）
どれ which one
なん／なに（何）what

ADJECTIVE

かんたんな（簡単な）easy
むずかしい（難しい）difficult

ADVERB

ちょっと slightly, a little
とても very much
まあまあ more or less

VERB

～です to be, copula in the polite/neutral affirmative
 present form (cf. ～だ (plain counterpart))
～じゃありません／～ではありません not to be,
 copula in the polite/neutral negative present form (cf.
 ～じゃない／～ではない (plain counterpart))

PARTICLE

～か sentence-final question particle
～から from ...
～は (wa) topic marker, as for ... *Exceptional pronunciation
～も also
～よ sentence-final emphasis particle

INTERJECTION

じゃあ then

OTHERS

いいえ no, wrong
～かた（～方）person (polite)（この方 this
 person) (cf. ひと）
～ご（～語）... language（日本語 Japanese
 language)
～じん（～人）... person (nationality)（日本人
 Japanese person)
そうですか Oh, I see./Really?
はい yes, right

CHAPTER THREE

Describing Things and People

Objectives:
- to describe things and people around you
- to learn how to introduce yourself
- to learn and use the grammar item ～の: ...'s (modifier maker) and ～ね: ..., *isn't it?* (sentence final confirmation marker)

Kanji and Vocabulary

1. Reading and Writing Kanji Characters

A) Let's read each of the following kanji words or phrases aloud several times.

はは
母 *one's own mother*   かあ お母さん *someone else's mother*
ちち
父 *one's own father*   とう お父さん *someone else's father*
あに
兄 *one's older brother*   にい お兄さん *someone else's brother*
だいがく
大学 *university*   だいがく 大学いん *graduate school*
おとこ ひと
男の人 *man*   おんな ひと 女の人 *woman*

B) In the boxes provided, write each kanji character following the correct stroke order.

母 はは・ボ *mother*	く 口 马 母 母 [5]

Example: 母 *one's mother,* お母さん *someone else's mother,* 母国語 *one's mother tongue*

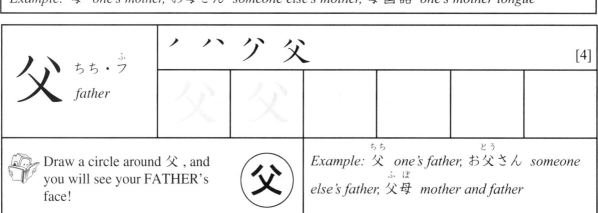

父 ちち・フ *father*	ノ ハ グ 父 [4]

Draw a circle around 父 , and you will see your FATHER's face!

父

Example: 父 *one's father,* お父さん *someone else's father,* 父母 *mother and father*

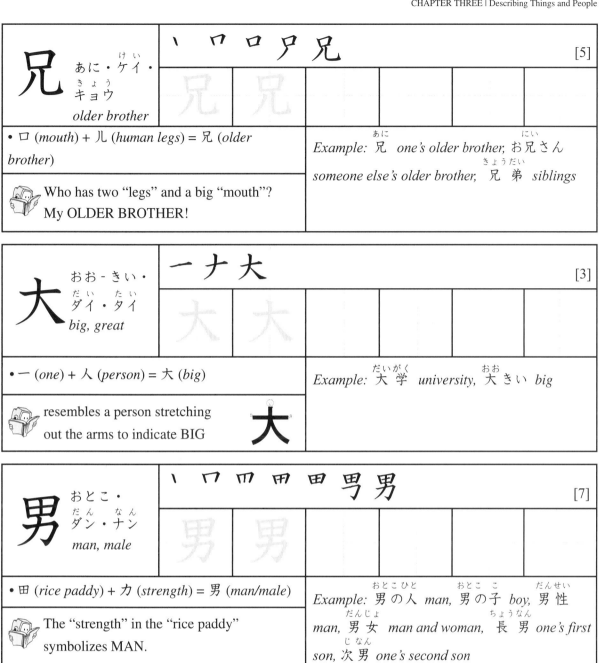

兄　あに・ケイ・キョウ　*older brother*

ヽ ロ ロ ア 兄　[5]

• 口 (*mouth*) + 儿 (*human legs*) = 兄 (*older brother*)

Who has two "legs" and a big "mouth"? My OLDER BROTHER!

Example: 兄 *one's older brother,* お兄さん *someone else's older brother,* 兄弟 *siblings*

大　おお-きい・ダイ・タイ　*big, great*

一 ナ 大　[3]

• 一 (*one*) + 人 (*person*) = 大 (*big*)

resembles a person stretching out the arms to indicate BIG

大

Example: 大学 *university,* 大きい *big*

男　おとこ・ダン・ナン　*man, male*

ヽ ロ 皿 田 田 甲 男　[7]

• 田 (*rice paddy*) + 力 (*strength*) = 男 (*man/male*)

The "strength" in the "rice paddy" symbolizes MAN.

Example: 男の人 *man,* 男の子 *boy,* 男性 *man,* 男女 *man and woman,* 長男 *one's first son,* 次男 *one's second son*

女　おんな・ジョ　*woman, female*

く 女 女　[3]

• く + ノ + 一 (*one*) = 女 (*female/woman*)

resembles a FEMALE

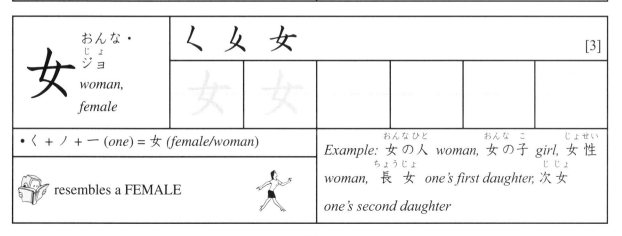

Example: 女の人 *woman,* 女の子 *girl,* 女性 *woman,* 長女 *one's first daughter,* 次女 *one's second daughter*

C) The following sentences include many kanji words without furigana. Test how well you've mastered the kanji characters by reading the sentences aloud on your own and translating them.

1. 山田さんのお父さんとお母さんはすう学の先生です。

2. 川口さんのお兄さんは大学いんの学生です。

3. 父と母は日本人です。

4. これはあの男の人の車です。それはあの女の人のです。

5. 私の兄は大学のぶん学の学生です。

D) Fill in the correct kanji characters in the boxes provided.

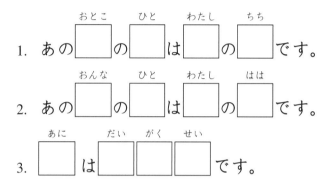

1. あの　[おとこ]　の　[ひと]　は　[わたし]　の　[ちち]　です。

2. あの　[おんな]　の　[ひと]　は　[わたし]　の　[はは]　です。

3. [あに]　は　[だい][がく][せい]　です。

2. Naming and Describing Things and People

A) Draw lines to match.

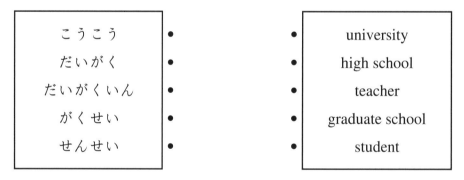

こうこう	•	•	university
だいがく	•	•	high school
だいがくいん	•	•	teacher
がくせい	•	•	graduate school
せんせい	•	•	student

B) These are the things you often carry. Do you know what they are called in Japanese? Write them down in hiragana.

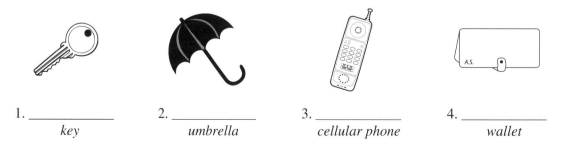

1. _____
   key

2. _____
   umbrella

3. _____
   cellular phone

4. _____
   wallet

C) Fill in the blanks in hiragana.

In Japanese, the humble form, such as 母 (はは), is often used when addressing one's own family members. But the polite form, such as お母さん (おかあ), should be used when addressing someone else's family members.

私の母
ともだちのお母さん

3. 私の _____
ともだちのお父さん

1. 私の _____
ともだちのお兄さん

4. 私のいもうと
ともだちの _____

Self

2. 私のあね
ともだちの _____

5. 私のおとうと
ともだちの _____

D) Fill in the blanks following the example so you can create an appropriate short conversation.

Example: A: おとうとです。
          B: ああ、おとうとさん ですか。

1. A: 母です。
    B: ああ、_____ ですか。

3. A: 兄です。
    B: ああ、_____ ですか。

2. A: 父です。
    B: ああ、_____ ですか。

4. A: あねです。
    B: ああ、_____ ですか。

E) Fill in the blanks following the example so you can create an appropriate short conversation.

Example: A: おとうとさんですか。
          B: はい、私のおとうと です。

1. A: お兄さんですか
    B: はい、私の _____ です。

3. A: お父さんですか
    B: はい、私の _____ です。

2. A: お母さんですか
    B: はい、私の _____ です。

4. A: おねえさんですか
    B: はい、私の _____ です。

Grammar

1. Noun 1 の Noun 2

In Japanese, a noun can be transformed into a modifier by adding の at the end of it. For example, in 日本語の先生 (*a Japanese language teacher*), 先生 is the referent (what's being referred to) and 日本語 is the modifier (the description for the referent). Please note that the referent should be placed after the modifier. If they are placed in the reversed order, the sentence has a completely different meaning. Unlike in the above example, 先生の日本語 means *the Japanese language spoken by the teacher*. In a sentence, there may be more than a modifier for a reference, such as 東京の大学の日本語の先生 (*a teacher of Japanese at a college in Tokyo*). The general rule to the correct sequence is to place the one with a broader meaning before that with a narrower meaning.

For each of the following, order the items provided to form a phrase that refers to the item represented in English.

1. { 日本人・学生・の }

   _____ (*a Japanese student*)

2. { 日本ご・こども・の }

   _____ (*the Japanese language spoken by children*)

3. { 車・兄・の }

   _____ (*my brother's car*)

4. { 車・ともだち・兄・の・の }

   _____ (*my brother's friend's car*)

5. { 先生・大学・日本ご・の・の }

   _____ (*a teacher of Japanese at the college*)

2. A は B です

As a referent may be referred to using many words with the particle の , a simple statement of the **A** は **B** です (A *is* B) structure can be pretty long. Please note that in this type of sentences, は is used only once while there can be more than one の .

Complete each sentence by filling in the blanks with は and の, then translate the sentence.

1. スミスさん ____ 日本ご ____ 学生です。

   Translation: _____

2. 山田さん ＿＿＿ 大学いん ＿＿＿ 学生です。

   Translation: ＿＿＿＿＿＿＿＿＿＿＿＿＿＿＿＿＿＿＿＿＿＿＿＿＿

3. 兄 ＿＿＿ ともだち ＿＿＿ お兄さん ＿＿＿ 先生です。

   Translation: ＿＿＿＿＿＿＿＿＿＿＿＿＿＿＿＿＿＿＿＿＿＿＿＿＿

4. 私 ＿＿＿ おとうと ＿＿＿ ともだち ＿＿＿ 日本ご ＿＿＿ 学生です。

   Translation: ＿＿＿＿＿＿＿＿＿＿＿＿＿＿＿＿＿＿＿＿＿＿＿＿＿

5. これ ＿＿＿ いもうと ＿＿＿ すう学 ＿＿＿ 本です。

   Translation: ＿＿＿＿＿＿＿＿＿＿＿＿＿＿＿＿＿＿＿＿＿＿＿＿＿

3. Dropping the Noun after の

A referent in a phrase with a modifier created by の can be omitted if it is contextually understood. In the example below, いす can be dropped from the subsequent sentence since it has been introduced before.

In each of the following, bracket the referent that can be omitted.

Example: 私のいすはこれです。山田さんの (いす) はそれです。

1. これは私のかぎです。それは山田さんのかぎです。
2. あれはすう学の本です。あれは日本ごの本です。
3. 私の兄の車はこれです。私の父の車はあれです。

Conversation and Usage

1. Describing People

Japanese people often compliment others on their appearance, clothing, talents and achievements. However, to stay modest, they do not compliment their own family members and often deny the compliments on themselves or on their family members.

Mr. Brown has just joined a new company and he is attending an informal party by the company. Listen carefully to his conversation with his new colleague, Mr. Yamamoto. Then answer the questions that follow.

ブラウン：あの男の人はだれですか。

山本　：本田さんです。営業部の部長のアシスタントです。

ブラウン：ああ、そうですか。

山本　　：とてもいい人ですよ。あとで、紹介しますね。

ブラウン：ああ、おねがいします。

　　　　　じゃあ、あの女の人はだれですか。

山本　　：私のいもうとです。

ブラウン：ああ、山本さんのいもうとさんですか。きれいですね。

山本　　：いいえ。

ブラウン：あとで、紹介してくださいね。

[***Unfamiliar words:*** 山本 family name, 本田 family name, 営業部 *sales division*, 部長 *division head*, アシスタント *assistant*, いい人 *nice person*, あとで *later*, 紹介する *to introduce*]

1. What division does Mr. Honda belong to?　_____

2. What is Mr. Honda's title?　_____

Note: The particle ね at the end of a sentence invites the listener's agreement.

2. Situational Response

In the following situations, what would you say in Japanese?

1. You are at a party with your friend. You see an unfamiliar woman at the corner of the room, and you want to ask your friend who she is.

   _____

2. Someone asked about your older brother. You want to say that he is a student of mathematics at a college in Osaka.

   _____

Listening Comprehension

Finding the Owners

You will hear a narrative about the following vehicles. Identify the owner of each vehicle and write it down in English in the space provided.

くるま
車

ばん
バン

とらっく
トラック

1. _____　　2. _____　　3. _____

Reading Comprehension

Introducing Oneself

The following is a self-introduction by Kevin Brown. Read it carefully, then answer the questions.

<ruby>私<rt>わたし</rt></ruby>はケビン・ブラウンです。<ruby>会社員<rt>かいしゃいん</rt></ruby>です。<ruby>出身<rt>しゅっしん</rt></ruby>はノースキャロライナです。<ruby>趣味<rt>しゅみ</rt></ruby>はテニスです。<ruby>家内<rt>かない</rt></ruby>は<ruby>日本人<rt>にほんじん</rt></ruby>です。<ruby>大学院生<rt>だいがくいんせい</rt></ruby>です。<ruby>家内<rt>かない</rt></ruby>の<ruby>専攻<rt>せんこう</rt></ruby>は<ruby>文学<rt>ぶんがく</rt></ruby>です。<ruby>家内<rt>かない</rt></ruby>の父は<ruby>高校<rt>こうこう</rt></ruby>の<ruby>数学<rt>すうがく</rt></ruby>の<ruby>教師<rt>きょうし</rt></ruby>です。<ruby>家内<rt>かない</rt></ruby>の母は<ruby>高校<rt>こうこう</rt></ruby>の<ruby>英語<rt>えいご</rt></ruby>の<ruby>教師<rt>きょうし</rt></ruby>です。

1. With the help of a dictionary, write down the meaning of the following words.

    (a) 趣味 (しゅみ shumi) _____

    (b) 家内 (かない kanai) _____

    (c) 教師 (きょうし kyoushi/kyōshi) _____

2. What sport does Kevin play? _____

3. What does Kevin's wife do? _____

Writing

Essay Writing

Write about yourself and your family in Japanese as much as you can. You can write your name in romaji or English for now.

_____

_____

_____

_____

_____

_____

New Vocabulary Reference List

NOUN

あに・おにいさん（兄・お兄さん）*older brother*
あね・おねえさん（姉・お姉さん）*older sister*
いもうと・いもうとさん（妹・妹さん）*younger sister*
おとうと・おとうとさん（弟・弟さん）*younger brother*
おとこのひと（男の人）*man*
おんなのひと（女の人）*woman*
かぎ（鍵）*key*
かさ（傘）*umbrella*
けいたいでんわ（携帯電話）*cellular phone*
こうこう（高校）*high school*
こども・こどもさん・おこさん（子供・子供さん・お子さん）*child*
さいふ（財布）*wallet*

だいがく（大学）*university*
だいがくいん（大学院）*graduate school*
ちち・おとうさん（父・お父さん）*father*
ともだち（友達）*friend*
はは・おかあさん（母・お母さん）*mother*

ADJECTIVE

かわいい（可愛い）*cute*
きれいな（綺麗な）*pretty, beautiful*
はんさむな（ハンサムな）*handsome*

PARTICLE

〜ね *..., isn't it?*（きれいですね。 *It's beautiful, isn't it?*）
〜の *...'s; of ...*（私の本 *my book*）

CHAPTER FOUR

Using Numbers and Katakana

Objectives:

- to read and write katakana characters
- to count up to 99,999 in Japanese
- to list nouns using と
- to learn the phrases for enquiring time, telephone numbers and prices

Katakana

Katakana consists of 46 characters and each forms the counterpart to a hiragana character, representing the same syllable sound. The only difference between katakana and hiragana is in the use of an elongation mark – for representing a long vowel. For example, りい in hiragana is written as リ– in katakana. Katakana is only used to write non-Chinese foreign names, loan words from the West and most of onomatopoeic expressions. (Chinese names and loan words can be written in either kanji or katakana.)

1. Reading and Writing Basic Katakana I

A) In the table below, identify the katakana counterpart for each hiragana character and practice writing it in the boxes provided, following the correct stroke order.

あ	ア		ア	ア				
い	イ		イ	イ				
う	ウ		ウ	ウ				
え	エ		エ	エ				
お	オ		オ	オ				

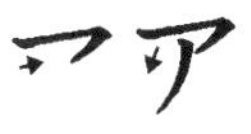

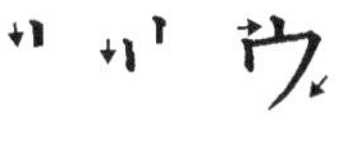

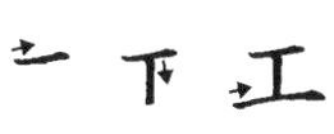

か	カ	ヮ カ	カ	カ				
き	キ	´ ≠ キ	キ	キ				
く	ク	´ ク	ク	ク				
け	ケ	´ ≠ ケ	ケ	ケ				
こ	コ	⁷ コ	コ	コ				

B) Convert the following hiragana characters to katakana.

  1. き : _____   2. う : _____   3. ご : _____   4. お : _____

2. Reading and Writing Basic Katakana II

A) In the table below, identify the katakana counterpart for each hiragana character and practice writing it in the boxes provided, following the correct stroke order.

さ	サ	ˉ ≠ サ	サ	サ				
し	シ	´ ⸴ シ	シ	シ				
す	ス	⁷ ス	ス	ス				
せ	セ	ˉ セ	セ	セ				
そ	ソ	´ ソ	ソ	ソ				
た	タ	´ ク タ	タ	タ				

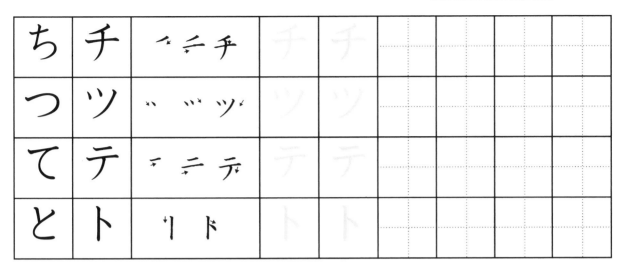

ち	チ	´ ニ チ	チ	チ				
つ	ツ	` `` ツ	ツ	ツ				
て	テ	´ ニ テ	テ	テ				
と	ト	´ ト	ト	ト				

B) Convert the following hiragana characters to katakana.

1. つ: _____　　　　2. そ: _____　　　　3. た: _____　　　　4. ぐ: _____

3. Reading and Writing Basic Katakana III

A) In the table below, identify the katakana counterpart for each hiragana character and practice writing it in the boxes provided, following the correct stroke order.

な	ナ	ー ナ	ナ	ナ				
に	ニ	´ ニ	ニ	ニ				
ぬ	ヌ	フ ヌ	ヌ	ヌ				
ね	ネ	´ ゛ ネ ネ	ネ	ネ				
の	ノ	ノ	ノ	ノ				
は	ハ	゛ ハ	ハ	ハ				
ひ	ヒ	ー ヒ	ヒ	ヒ				

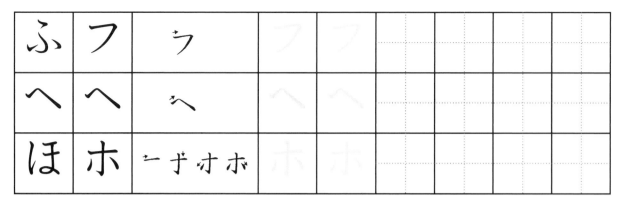

B) Draw lines to match the katakana words with their meanings.

セーター	•		•	bus
バス	•		•	test
テスト	•		•	sweater
ソーセージ	•		•	sausage

4. Reading and Writing Basic Katakana IV

A) In the table below, identify the katakana counterpart for each hiragana character and practice writing it in the boxes provided, following the correct stroke order.

ゆ	ユ	ヲ ユ							
よ	ヨ	ヲ ヲ ヨ							

B) Do you know the meaning of these katakana words? Write them down in the blanks provided.

1. メニュー: _____

2. ネクタイ: _____

3. サッカー: _____

4. スカート: _____

5. Reading and Writing Basic Katakana V

A) In the table below, identify the katakana counterpart for each hiragana character and practice writing it in the boxes provided, following the correct stroke order.

ら	ラ	﹃ ラ							
り	リ	リ リ							
る	ル	ﾉ ル							
れ	レ	レ							
ろ	ロ	ﾉ ﾛ ロ							
わ	ワ	ﾉ ウ							
を	ヲ	﹄ ﹃ ヲ							
ん	ン	﹀ ン							

B) Draw lines to match, then read the country names aloud.

アメリカ	• •	Australia
フランス	• •	Singapore
オーストラリア	• •	Canada
シンガポール	• •	The USA
イギリス	• •	Egypt
カナダ	• •	France
ドイツ	• •	Germany
スペイン	• •	England
ブラジル	• •	Spain
タイ	• •	Brazil
エジプト	• •	Thai

Kanji and Vocabulary

1. Reading and Writing Kanji Characters I

A) Let's read each of the following kanji words or phrases aloud several times.

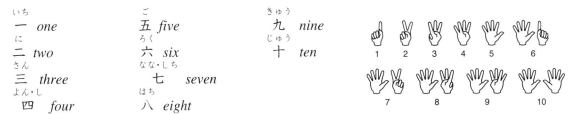

いち 一 *one*	ご 五 *five*	きゅう 九 *nine*
に 二 *two*	ろく 六 *six*	じゅう 十 *ten*
さん 三 *three*	なな・しち 七 *seven*	
よん・し 四 *four*	はち 八 *eight*	

B) In the boxes provided, write each kanji character following the correct stroke order.

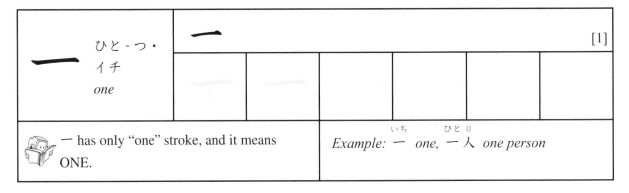

	ひと‐つ・ イチ *one*	一						[1]

— has only "one" stroke, and it means ONE.	*Example:* 一 *one,* 一人 *one person*

二 ふた - つ・二 *two*	一 二				[2]

二 has "two" strokes, and it means TWO.

Example: 二 (に) *two,* 二 (ふた) つ *two pieces*

三 みっ - つ・サン *three*	一 二 三				[3]

三 has "three" strokes, and it means THREE.

Example: 三 (さん) *three,* 三 (みっ) つ *three pieces*

四 よっ - つ・よん・よ・シ *four*	丨 冂 冈 四 四				[5]

• As its variant pronunciation (し) sounds like the kanji word 死 (し), which means *death,* 四 (*four*) is considered an unlucky number in Japan.

resembles a window with the curtains tied to both sides

Example: 四 (よん) *four,* 四 (し) 月 (がつ) *April*

五 いつ - つ・ゴ *five*	一 丆 五 五				[4]

五 has only four strokes, but it looks like having FIVE lines in all.

Example: 五 (ご) *five*

六 むっ - つ・ロク・ロッ *six*	丶 亠 六 六				[4]

• 亠 (*lid*) + 八 (*eight*) = 六 (*six*)

Example: 六 (ろく) *six*

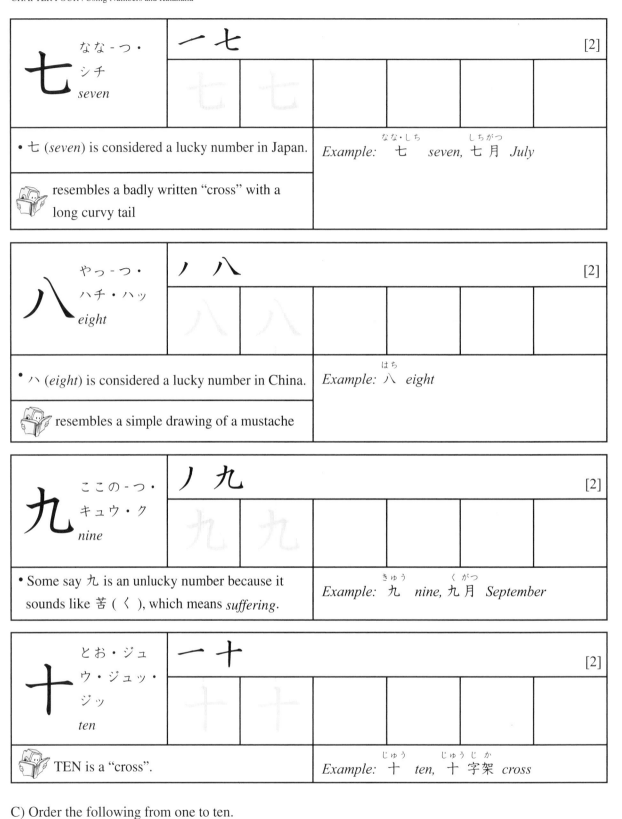

七 なな-つ・シチ *seven*

一 七

七 七

• 七 (*seven*) is considered a lucky number in Japan.

resembles a badly written "cross" with a long curvy tail

Example: 七 *seven,* 七月 *July*

八 やっ-つ・ハチ・ハッ *eight*

ノ 八

八 八

• 八 (*eight*) is considered a lucky number in China.

resembles a simple drawing of a mustache

Example: 八 *eight*

九 ここの-つ・キュウ・ク *nine*

ノ 九

九 九

• Some say 九 is an unlucky number because it sounds like 苦 (く), which means *suffering*.

Example: 九 *nine,* 九月 *September*

十 とお・ジュウ・ジュッ・ジッ *ten*

一 十

十 十

TEN is a "cross".

Example: 十 *ten,* 十字架 *cross*

C) Order the following from one to ten.

三 ・ 五 ・ 六 ・ 十 ・ 七 ・ 一 ・ 四 ・ 二 ・ 八 ・ 九

2. Reading and Writing Kanji Characters II

A) Let's read each kanji word or phrase aloud several times, then check how well you can remember what it means.

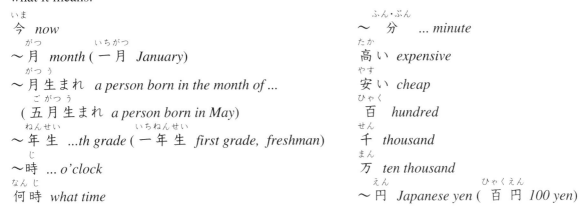

いま
今 *now*

がつ　　　　　いちがつ
〜月 *month* (一月 *January*)

がつう
〜月生まれ *a person born in the month of ...*

ごがつう
(五月生まれ *a person born in May*)

ねんせい　　　　　　いちねんせい
〜年生 *...th grade* (一年生 *first grade, freshman*)

じ
〜時 *... o'clock*

なんじ
何時 *what time*

ふん・ぶん
〜 分 *... minute*

たか
高い *expensive*

やす
安い *cheap*

ひゃく
百 *hundred*

せん
千 *thousand*

まん
万 *ten thousand*

えん　　　　　　ひゃくえん
〜円 *Japanese yen* (百円 *100 yen*)

B) In the boxes provided, write each kanji character following the correct stroke order.

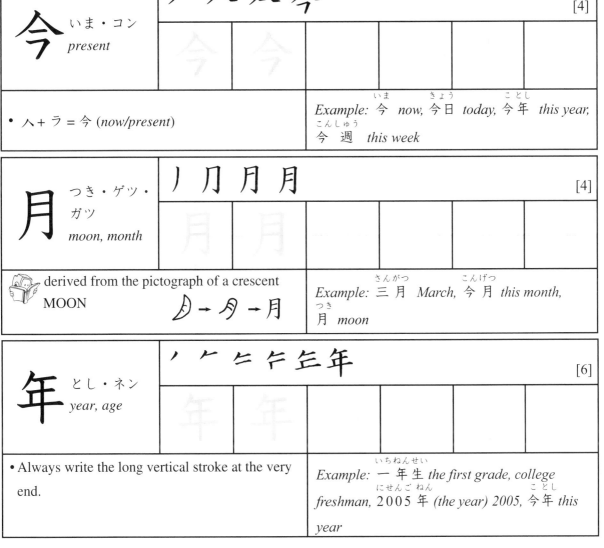

今 いま・コン *present*	ノ 人 ^ 今 [4]
• 人 + ラ = 今 (*now/present*)	Example: 今 *now*, 今日 *today*, 今年 *this year*, 今週 *this week*

月 つき・ゲツ・ガツ *moon, month*	ノ 刀 月 月 [4]
derived from the pictograph of a crescent MOON　月 → 月 → 月	Example: 三月 *March*, 今月 *this month*, 月 *moon*

年 とし・ネン *year, age*	ノ 亠 亠 仁 伝 年 [6]
• Always write the long vertical stroke at the very end.	Example: 一年生 *the first grade, college freshman*, 2005年 *(the year) 2005*, 今年 *this year*

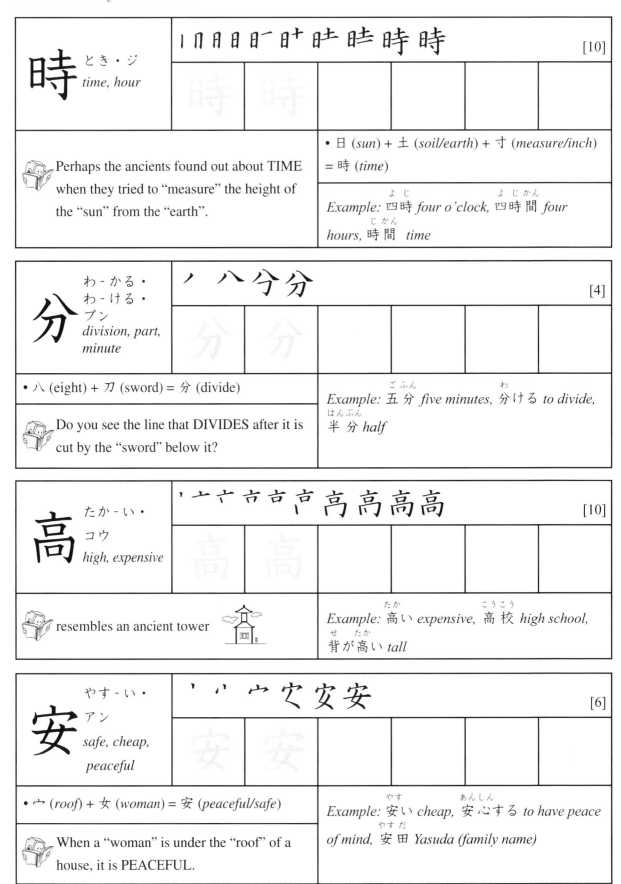

時 とき・ジ
time, hour

１ 冂 冂 日 日 昨 昨 昨 時 時 [10]

Perhaps the ancients found out about TIME when they tried to "measure" the height of the "sun" from the "earth".

• 日 (*sun*) + 土 (*soil/earth*) + 寸 (*measure/inch*) = 時 (*time*)

Example: 四時 *four o'clock*, 四時間 *four hours*, 時間 *time*

分 わ-かる・わ-ける・ブン
division, part, minute

ノ 八 分 分 [4]

• 八 (*eight*) + 刀 (*sword*) = 分 (*divide*)

Do you see the line that DIVIDES after it is cut by the "sword" below it?

Example: 五分 *five minutes*, 分ける *to divide*, 半分 *half*

高 たか-い・コウ
high, expensive

' 亠 亠 古 古 占 高 高 高 高 [10]

resembles an ancient tower

Example: 高い *expensive*, 高校 *high school*, 背が高い *tall*

安 やす-い・アン
safe, cheap, peaceful

' 宀 宀 宀 安 安 [6]

• 宀 (*roof*) + 女 (*woman*) = 安 (*peaceful/safe*)

When a "woman" is under the "roof" of a house, it is PEACEFUL.

Example: 安い *cheap*, 安心する *to have peace of mind*, 安田 *Yasuda (family name)*

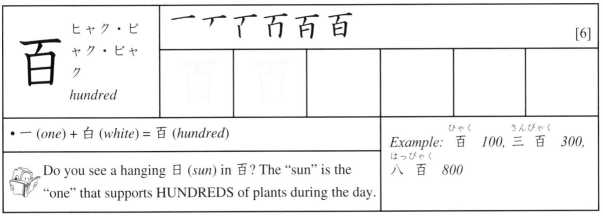

百 ヒャク・ピャク・ビャク *hundred*

一 ァ ァ 百 百 百 [6]

• 一 (*one*) + 白 (*white*) = 百 (*hundred*)

Do you see a hanging 日 (*sun*) in 百? The "sun" is the "one" that supports HUNDREDS of plants during the day.

Example: 百 (ひゃく) *100,* 三百 (さんびゃく) *300,* 八百 (はっぴゃく) *800*

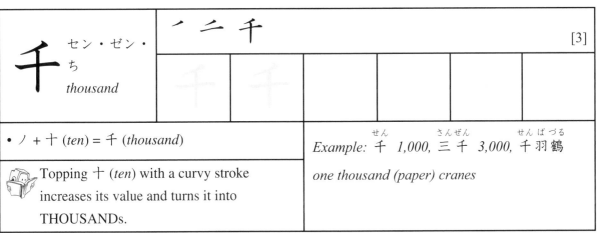

千 セン・ゼン・ち *thousand*

ノ ニ 千 [3]

• ノ + 十 (*ten*) = 千 (*thousand*)

Topping 十 (*ten*) with a curvy stroke increases its value and turns it into THOUSANDs.

Example: 千 (せん) *1,000,* 三千 (さんぜん) *3,000,* 千羽鶴 (せんばづる)

one thousand (paper) cranes

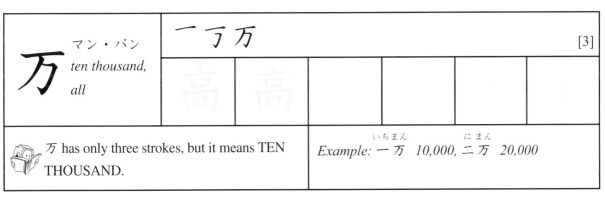

万 マン・バン *ten thousand, all*

一 ヮ 万 [3]

• 万 has only three strokes, but it means TEN THOUSAND.

Example: 一万 (いちまん) *10,000,* 二万 (にまん) *20,000*

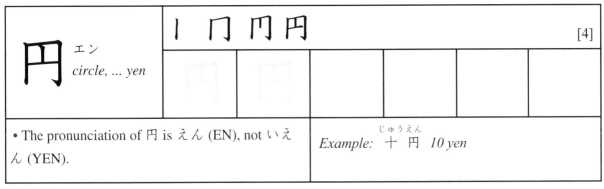

円 エン *circle, ... yen*

丨 冂 冂 円 [4]

• The pronunciation of 円 is えん (EN), not いえん (YEN).

Example: 十円 (じゅうえん) *10 yen*

C) Fill in the boxes with suitable kanji characters.

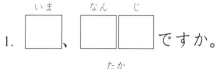

1. ⬚（いま）、⬚⬚（なん・じ）ですか。

2. ちょっと⬚（たか）いです。

3. まあまあ⬚（やす）いです。

4. 私は⬚⬚⬚（し・がつ・う）まれです。

3. Pronouncing Number Phrases

Write the pronunciation of the underlined numbers or phrases in hiragana.

1. 山田さんのでんわばんごうは <u>721-4281</u> です。 _____

2. ようこさんは大学の<u>3年生</u>です。 _____

3. たけしさんはこうこうの<u>2年生</u>です。 _____

4. このくつは<u>3万円</u>です。 _____

5. このテレビは <u>59,600</u> 円です。 _____

6. このカメラは<u>五万円</u>です。 _____

4. Telling the Time

What time is it? Write down in hiragana.

| 08:37 | 07:17 | 10:45 | 09:02 |

1. _____　　2. _____　　3. _____　　4. _____

Grammar

Listing Nouns Using と

と is a particle used in listing items. In a sentence, it should be placed after each listed item except the last one, for example, カメラと、ラジオと、テレビを下さい (*Please give me a camera, a radio, and a TV*).

Pretend that you are in a store and you want to buy the following items. What would you say in each of the following?

1. りんご (*apple*), バナナ (*banana*)

_____

2. ノート *(notebook)*, えんぴつ *(pencil)*, けしゴム *(eraser)*

_____

3. 30 円のきって *(¥30 stamp)*, 50 円のきって *(¥50 stamp)*

_____

Conversation and Usage

1. Asking about Time

The phrase to ask about time is 今、何時ですか .

A man and a woman are talking at the bus stop. Listen to their conversation carefully and answer the questions that follow in Japanese.

女 の 人 ： すみません。今、何時ですか。

男 の 人 ： 2 時 15 分です。

女の人 ： ああ、そうですか。どうも。

男の人 ： いいえ。

女の人 ： あのう、次のさくらまち行きのバスは何時ですか？

男の人 ： すみません。ちょっとわかりません。

女の人 ： ああ。じゃあ、いしかわまち行きのバスは？

男人 ： 2 時 35 分です。

女の人 ： ああ、そうですか。

[***Unfamiliar words:*** 次の *next,* 〜行き *bound for ...*]

Note: わかりません literary means *I don't understand*, but it also means *I don't know*.

1. What time does the next bus bound for Ishikawa-machi arrive?

   _____

2. How long does the woman have to wait in order to take the next bus for Ishikawa-machi?

   _____

2. Asking for Prices

"How much" is いくらですか in Japanese. When you want to buy something, just say 〜を下さい or 〜をおねがいします, which means *Please give it to me*.

Takeshi is checking out some prices in a stationery store. Listen carefully to his conversation with the store clerk and then answer the questions that follow.

たけし　　：すみません。この筆（ふで）はいくらですか。

てんいん：それは 2,000 円（えん）です。

たけし　　：ああ、そうですか。じゃあ、この筆（ふで）と、その 硯（すずり）を下（くだ）さい。

てんいん：はい。消費税（しょうひぜい）を入（い）れて、6,975 円です。

たけし　　：10,000 円から、お願（ねが）いします。

てんいん：はい。じゃあ、おつりは 3,025 円（えん）ですね。どうぞ。

たけし　　：どうも。

てんいん：どうもありがとうございます。

[**Unfamiliar words:** 筆（ふで） *(calligraphy) brush*, 硯（すずり） *inkstone/ink slab*, 消費税（しょうひぜい）を入（い）れて *including consumption tax*, おつり *change*]

1. What did Takeshi buy?　　　_____

2. How much did Takeshi pay?　　_____

3. Situational Response

In the following situations, what would you say in Japanese?

1. You are at a waiting room in a hospital. You want to know what time it is, but you don't have a watch. The person who is sitting next to you has a watch.

   _____

2. You have just made an appointment to meet Ms. Yamada next Sunday. You are thinking of getting her phone number just in case.

   _____

3. You want to get in touch with Mr. Smith, but you don't have his phone number. You want to ask Ms. Yamada whether she has it.

   _____

Listening Comprehension

1. Taking Down the Telephone Numbers

 Listen carefully as the telephone numbers of the following people are read out to you. Take down the numbers and fill in the blanks correctly.

1. たかはしさん (さっぽろ)

 _____

2. もりさん (とうきょう)

 _____

3. たかはしさん (おおさか)

 _____

4. たかださん (ふくおか)

 _____

2. Matching the Age and Grade Level

 You will hear the age and grade level of various people. Listen to the information carefully, then draw lines to match.

15 さい ●		● こうこう 1 年生
17 さい ●		● こうこう 2 年生
18 さい ●	みゆきさん	● こうこう 3 年生
19 さい ●		● 大学 1 年生
21 さい ●		● 大学 2 年生
22 さい ●	たけしさん	● 大学 3 年生
23 さい ●		● 大学 4 年生
24 さい ●		● 大学いんの 1 年生
28 さい ●	さちこちゃん	● 大学いんの 2 年生
30 さい ●		
31 さい ●		
32 さい ●	ひろこさん	

Reading Comprehension

Checking Out A Car-renting Advertisement

Below is an advertisement by a car-renting company on a special offer. Study it carefully, then answer the questions.

エコノミーレンタカー　ハワイ

Hawaii Economy Rent-A-Car	1 日 (24 時間) レンタル料金	ウイークリー (5-7 日間) レンタル料金
エコノミー　4 ドアー	¥4,300	¥18,000
コンパクト　4 ドアー	¥4,800	¥20,100
ミニバン	¥8,400	¥34,900
ジープ	¥8,400	¥34,900
SUB	¥8,400	¥34,900

1. Which location does this offer apply to? _____

2. How much do they charge for renting a 4-door compact car for one day? _____

3. How much do they charge for renting a mini-van for one week? _____

Writing

Creating a Business Card

A Japanese business card is designed either vertically or horizontally. It typically contains one's name, affiliated company or institution, title, address, telephone/fax number, and e-mail address.

Example:

ABC, Co. Lit.

ケント・ブラウン

〒110 東京都台東区松井町 3-3
TEL: (03)3835-1111　　E-mail: kent@abc.com

Complete the following to make a Japanese business card for yourself. Write your name in katakana.

Affiliation: _____

Name _____

Address: _____

Telephone: _____　E-mail: _____

New Vocabulary Reference List

NOUN

いま（今）*now*

きゃく（客）*customer, guest*

ごご（午後）*p.m., afternoon*

ごぜん（午前）*a.m.*

せん（千）*thousand*

テレビ *TV*

てんいん（店員）*store clerk*

でんわ（電話）*telephone*

でんわばんごう（電話番号）*telephone number*

ひゃく（百）*hundred*

まん（万）*ten thousand*

れい／ゼロ（零・ゼロ・0）*zero*

カメラ *camera*

ラジオ *radio*

QUESTION WORD

いくら *how much*

ADJECTIVE

いい *fine, good* (irregular adjective)

たかい（高い）*expensive, tall, high*

やすい（安い）*cheap, inexpensive*

COUNTER

〜えん（〜円）... *yen (¥)*

〜がつ（〜月）*the months of the year (e.g. 一月 January)*

〜さい（〜オ／〜歳）*a counter for age, ... years old*

〜じ（〜時）... *o'clock*

〜ドル ... *dollars ($)*

〜ねんせい（〜年生）...*th grade*（一年生 *first grade, freshman*）

〜ふん／〜ぷん（〜分）*minutes*

PARTICLE

〜と *and*

OTHERS

〜がつうまれ（〜月生まれ）*a person born in the month of ...*

〜はん（〜半）*half*

ください *Give me ...*

（本を下さい *Give me the book, please.*）

ぜんぶで（全部で）*all together*

CHAPTER FIVE

Coming and Going

Objectives:
- to name common fun places and institutions
- to learn simple phrases for making plans
- to learn and use the verb forms (〜る, 〜ない, 〜ます, 〜ません) for plan/informal speech style and polite/neutral speech style

Kanji and Vocabulary

1. Reading and Writing Kanji Characters

A) Let's read each kanji word or phrase aloud several times, then check how well you can remember what it means.

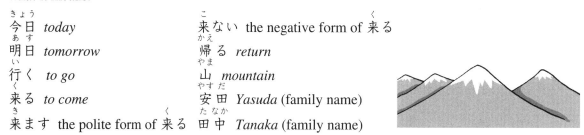

今日 *today*
明日 *tomorrow*
行く *to go*
来る *to come*
来ます *the polite form of* 来る

来ない *the negative form of* 来る
帰る *return*
山 *mountain*
安田 *Yasuda* (family name)
田中 *Tanaka* (family name)

B) In the boxes provided, write each kanji character following the correct stroke order.

| 明 あか‐るい・あ‐ける・メイ *bright, light* | 丨 冂 月 日 旳 明 明 明 [8] |
| 明 | |

- 日 (*sun*) + 月 (*moon*) = 明 (*bright*)

When the "sun" and the "moon" are placed side by side, will it be very BRIGHT?

Example: 明日 *tomorrow,* 明け方 *dawn,* 明るい *bright,* 明治時代 *the Meiji Era*

| 行 い‐く・おこな‐う・コウ・ギョウ *go, conduct, line, column* | ノ ク 彳 彳 行 行 [6] |
| 行 | |

行 appears to have two paths where one can GO and walk on them.

Example: 行く *to go,* 行動 *action/conduct,* 行儀 *manner/behavior;* 銀行 *bank*

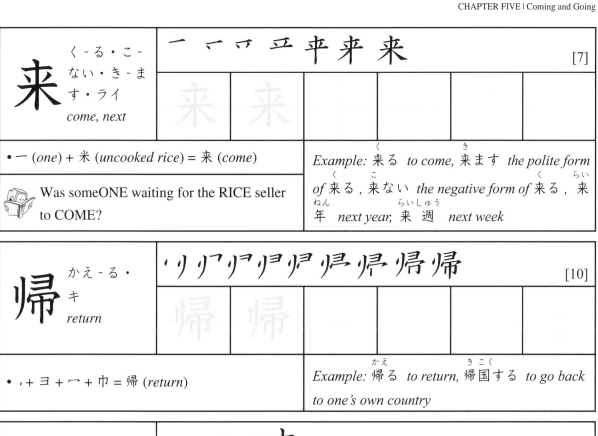

来 く‐る・こ‐ ない・き‐ま す・ライ
come, next

一 ← ⼇ ⼕ 平 来 来 [7]

• 一 (*one*) + 米 (*uncooked rice*) = 来 (*come*)

Was someONE waiting for the RICE seller to COME?

Example: 来る *to come,* 来ます *the polite form of* 来る *,* 来ない *the negative form of* 来る *,* 来年 *next year,* 来週 *next week*

帰 かえ‐る・ キ
return

'丿 刂ˀ 刂ˀ 刂ᵌ 刂ᵌ 帰 帰 帰 帰 [10]

• ⼃ + ヨ + ⼌ + 巾 = 帰 (*return*)

Example: 帰る *to return,* 帰国する *to go back to one's own country*

中 なか・チュウ・ ジュウ
middle, inside

⼂ ⼍ ⼝ 口 中 [4]

• 口 (*mouth*) + | = 中 (*middle*)

Who has a "mouth" that is divided by a vertical line in the MIDDLE?

Example: 田中 *Tanaka (family name),* 中 *inside,* 中国 *China,* 中学校 *middle school,* 一年中 *all year around*

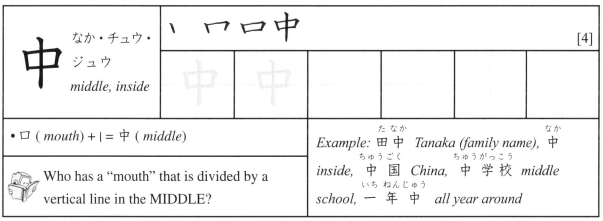

C) Let's read each sentence aloud. Do you know what it means?

1. 田中さんと川口さんは大学の日本ごのクラスのアシスタントです。
2. 安田さんと山田さんは今日うちに来ます。
3. スミスさんは来るつもりですか。来ないつもりですか。
4. 明日は山に行きます。うみには行きません。

D) Fill in the boxes with suitable kanji characters.

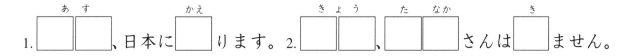

あ す　　　　　　　 かえ　　　　　　 きょう　　　 た なか　　　　　 き
1. ☐☐、日本に☐ります。 2. ☐☐、☐☐さんは☐ません。

E) From the list provided below, pair up any two kanji characters to form three compound words.

日・今・明・本　　1. ☐☐　　2. ☐☐　　3. ☐☐

2. Naming Fun Places

Hidden in the puzzle box below are the names of seven fun places which you would go in the evening, on weekends or whenever you are free. Can you find and list them? The names may be read horizontally or vertically.

1. _____

2. _____

3. _____

4. _____

5. _____

6. _____

7. _____

ば	こ	や	ま	ど
え	う	み	い	う
い	さ	し	ざ	ぶ
が	く	み	か	つ
か	ほ	ん	や	え
ん	こ	う	え	ん

3. Naming Common Institutions

Write down where you can find each item below.

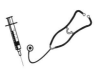

1. ゆう _____

2. びょ _____

3. ぎ _____

Grammar

Japanese has three speech styles: the plain/informal speech style used with one's social insiders and social subordinates, the polite/neutral speech style used with others to show a moderate degree of respect, and the formal speech style used to show the highest degree of politeness and respect. These styles are manifested not only in the choice of words but also in verb forms. Let's look at the verb forms used in the plain/informal and polite/neutral speech styles. For plain/informal speech style, verbs should be in their plain form—their forms as listed in the dictionary or added with ない for present tense. For polite/neutral speech style, one should use the verbs in their polite form—added with the polite suffix ます (affirmative) or ません (negative) for present tense.

1. 〜ます

 Following the examples, conjugate each verb to its polite present affirmative form using the suffix ます. For verbs whose classes are unclear from their ending sounds, their classes are specified.

Example: たべる *to eat* ⟶ <u>たべ</u>ます (If the verb is a ru-verb, drop ru and add ます.)

よむ *to read* ⟶ <u>よみ</u>ます (If the verb is an u-verb, drop u, add i, and then add ます.)

1. かく *to write* ⟶ _____ ます
2. およぐ *to swim* ⟶ _____ ます
3. しぬ *to die* ⟶ _____ ます
4. かう *to buy* ⟶ _____ ます
5. まつ *to wait* ⟶ _____ ます
6. ねる *to sleep* (ru-verb) ⟶ _____ ます
7. とる *to take* ⟶ _____ ます
8. みる *to watch* (ru-verb) ⟶ _____ ます
9. とぶ *to fly* ⟶ _____ ます
10. はなす *to speak* ⟶ _____ ます
11. する *to do* (irregular) ⟶ _____ ます
12. くる *to come* (irregular) ⟶ _____ ます

Note:

- Japanese regular verbs in the dictionary form (what is listed in the dictionary) may end in る, く, ぐ, す, む, ぬ, ぶ, う, or つ, and are classified into ru-verbs and u-verbs.
  - If a verb ends in る and the preceding vowel is e or i, it can be a ru-verb or an u-verb, and you have to memorize them.
  - If a verb ends in る and the preceding vowel is a, u, or o, it is always an u-verb.
  - If a verb ends in any syllable other than る, it is always an u-verb.
- する and くる are irregular verbs, and they become します and きます, respectively.
- In Japanese, the present tense specifies only the future and habitual actions, and it doesn't indicate on-going or progressing actions.

2. 〜ません

Just by replacing ます in the polite present affirmative form of a verb with ません, you can instantly create its negative counterpart.

 Following the example, answer each question in negative. In your answer, you can drop all the phrases except the verb.

Example: 日本に行きますか。　—いいえ、行きません。

1. ゆうびんきょくに行きますか。　　—いいえ、_____。
2. 今日はうちに帰りますか。　　—いいえ、_____。

3.　こんばんはカラオケに行きますか。　　　—いいえ、＿＿＿＿＿＿＿＿＿＿＿＿＿＿＿＿＿＿。

4.　山田さんはここに来ますか。　　　　　　—いいえ、＿＿＿＿＿＿＿＿＿＿＿＿＿＿＿＿＿＿。

5.　明日大学に行きますか。　　　　　　　　—いいえ、＿＿＿＿＿＿＿＿＿＿＿＿＿＿＿＿＿＿。

Note: To indicate where you are going, use particle に, which is equivalent to preposition "to" in English. However, unlike "to" in English, "に" should be placed after the destination, as in "とうきょうに".

3. 〜ない

A) Following the examples, conjugate each verb to its plain present negative form that ends in ない.

Example: たべる *to eat* (ru-verb) ⟶ たべない (If the verb is a ru-verb, drop ru and add ない .)

よむ *to read* ⟶ よまない (If the verb is an u-verb, drop u, add a, and then add ない .)

1.　かく *to write* ⟶ ＿＿＿＿＿ない
2.　のむ *to drink* ⟶ ＿＿＿＿＿ない
3.　およぐ *to swim* ⟶ ＿＿＿＿＿ない
4.　しぬ *to die* ⟶ ＿＿＿＿＿ない
5.　かう *to buy* ⟶ ＿＿＿＿＿ない
6.　まつ *to wait* ⟶ ＿＿＿＿＿ない
7.　ねる *to sleep* (ru-verb) ⟶ ＿＿＿＿＿ない
8.　とる *to take* ⟶ ＿＿＿＿＿ない
9.　みる *to watch* (ru-verb) ⟶ ＿＿＿＿＿ない
10.　とぶ *to fly* ⟶ ＿＿＿＿＿ない
11.　はなす *to speak* ⟶ ＿＿＿＿＿ない
12.　する *to do* (irregular) ⟶ ＿＿＿＿＿ない
13.　くる *to come* (irregular) ⟶ ＿＿＿＿＿ない

Note:

- Watch out for the verbs which end in う. The negative form of かう is かわない, and NOT かあない. This type of verb includes the hidden consonant w, which is manifested only when followed by the vowel a.
- する and くる are irregular, and they become しない and こない, respectively.

B) Fill in the blanks with the correct form of verbs.

Example: 帰る ・帰らない ・帰ります ・帰りません

1.　来る　　・＿＿＿＿＿＿＿＿　・＿＿＿＿＿＿＿＿　・＿来ません＿
2.　行く　　・＿＿＿＿＿＿＿＿　・＿行きます＿　・＿＿＿＿＿＿＿＿
3.　うたう　・＿＿＿＿＿＿＿＿　・＿＿＿＿＿＿＿＿　・＿うたいません＿
4.　わかる　・＿わからない＿　・＿＿＿＿＿＿＿＿　・＿＿＿＿＿＿＿＿

4. あまり／ぜんぜん／よく

The frequency adverbs あまり ((*not*) *very often*) and ぜんぜん (*never*) must be used with a negative verb. By contrast, よく (*often*) is used with an affirmative verb.

Form grammatical sentences following the example.

Example: デパート・あまり ⟶ デパートにはあまり行きません。

1. レストラン・あまり ⟶ _____。
2. いざかや・ぜんぜん ⟶ _____。
3. カラオケ・よく ⟶ _____。
4. 本や・あまり ⟶ _____。

Note: Particles such as は and も can follow a grammatical particle such as に.

Conversation and Usage

1. Making Plans for Tonight

In an informal conversation, the question particle か is either omitted or replaced by の, and はい (*yes*) and いいえ (*no*) are replaced by うん and うんんん, respectively. Particles and the copula です are also frequently omitted.

Two roommates are discussing their plans for the evening. Listen to their conversation carefully (paying attention to the intonation) and answer the questions that follow.

ゆきこ ： 今晩バイトに行く？

あきこ ： うんんん、行かない。

ゆきこ ： ああ、そう。

あきこ ： うん。

ゆきこ ： じゃあ、今晩テニス部の飲み会に来る？

あきこ ： どこ？

ゆきこ ： くろふね。

あきこ ： いいの？

ゆきこ ： いいよ。

あきこ ： 何時？

ゆきこ ： 7時。

あきこ　：あ、そう。

ゆきこ　：ああ、会費は 3,000 円よ。

あきこ　：えっ、高い！

ゆきこ　：そう？でも、すしの食べ放題よ！

あきこ　：うん。でも、私、行かない。ごめん。

[**Unfamiliar words:** バイト (= アルバイト) *part-time job,* テニス部 *tennis club,* 飲み会 *party (with alcohol),* 会費 *participation fee,* すしの食べ放題よ！ *You can eat sushi as much as you like,* ごめん *an informal short version of* ごめんなさい *(I'm sorry.)*]

1. Will Akiko go to work tonight?　＿＿＿＿＿＿＿＿＿＿＿＿＿＿

2. Where is Yukiko going tonight?　＿＿＿＿＿＿＿＿＿＿＿＿＿＿

3. Is Akiko going to the same place as Yukiko tonight? Why?　＿＿＿＿＿＿＿＿＿＿

2. Situational Response

In the following situations, what would you say in Japanese?

1. You are talking with Kenji, and you want to ask him if he will go to class today.

　＿＿＿＿＿＿＿＿＿＿＿＿＿＿＿＿＿＿＿＿＿＿＿＿＿＿＿＿＿＿＿＿＿＿

2. You are talking with Tomoko. You would like to ask her whether she often goes to Izakaya.

　＿＿＿＿＿＿＿＿＿＿＿＿＿＿＿＿＿＿＿＿＿＿＿＿＿＿＿＿＿＿＿＿＿＿

3. You are with Takeshi, and you have just thought of going to a restaurant with him tonight.

　＿＿＿＿＿＿＿＿＿＿＿＿＿＿＿＿＿＿＿＿＿＿＿＿＿＿＿＿＿＿＿＿＿＿

4. Your friend has just suggested going to the bookstore, and you want to go there with him.

　＿＿＿＿＿＿＿＿＿＿＿＿＿＿＿＿＿＿＿＿＿＿＿＿＿＿＿＿＿＿＿＿＿＿

Note: When you want to make a suggestion nicely or politely, ask by using the negative question with ませんか. For example, 本やに行きませんか means *Why don't we go to the bookstore?*. To say "Let's do ...", use ましょう; as in 本やに行きましょう *Let's go to the bookstore.*

Listening Comprehension

About the Places to Go

Listen carefully to the narrative on the CD and determine whether the following statements are true or false.

1. This person often goes to a bookstore.　　(True • False)

2. This person often goes to a library.　　(True • False)

3. This person often goes to a movie theater.　　(True • False)

Reading Comprehension

1. Reading a Timetable

JR東海道新幹線　新大阪方面下り（東京～新大阪）［平日］

列車番号		1A	9201A	597A	41A	561A	9171A	361A	3A	9303A	531A
列車名		[新幹線] のぞみ 1号	[新幹線] のぞみ 201号	[新幹線] こだま 597号	[新幹線] のぞみ 41号	[新幹線] こだま 561号	[新幹線] のぞみ 171号	[新幹線] ひかり 361号	[新幹線] のぞみ 3号	[新幹線] のぞみ 303号	[新幹線] こだま 531号
東京	発	06:00	06:05		06:20	06:23	06:26	06:36	06:50	06:53	06:56
品川	発	06:06	06:12		06:27	06:30	06:34	レ	06:58	07:01	07:04
新横浜	発	06:18	06:24		06:39	06:42	06:46	06:53	07:09	07:13	07:15
小田原	発	レ	レ		レ	07:02	レ	07:10	レ	レ	07:37
熱海	発	レ	レ		レ	07:12	レ	レ	レ	レ	07:47
三島	着	レ	レ	—	レ	07:21	レ	レ	レ	レ	07:54
〃	発	レ	レ	—	レ	07:27	レ	レ	レ	レ	08:00
新富士	発	レ	レ		レ	07:43	レ	レ	レ	レ	08:10
静岡	着	レ	レ	—	レ	07:55	レ	レ	レ	レ	08:22
〃	発	レ	レ	06:44	レ	07:58	レ	レ	レ	レ	08:25
掛川	発	レ	レ	06:59	レ	08:14	レ	レ	レ	レ	08:44
浜松	着	レ	レ	07:10	レ	08:25	レ	レ	レ	レ	08:56
〃	発	レ	レ	07:13	レ	08:31	レ	レ	レ	レ	08:59
豊橋	発	レ	レ	07:29	レ	08:51	レ	レ	レ	レ	09:18
三河安城	発	レ	レ	07:44	レ	09:07	レ	レ	レ	レ	09:34
名古屋	着	07:39	07:47	07:56	08:02	09:19	08:09	08:22	08:33	08:36	09:46
〃	発	07:40	07:48	07:58	08:03	—	08:11	08:24	08:34	08:38	09:48
岐阜羽島	発	レ	レ	08:13	レ		レ	08:37	レ	レ	09:59
米原	発	レ	レ	08:30	レ		レ	08:57	レ	レ	10:19
京都	着	08:16	08:24	08:55	08:40	—	08:47	09:20	09:11	09:14	10:40
〃	発	08:17	08:25	08:56	08:41	—	08:48	09:21	09:12	09:16	10:41
新大阪	着	08:30	08:40	09:13	08:56		09:02	09:36	09:27	09:30	10:56

しんかんせん
新 幹 線 is a network of high-speed railway lines in Japan. One of them is the じぇーあーるとうかいどうしんかんせん JR 東海道新幹線 which runs between とうきょう 東京 and しんおおさか 新大阪, going through しながわ 品川, しんよこはま 新横浜, おだわら 小田原, あたみ 熱海, みしま 三島, しんふじ 新富士, しずおか 静岡, かけがわ 掛川, はままつ 浜松, とよはし 豊橋, みかわあん じょう 三河安城, なごや 名古屋, ぎふはしま 岐阜羽島, まいばら 米原 and きょうと 京都. There are three types of trains operating on this line: from the fastest to slowest, they are のぞみ, ひかり and こだま. Here is a timetable of the trains on service. Study it carefully, then answer the following questions.

1. How long does こだま take to arrive at Shin-Osaka when it leaves Tokyo at 6:20 a.m.?

2. How long does こだま take to arrive at Shin-Osaka when it departs Tokyo at 6:56 a.m.?

_____

3. If you want to arrive at 静岡 before 8 a.m., which 新幹線 is the latest one you can take from Tokyo?

_____

2. Planning for Tomorrow and The Day After Tomorrow

Read the following passage and answer the questions.

明日はバイトに行きます。それから、としょかんに行きます。それから、スーパーマーケットに行きます。あさってはバイトに行きません。としょかんにも行きません。でも、デパートに行きます。

[**Unfamiliar words:** あさって *the day after tomorrow,* バイト (or アルバイト) *part-time job,* それから *and then*]

1. Where is this person going tomorrow? _____

2. Where is this person going the day after tomorrow? _____

Writing

Essay Writing

Write about where you plan to go tomorrow and the day after tomorrow.

_____

_____

_____

_____

_____

_____

_____

_____

New Vocabulary Reference List

NOUN

あす（明日）・あした *tomorrow*

いざかや（居酒屋）*Izakaya bar (casual Japanese-style bar)*

うち（家）*house, home*

うみ（海）*sea, ocean*

えいがかん（映画館）*movie theater*

カラオケ *karaoke*

きょう（今日）*today*

ぎんこう（銀行）*bank*

クラス *class*

こうえん（公園）*park*

こんばん（今晩）*this evening, tonight*

しゅうまつ（週末）*weekend*

デパート *department store*

どうぶつえん（動物園）*zoo*

びょういん（病院）*hospital*

ほんや（本屋）*bookstore*

やま（山）*mountain*

ゆうがた（夕方）*early evening, dusk*

ゆうびんきょく（郵便局）*post office*

レストラン *restaurant*

PRONOUN

あそこ *over there*

ここ *here*

そこ *there (near you)*

QUESTION WORD

どこ *where*

ADJECTIVE

ひまな（暇な）*not busy, free*

ADVERB

あまり（〜ない）*(not) often, (not) much*

ぜんぜん（〜ない）*(not) at all*

ときどき（時々）*sometimes*

よく *often, well*

VERB (U-verb)

いく（行く）*to go*

うたう（歌う）*to sing*

かえる（帰る）*to return to one's home, country, or base*

わかる（分かる）*to understand, to know*

VERB (Irregular Verb)

くる（来る）*to come*

CONJUNCTION

でも *but, however*

PARTICLE

〜に *to ...*

OTHERS

〜ます *polite present affirmative suffix for verbs*

〜ません *polite present negative suffix for verbs*

CHAPTER SIX

Describing Daily-life Activities

Objectives:

- to name different forms of transportation, favorite pastime activities and common food items
- to learn simple phrases for ordering foods
- to learn and use the past verb forms (ました, ませんでした)
- to learn and use particles で, が and を

Kanji and Vocabulary

1. Reading and Writing Kanji Characters I

A) Let's read each kanji word or phrase aloud several times, then check how well you can remember what it means.

でん車 *train*
じてん車 *bicycle*
歩いて *by walking, on foot*
飲む *to drink*
作る *to make*

買う *to buy*
食べる *to eat*
書く *to write*
使う *to use*
見る *to look at*

B) In the boxes provided, write each kanji character following the correct stroke order.

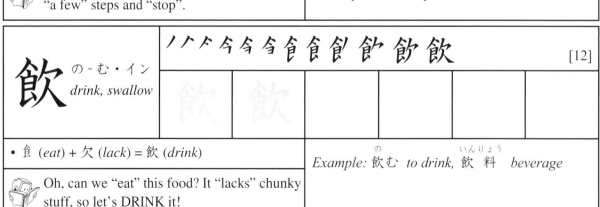

歩 ある-く・あゆ-む・ホ・ポ walk	丨 丨ㅏ 丨ㅏ 止 步 步 步 歩 [8]
• 止 (*to stop*) + 少 (*a few*) = 歩 (*walk*)	*Example:* 歩く *to walk,* 歩いて *on foot,* 一歩 *one step,* 歩行者 *pedestrian*
When a baby learns to WALK, it often goes "a few" steps and "stop".	

飲 の-む・イン drink, swallow	ノ 𠂉 𠂉 今 今 今 食 食 飮 飲 飲 飲 [12]
• 食 (*eat*) + 欠 (*lack*) = 飲 (*drink*)	*Example:* 飲む *to drink,* 飲料 *beverage*
Oh, can we "eat" this food? It "lacks" chunky stuff, so let's DRINK it!	

食

た-べる・ショク
eat, food

ノ 人 へ 今 今 今 食 食 食 [9]

- へ + 良 (good) = 食 (food)

It is "good" to EAT under the "tent" because we don't want to have inchworms in our FOOD (taking へ as a "tent").

Example: 食べる *to eat*, 食堂 *dining room/restaurant*, 食事 *meal*, 日本食 *Japanese foods*

書

か-く・ショ
write, book, document

フ ヲ ヲ ヨ 聿 聿 書 書 書 書 [10]

聿 shows a hand ヨ holding a brush (大). When combined with 日 (sun/day), it suggests WRITE "daily" and we will end up with DOCUMENTS and BOOKS.

Example: 書く *to write*, 書道 *calligraphy*, 教科書 *textbook*

作

つく-る・サク・サ
make, produce

ノ イ イ 个 作 作 作 作 [7]

- イ (person) + 乍 = 作 (make/produce)

With a "saw", a "person" is able to MAKE or PRODUCE something (taking 乍 as a "saw").

Example: 作る *to make*, 作文 *composition (writing)*, 操作 *operation*

使

つか-う・シ
use, servant

ノ イ 亻 仁 仁 佢 佢 使 使 [8]

- イ (person) + 吏 (official) = 使 (servant)

That "person" is the SERVANT of an "official".

Example: 使う *to use*

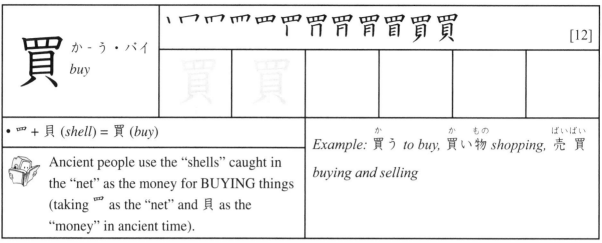

買 か‐う・バイ buy

ノ 冂 冂 罒 罒 罒 罒 罒 胃 胃 買 買 [12]

• 罒 + 貝 (shell) = 買 (buy)

Ancient people use the "shells" caught in the "net" as the money for BUYING things (taking 罒 as the "net" and 貝 as the "money" in ancient time).

Example: 買う *to buy,* 買い物 *shopping,* 売買 *buying and selling*

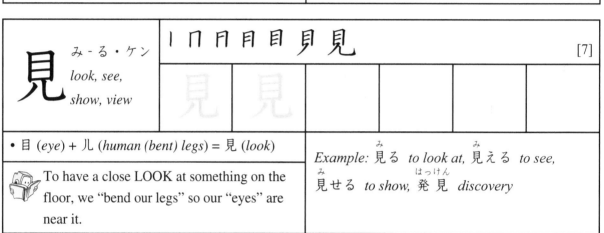

見 み‐る・ケン look, see, show, view

｜ 冂 冂 目 目 目 見 見 [7]

• 目 (eye) + 儿 (human (bent) legs) = 見 (look)

To have a close LOOK at something on the floor, we "bend our legs" so our "eyes" are near it.

Example: 見る *to look at,* 見える *to see,* 見せる *to show,* 発見 *discovery*

C) Draw lines to match.

| 買う | 見る | 食べる | 飲む | 書く |

2. Reading and Writing Kanji Characters II

A) Let's read each kanji word or phrase aloud several times. Circle the characters you have learned before.

〜時間 ... *hours*

〜分(間) or 〜分(間) ... *minutes*

晩 *evening*

昨日 *yesterday*

朝 *morning*　　　今朝 *this morning*
あさ　　　　　　けさ

昼 *noon*　　　今晩 *this evening*
ひる　　　　　　こんばん

B) In the boxes provided, write each kanji character following the correct stroke order.

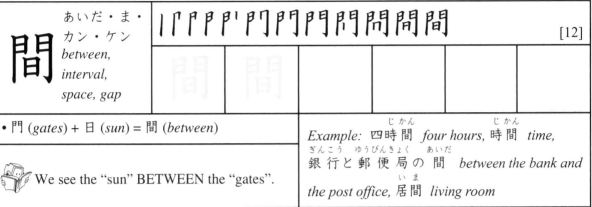

間 あいだ・ま・カン・ケン *between, interval, space, gap*	｜ 冂 冂 冂 冃 門 門 門 門 閇 閇 間 [12]

• 門 (*gates*) + 日 (*sun*) = 間 (*between*)

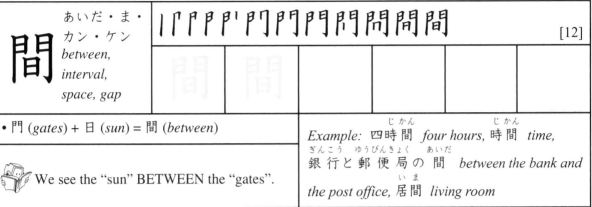 We see the "sun" BETWEEN the "gates".

Example: 四時間 *four hours*, 時間 *time*,
じかん　　　　　　じかん
銀行と郵便局の 間 *between the bank and*
ぎんこう　ゆうびんきょく　あいだ
the post office, 居間 *living room*
いま

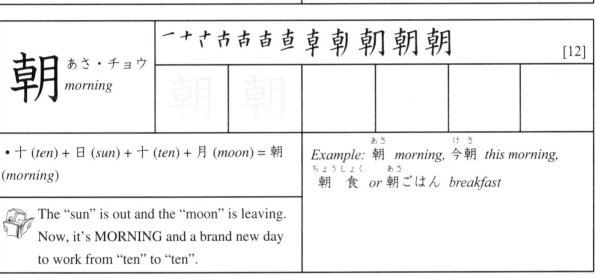

朝 あさ・チョウ *morning*	一 十 六 古 古 古 直 卓 朝 朝 朝 朝 [12]

• 十 (*ten*) + 日 (*sun*) + 十 (*ten*) + 月 (*moon*) = 朝 (*morning*)

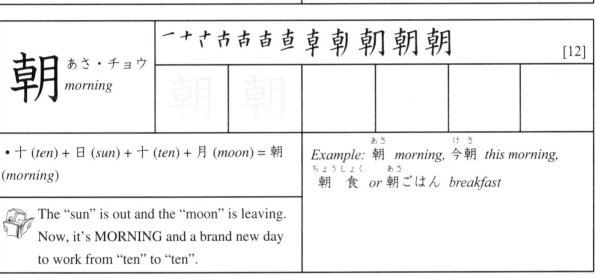 The "sun" is out and the "moon" is leaving. Now, it's MORNING and a brand new day to work from "ten" to "ten".

Example: 朝 *morning*, 今朝 *this morning*,
あさ　　　けさ
朝 食 *or* 朝ごはん *breakfast*
ちょうしょく　あさ

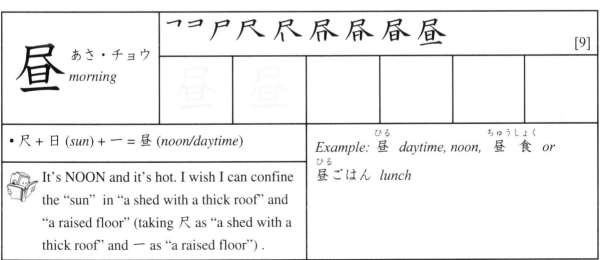

昼 あさ・チョウ *morning*	フ コ ユ 尸 尺 尺 尽 昼 昼 [9]

• 尺 + 日 (*sun*) + 一 = 昼 (*noon/daytime*)

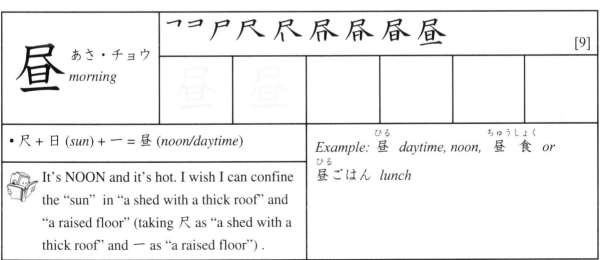 It's NOON and it's hot. I wish I can confine the "sun" in "a shed with a thick roof" and "a raised floor" (taking 尺 as "a shed with a thick roof" and 一 as "a raised floor").

Example: 昼 *daytime, noon*, 昼 食 *or*
ひる　　　　　　ちゅうしょく
昼ごはん *lunch*
ひる

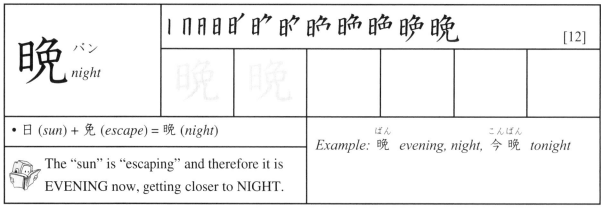

晩 バン night

一 ∩ 日 日 日' 日免 日免 日免 晚 晚 晚 [12]

• 日 (*sun*) + 免 (*escape*) = 晩 (*night*)

The "sun" is "escaping" and therefore it is EVENING now, getting closer to NIGHT.

Example: 晩 *evening, night,* 今晩 *tonight*
(ばん) (こんばん)

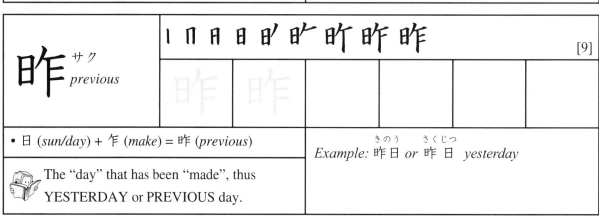

昨 サク previous

一 ∩ 日 日 日' 日乍 昨 昨 昨 [9]

• 日 (*sun/day*) + 乍 (*make*) = 昨 (*previous*)

The "day" that has been "made", thus YESTERDAY or PREVIOUS day.

Example: 昨日 *or* 昨日 *yesterday*
(きのう) (さくじつ)

C) How well do you remember the kanji you've learned so far? To find out, let's read the following passages aloud.

1. 私は歩いて大学に行きます。10分ぐらいです。田中さんは車で大学に行きます。1時間ぐらいかかります。山田さんはじてん車と、でん車で行きます。1時間20分ぐらいかかります。

2. 今朝は朝ごはんを食べませんでした。昼ごはんはサラダを食べました。今晩はたくさん食べるつもりです。今晩の晩ごはんはてんぷらです。私が作ります。ビールも飲みます。昨日の晩もビールを飲みました。

3. 昨日はくつを買いました。それから、えいがを見ました。

4. かんじをたくさん書きました。ペンを使いました。

D) Fill in the correct kanji characters in the boxes provided.

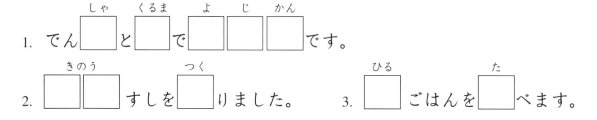

1. でん □（しゃ）と □（くるま）で □（よ）□（じ）□（かん）です。

2. □（きの）□（う）すしを □（つく）りました。　3. □（ひる）ごはんを □（た）べます。

E) List as many kanji characters as you can that have

1. 日 as a component, for example 間 .

_____

2. 月 as a component.

_____

3. イ as a component.

_____

F) おくりがな

おくりがな is the hiragana character representing inflectional ending that is added at the end of a kanji character. For example, い in 高い (*expensive*) and う in 買う (*to buy*) are おくりがな . You need to remember what おくりがな is needed for each kanji word. For example, which is correct, 食べる or 食る ? The おくりがな needed in this case is べる , so 食べる is correct. Which is correct, 使う or 使かう ? The おくりがな needed in this case is う , so 使う is correct.

Add おくりがな to each kanji character following the example.

Example: 食 ___べる___ *to eat*

1.	書 _____ *to write*	4.	作 _____ *to make*	7.	飲 _____ *to drink*
2.	買 _____ *to buy*	5.	行 _____ *to go*	8.	見 _____ *to look at*
3.	使 _____ *to use*	6.	歩 _____ *to walk*		

3. Naming Different Forms of Transportation

Draw lines to match.

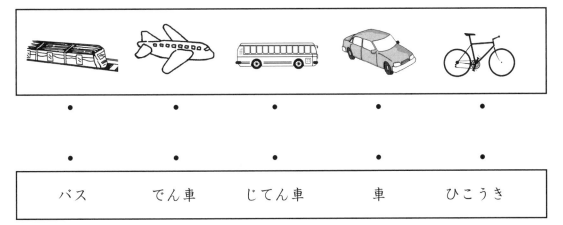

バス　　　　でん車　　　じてん車　　　車　　　ひこうき

4. Learn about Pastime Activities

Fill in the blanks with the words listed below.

{うた・ざっし・えいが・てがみ}

1. 兄はよく＿＿＿＿＿＿＿＿を読みます。　　3. 私はしゅうまつ＿＿＿＿＿＿を見ます。

2. ひまな時、＿＿＿＿＿＿を書きます。　　4. カラオケ・ボックスで＿＿＿＿＿＿を
　　　　　　　　　　　　　　　　　　　　　　　うたいます。

Grammar

1. Present/Past

The past counterparts of ます and ません are ました and ませんでした, respectively. They follow the verbs in the stem form and express the past action or habit.

Following the example, answer each question in negative, paying attention to the tense.

Example: A: てんぷらを食べましたか。

B: いいえ、食べませんでした。

1. A: おさけを飲みましたか。

   B: いいえ、＿＿＿＿＿＿＿＿＿＿＿＿＿＿＿＿＿。

2. A: ギャンブルをしますか。

   B: いいえ、＿＿＿＿＿＿＿＿＿＿＿＿＿＿＿＿＿。

3. A: ざっしを買いましたか。

   B: いいえ、＿＿＿＿＿＿＿＿＿＿＿＿＿＿＿＿＿。

4. A: よくテレビを見ますか。

   B: いいえ、＿＿＿＿＿＿＿＿＿＿＿＿＿＿＿＿＿。

5. A: 私の車を使いましたか。

   B: いいえ、＿＿＿＿＿＿＿＿＿＿＿＿＿＿＿＿＿。

2. Particle で

The noun marked by the particle で shows how an action takes place, specifying the instrument, method, mean, form of transportation used and location of an activity.

Fill in the blanks using で or に.

1. ゆきこさんはアメリカ＿＿＿来ます。

2. ゆきこさんはアメリカ＿＿＿べんきょうします。

3. 父はよくレストラン＿＿＿行きます。

4. 父はよくレストラン＿＿＿食べます。

5. スミスさんはうち ＿＿＿ 帰りました。

6. ペン ＿＿＿ てがみを書きます。

7. フォークとナイフ ＿＿＿ ステーキを食べます。

8. 日本のアニメは日本ご ＿＿＿ 見ます。

3. Particle が/を and Transitive/Intransitive Verbs

The particle が marks the subject and the particle を marks the direct object in a sentence.

In the following sentences, fill in the blanks with appropriate noun phrases from Box A and particles from Box B. There will be more than one answer.

Example: 兄がすしを食べました。

1. 父が ＿＿＿＿＿＿＿＿＿ 書きました。

2. おとうとが ＿＿＿＿＿＿＿ 使いました。

3. いもうとは ＿＿＿＿＿＿＿ ねました。

4. ＿＿＿＿＿＿＿＿＿ 来ました。

5. 私は ＿＿＿＿＿＿＿＿＿ 行きました。

6. マイクさんは昨日 ＿＿＿＿＿＿＿＿
   べんきょう
   勉 強 しました。

Box A		**Box B**
山田さん	兄	が
てがみ	すし	
ねこ	大学	に
私のじてん車	としょかん	
母のベッド	日本ご	で
まんねんひつ	車	
(fountain pen)	ここ	を

Note: In English, the subject is the noun (phrase) right before the verb and the direct object is the noun (phrase) right after the verb. To give you an idea of what a subject or a direct object is, let's consider this sentence "Mary invites her friend to her house for dinner every Sunday". There are 5 noun phrases in this sentence, namely, "Mary", "her friend", "her house", "dinner", and "every Sunday", but "Mary" is the only subject and "her friend" is the only direct object. A subject is normally present in any English sentence, but a direct object is present only if the verb is a transitive verb such as "to invite". For example, there is no direct object in the sentence "Mary runs with her friend on Sundays". Here, the noun phrase (her friend) after the verb is not a direct object because it is not immediately after the verb and the verb "run" is not a transitive verb but an intransitive verb.

4. Particles

In each of the following, form a sentence by adding an appropriate particle. Do not use は or も.

Example: としょかん・勉強 しました ⟶　　としょかんで勉強 しました。

1. 車・買いました　　⟶　　_____

2. 兄・車・買いました　　⟶　　_____

3. 車・兄・買いました　　⟶　　_____

4. じてん車・大学・行きました　　⟶　　_____

5. て・すし・食べました　　⟶　　_____

6. 日本・日本ご・勉 強 しました　　⟶　　_____

7. 兄・ここ・来ました　　⟶　　_____

Conversation and Usage

1. Sharing Personal Information

In a conversation, ～んです is often added at the end of a sentence to make the conversation more interactive.

Listen to the conversation between Kenji and his female colleague Shizuka on the CD, and specify if each of the following statements is "true" or "false".

けんじ 　：あしたの土曜日、いっしょに映画を見ませんか？

しずか 　：うんん、ちょっと。

けんじ 　：あしたは 忙 しいんですか。

しずか 　：あしたは松坂屋に行くんです。ウエディングドレスを見るんです。

けんじ 　：えっ？

しずか 　：私、6月に結婚するんです。

けんじ 　：えっ？本当ですか。

しずか 　：ええ。

けんじ 　：お相手は？

しずか 　：相手は同じ会社の人です。

けんじ 　：えっ？

しずか 　：山下さんです。

けんじ 　：えっ？ぼくのアシスタントの山下？

しずか　：ええ。

けんじ　：本当ですか？

しずか　：ええ。

けんじ　：ああ、そうですか。おめでとうございます。

しずか　：ありがとうございます。

けんじ　：式は？

しずか　：式はハワイで挙げるつもりです。

けんじ　：ああ。

[**Unfamiliar words:** 忙しい *busy*, 松坂屋 *Matsuzakaya (A well-known Japanese department store)*, ウエディングドレス *wedding gown*, 結婚する *to get married*, 本当 *truth*, 相手 *partner*, 同じ *same*, 会社 *company*, おめでとうございます。 *Congratulations*, 式 *ceremony*, 挙げる *to have (a ceremony)*]

1. Shizuka will go to see a movie with Kenji tomorrow.　　　(True • False)
2. Kenji is Shizuka's fiancé's assistant.　　　(True • False)
3. Shizuka will get married in June.　　　(True • False)

Note:　Always add つもりです at the end of the sentence to mean "I plan to do ...", and the verbs must be in the plain form.

Examples: 結婚式に行くつもりです。　*I plan to go to the wedding ceremony.*

結婚式に行かないつもりです。　*I plan not to go to the wedding ceremony.*

2. Ordering at the Fast Food Restaurant

A customer is ordering food from a store clerk at a fast food restaurant. Listen to their conversation carefully and answer the questions that follow.

店員　：いらっしゃいませ。ご注文は？

客　　：チーズバーガーを一つと、テリヤキバーガーを二つと、コーラを一つと、オレンジジュースを二つお願いします。

店員　：はい。チーズバーガーをおーつと、テリヤキバーガーをお二つと、コーラをおーつと、オレンジジュースをおーつですね。

客　　：いいえ、オレンジジュースは二つです。

店員　：あ、失礼いたしました。

[**Unfamiliar words:** ご 注 文 は ? *How about your order?,* テリヤキバーガー *teriyaki burger,* 失 礼 いたしました *I am sorry.*]

1. How many cheese burgers were ordered? _____

2. How many teriyaki burgers were ordered? _____

3. What beverages were ordered? How many for each? _____

3. Situational Response

In the following situations, what would you say in Japanese?

1. You want to ask your classmate (田中さん) how he commutes to school.

_____

2. You want to ask your friend (山田さん) what she usually does when she is free.

_____

3. At a party, you met an American student (トム Tom) who speaks very fluent Japanese. You want to ask him where he studied Japanese.

_____

Listening Comprehension

Commuting to College

Takako is a college student. She goes to her college by taking the Yamanote Line (山手線). Listen to her narrative on the CD, and answer the questions in English. You may encounter unfamiliar words in this exercise.

1. From what railway station does she take the Yamanote Line to her college?

_____

2. At what railway station does she get off the Yamanote Line when she goes to her college?

_____

3. How long does it take from her home to her college, door to door?

_____

Reading Comprehension

Reading a Menu

The following is a menu of a fast food restaurant. Study it carefully and answer the questions.

ハンバーガー メニュー	ハンバーガー	¥250
	ビッグバーガー	¥280
	チーズバーガー	¥280
	ダブルチーズバーガー	¥290
	テリヤキバーガー	¥280
	テリヤキチキンバーガー	¥290
	フィッシュバーガー	¥290
ドリンクメニュー	コールドドリンク	
	コーラ	(S) ¥100　(M) ¥180　(L) ¥200
	ジンジャエール	(S) ¥100　(M) ¥180　(L) ¥200
	メロンソーダ	(S) ¥100　(M) ¥180　(L) ¥200
	オレンジジュース	¥100
	アップルジュース	¥100
	アイスティー(レモン・ミルク)	(S) ¥100　(M) ¥180　(L) ¥200
	アイスコーヒー	(S) ¥100　(L) ¥200
	シェイク(バニラ・ ストロベリー・チョコレート)	(S) ¥100　(L) ¥200
	ホットドリンク	
	ホットティー(レモン・ミルク)	¥180
	ブレンドコーヒー	(S) ¥100　(L) ¥200
	ホットココア	¥180
サイドメニュー	サラダ	¥200
	フライポテト	(S) ¥200　(M) ¥250　(L) ¥300
	チキンナゲット	¥200
セットメニュー	ハンバーガーセット	¥600 ＋ドリンク＆フライポテト (M)
	ビッグバーガーセット	¥630 ＋ドリンク＆フライポテト (M)
	チーズバーガーセット	¥630 ＋ドリンク＆フライポテト (M)
+	ダブルチーズバーガーセット	¥640 ＋ドリンク＆フライポテト (M)
	テリヤキバーガーセット	¥630 ＋ドリンク＆フライポテト (M)
	テリヤキチキンバーガーセット	¥640 ＋ドリンク＆フライポテト (M)
	フィッシュバーガーセット	¥640 ＋ドリンク＆フライポテト (M)

1. How much is a teriyaki burger?   ¥ _____

2. How much is a medium-sized coke?   ¥ _____

3. How much is medium-sized French fries?   ¥ _____

4. How much can you save if you order the above
    three items, one of each, as a set menu?   ¥ _____

Writing

Making a Shopping List

Make a list of the things you need to get in your next trip to the supermarket. For items you do not know what they are called in Japanese, list them in katakana.

ショッピングリスト

_____

_____

_____

_____

_____

_____

_____

_____

_____

New Vocabulary Reference List

NOUN

あさ（朝）morning

あさごはん（朝御飯）breakfast

アパート apartment

えいが（映画）movie, film

きのう（昨日）yesterday

けさ（今朝）this morning

ごはん（ご飯）cooked rice, meal

ざっし（雑誌）magazine

じてんしゃ（自転車）bicycle

しんぶん（新聞）newspaper

スプーン spoon

ちかてつ（地下鉄）subway

ていしょく（定食）set menu

てがみ（手紙）letter

でんしゃ（電車）(electric) train

はし・おはし（箸・お箸）chopsticks

ばん（晩）evening, night

ばんごはん（晩御飯）supper, dinner

ひこうき（飛行機）airplane

ひる（昼）noon, daytime

ひるごはん（昼御飯）lunch

プール swimming pool

みそしる（味噌汁）miso soup

ようふく（洋服）clothes

ADJECTIVE

たいへんな（大変な）hard, excessive, (trouble/
work) intensive

ADVERB

いつも always, all the time

たいてい usually, in general

VERB (Ru-Verb)

たべる（食べる）to eat

みる（見る）to watch, to look at

VERB (U-Verb)

あるく（歩く）to walk

およぐ（泳ぐ）to swim

かう（買う）to buy

かかる to cost, to take

かく（書く）to write

つかう（使う）to use

つくる（作る）to make

ねる（寝る）to go to bed, to sleep

のむ（飲む）to drink

ひく（弾く）to play (string instruments and
keyboards)

ふく（吹く）to blow, to play (wind instruments)

よむ（読む）to read

IRREGULAR VERB

する to do

べんきょうする（勉強する）to study

CONJUNCTION

それから and then, in addition

PARTICLE

〜で by ..., in ..., at ..., with ...

〜が subject marker

〜を direct object marker

COUNTER

〜じかん（〜時間）... hours

〜ふん（かん）／〜ぷん（かん）（〜分（間））...
minutes (the duration of time)

OTHERS

〜ぐらい／〜くらい approximately ..., about ...

〜つもりです to plan to do ...

〜ました polite past affirmative suffix for verbs

〜ませんでした polite past negative suffix for
verbs

〜んです It is the case that ... .

あるいて（歩いて）on foot, by walking

どれぐらい approximately how long/much/many

ひとつ（一つ）one (piece)

ふたつ（二つ）two (pieces)

CHAPTER SEVEN

Location of People and Things

Objectives:
- to name various common buildings, the things in a room and compass directions
- to learn simple phrases for calling a store and looking for direction
- to learn and use the grammar items ある, いる, いらっしゃる, relative location terms and particles に and で

Kanji and Vocabulary

1. Reading and Writing Kanji Characters I

A) Let's read each kanji word or phrase aloud several times, then check how well you can remember what it means.

木 *tree*
（あいだ）
間 *between*
（ちか）
近く *near*
（うえ）
上 *top*

（した）
下 *bottom*
（なか）
中 *middle*
（みぎ）
右 *right*
（ひだり）
左 *left*

B) In the boxes provided, write each kanji character following the correct stroke order.

| 木 | き・(ぎ)・モク・ボク tree, wood | 一 十 才 木 [4] |

• This character is also a component in many other characters such as 森 (*forest*), 休 (*to rest*), 枚 (counter for flat items) and 楽 (*fun*).

 resembles a TREE　　　*Example:* 木 (き) *tree*, 木曜日 (もくようび) *Thursday*

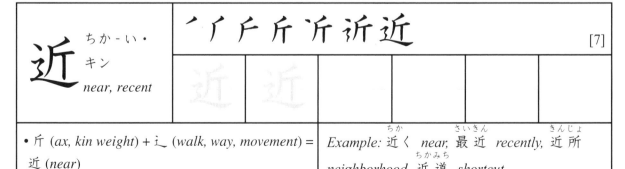

| 近 | ちか-い・キン near, recent | ノ 丶 厂 斤 斤 斤 近 近 [7] |

• 斤 (*ax, kin weight*) + 辶 (*walk, way, movement*) = 近 (*near*)

Example: 近く (ちか) *near*, 最近 (さいきん) *recently*, 近所 (きんじょ) *neighborhood*, 近道 (ちかみち) *shortcut*

 When you "walk" with a heavy "weight", you will not reach far, but end up somewhere NEAR.

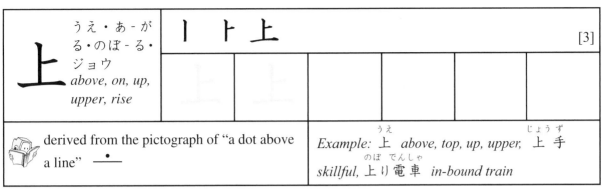

上　うえ・あ-が　る・のぼ-る・　ジョウ　*above, on, up, upper, rise*

｜　卜　上　[3]

derived from the pictograph of "a dot above a line" ――•――

Example: 上 *above, top, up, upper,* 上手 *skillful,* 上り電車 *in-bound train*

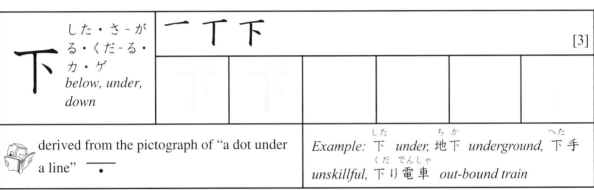

下　した・さ-が　る・くだ-る・　カ・ゲ　*below, under, down*

一　丁　下　[3]

derived from the pictograph of "a dot under a line" ――•――

Example: 下 *under,* 地下 *underground,* 下手 *unskillful,* 下り電車 *out-bound train*

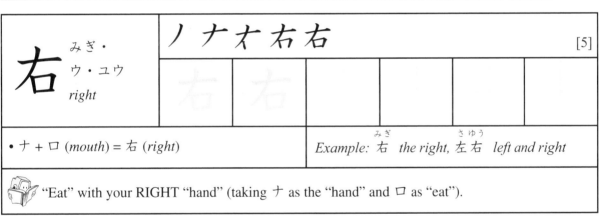

右　みぎ・　ウ・ユウ　*right*

ノ　ナ　オ　ナ　右　右　[5]

• ナ + 口 (*mouth*) = 右 (*right*)

Example: 右 *the right,* 左右 *left and right*

"Eat" with your RIGHT "hand" (taking ナ as the "hand" and 口 as "eat").

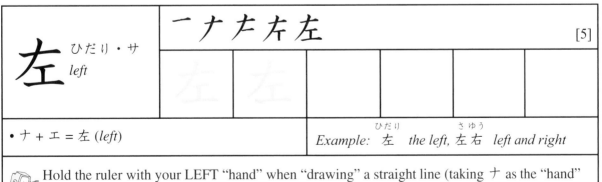

左　ひだり・サ　*left*

一　ナ　ナ　左　左　[5]

• ナ + エ = 左 (*left*)

Example: 左 *the left,* 左右 *left and right*

Hold the ruler with your LEFT "hand" when "drawing" a straight line (taking ナ as the "hand" and エ as doing manual work such as "drawing").

C) Fill in the boxes with appropriate kanji characters.

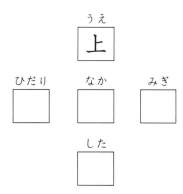

2. Reading and Writing Kanji Characters II

A) Let's read each kanji word or phrase aloud several times.

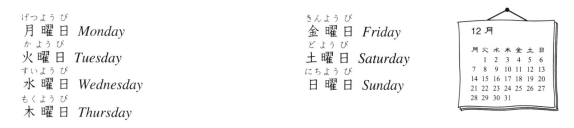

月曜日 *Monday*
げつようび

火曜日 *Tuesday*
かようび

水曜日 *Wednesday*
すいようび

木曜日 *Thursday*
もくようび

金曜日 *Friday*
きんようび

土曜日 *Saturday*
どようび

日曜日 *Sunday*
にちようび

B) In the boxes provided, write each kanji character following the correct stroke order.

曜 ヨウ *days of a week*

丨 冂 冃 日 日' 日⁷ 日⁷ 日ヲ 日ヲ 日ヨ 日ヲ 明 明 晔 晔 晔 曜 曜 [18]

• 日 (*day/sun*) + 羽 (*wings*) + 隹 (*bird*) = 曜 (*days of a week*)

Example: 月曜日 *Monday*
げつようび

The DAYS pass by as quickly as a flying "bird" with large "wings".

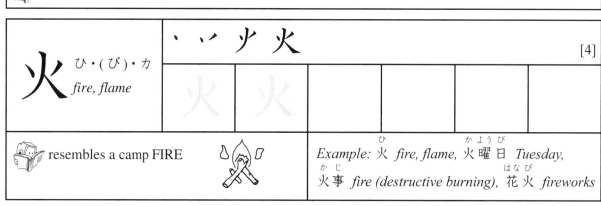

火 ひ・(び)・カ *fire, flame*

丶 ⺊ ⺌ 火 [4]

resembles a camp FIRE

Example: 火 *fire, flame*, 火曜日 *Tuesday*,
ひ　　　　　　　　かようび

火事 *fire (destructive burning)*, 花火 *fireworks*
かじ　　　　　　　　　　はなび

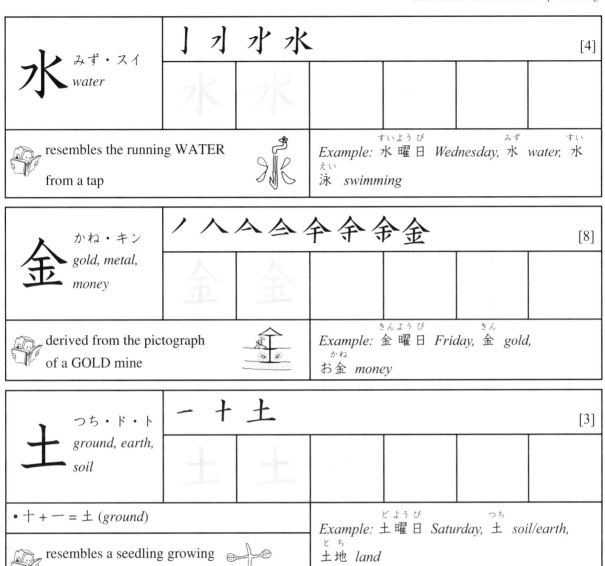

水 みず・スイ *water*

丿 刁 汀 水 [4]

resembles the running WATER from a tap

Example: 水曜日 *Wednesday,* 水 *water,* 水 泳 *swimming*

金 かね・キン *gold, metal, money*

丿 人 人 今 全 全 金 金 [8]

derived from the pictograph of a GOLD mine

Example: 金曜日 *Friday,* 金 *gold,* お金 *money*

土 つち・ド・ト *ground, earth, soil*

一 十 土 [3]

• 十 + 一 = 土 (*ground*)

resembles a seedling growing on the SOIL

Example: 土曜日 *Saturday,* 土 *soil/earth,* 土地 *land*

C) Draw lines to match.

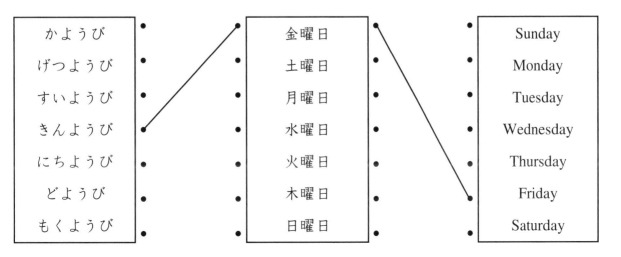

かようび	金曜日	Sunday
げつようび	土曜日	Monday
すいようび	月曜日	Tuesday
きんようび	水曜日	Wednesday
にちようび	火曜日	Thursday
どようび	木曜日	Friday
もくようび	日曜日	Saturday

D) The following passage contains many katakana and kanji characters you've learned so far. Let's read it aloud.

私のうちはこうえんと、としょかんの間にあります。川の近くです。さくらの木がたくさんあります。四月はとてもきれいです。うちから大学まででん車で1時間かかります。車では1時間45分かかります。大学には火曜日と木曜日に行きます。今日は水曜日ですから、大学に行きません。あしたはすう学のクラスです。今晩はすう学のしゅくだいをするつもりです。

3. Naming Common Buildings

Write the names of these buildings in Japanese.

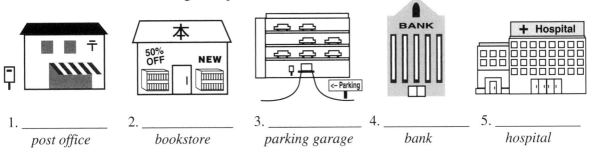

1. _____   2. _____   3. _____   4. _____   5. _____
   post office   *bookstore*   *parking garage*   *bank*   *hospital*

4. Naming Directions

Fill in the boxes with the correct directions.

North

West

East
ひがし

South

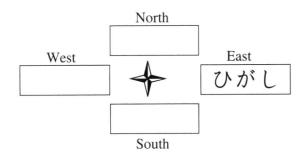

5. Naming the Things in a Room

Can you name these items in Japanese?

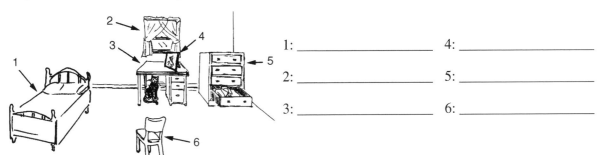

1: _____   4: _____

2: _____   5: _____

3: _____   6: _____

Grammar

1. ある・いる・いらっしゃる

To express the location (Y) of something (X), you say X は Y にあります. If X can move by itself, such as a person or an animal, replace あります with います. If X is a person you should pay respect to, replace います with いらっしゃいます.

Following the example, make a sentence to express the location of the item listed for each question.

Example: ゆうびんきょく・あそこ ⟶ ゆうびんきょくはあそこにあります。

1. じしょ・ここ ⟶ _____

2. さくらの木・あそこ ⟶ _____

3. 私の犬・そこ ⟶ _____
   はは
4. 母・うち ⟶ _____
   か あ
5. 山田さんのお母さん・あそこ ⟶ _____

2. Relative Location

In Japanese, the relative location is expressed by a relative location term such as 上 (top area) along with a reference item marked by the particle の. For example, つくえの上 means *the top of the desk*.

Following the example, state the relative location of the ball in each question.

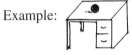
Example: 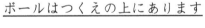 ボールはつくえの上にあります

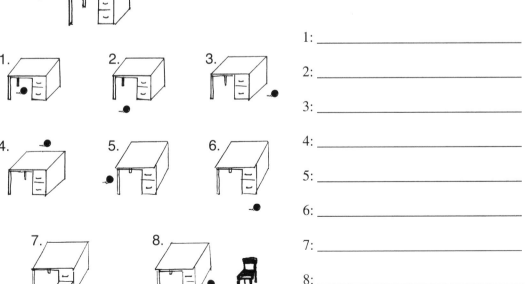

1: _____

2: _____

3: _____

4: _____

5: _____

6: _____

7: _____

8: _____

3. Particles に and で

Both particles に and で are used for marking locations; but で marks the location of an activity, while に marks the destination or location of an existence. Please note that に and で may be used to mark exactly the same noun, such as としょかん in the examples below—which to use depends on the verb. All the three sentences below are grammatical.

- 山田さんはとしょかんに行きます。 *Ms. Yamada goes to the library.*
- 山田さんはとしょかんでべんきょうします。 *Ms. Yamada studies at the library.*
- 山田さんはとしょかんにいます。 *Ms. Yamada is at the library.*

Fill in the blanks with に or で.

1. うちのねこはテーブルの下 ＿＿＿ 食べます。

2. ねこはテーブルの下 ＿＿＿ います。

3. テレビのリモコンはソファーの上 ＿＿＿ あります。 (リモコン *remote controller*)

4. 昨日は車でディズニーランド ＿＿＿ 行きました。

5. かぎはドアのまえのマットの下 ＿＿＿ あります。

6. 兄は今大学 ＿＿＿ います。

7. 私は大学のとしょかん ＿＿＿ しんぶんをよみます。

4. Location of People and Things

For stating the location of a specific item, always treat it as a topic by marking it with は . This ensures the item to remain as an old piece of information to both the speaker and listener who know of its existence, while highlighting its location as a new piece of information

For each question, rearrange the items provided to form a sensible sentence.

1. {います・山田さん・ぎんこう・に・は}

＿＿＿＿＿＿＿＿＿＿＿＿＿＿＿＿＿＿＿＿＿＿＿＿＿＿＿＿＿＿＿＿

2. {あります・車・ちゅうしゃじょう・は・に}

＿＿＿＿＿＿＿＿＿＿＿＿＿＿＿＿＿＿＿＿＿＿＿＿＿＿＿＿＿＿＿＿

3. {あります・つくえ・しゃしん・は・上・の・に}

＿＿＿＿＿＿＿＿＿＿＿＿＿＿＿＿＿＿＿＿＿＿＿＿＿＿＿＿＿＿＿＿

4. {あります・レストランは・えき・みなみ・に・の}

＿＿＿＿＿＿＿＿＿＿＿＿＿＿＿＿＿＿＿＿＿＿＿＿＿＿＿＿＿＿＿＿

Conversation and Usage

1. Calling the Store

In commercial context especially at a store or restaurant, store clerks use very polite business-like expressions and sentence endings. The most obvious examples are ございます and 〜でございます, which are the super-polite versions of あります and 〜です, respectively.

You will hear a telephone conversation between a customer and a store clerk at a computer store. Listen carefully, then answer the questions that follow.

店員　：いつもお世話になっております。コンピューター・ジャパンでございます。

客　　：あのう、来週のノートパソコンのセールは何曜日からですか。

店員　：火曜日からでございます。

客　　：ああ、月曜日じゃないんですね。

店員　：はい。火曜日から木曜日まででございます。

客　　：すべてのノートパソコンが 10% オフなんですよね。

店員　：はい。

客　　：ソニーのも、NEC のもですよね？

店員　：申し訳ございませんが、ソニーのと、NEC のは今在庫がございません。

客　　：あ、そうですか。どうも。

店員　：はい。宜しくお願い致します。

[**Unfamiliar words:** いつもお世話になっております *Thank you for your continuous patronage,* 来週 *next week,* ノートパソコン *notebook-type personal computer,* セール *sale,* すべての *all,* 10% オフ *10% off,* 申し訳ございませんが、... *I am sorry, but ...,* 在庫 *stock,* 宜しくお願い致します (= 宜しくお願いします)]

1. When does the sale start? _____
2. When does the sale end? _____
3. What items does the discount apply to? _____

Note: Particles から and まで express the starting point and ending point in terms of time, place and others.

- 3時から5時までべんきょうします。　*I will study from 3 o'clock to 5 o'clock.*
- うちから大学まで歩きます。　*I will walk from home to the university.*
- 38 ページから 59 ページまで読みま。　*I will read from page 38 to page 59.*

2. Looking for the Toilet

Toilets (bathrooms) are called お手洗い, トイレ, おトイレ, or 便所 in Japanese. 便所 is less
frequently used than the others. To ask where the toilet is for example, just say トイレはどこにありま
すか.

 A mother with her 7-year-old son is talking to a sales clerk of a department store in Japan. She is
finding out where the toilet is as her son needs to use it. Listen to their conversation carefully, then
answer the questions that follow.

女の人 ： すみません。

店員 ： はい。

女の人 ： トイレはどこにありますか。

店員 ： 3階の階段のそばに女性用がございます。

女の人 ： 男性用は？

店員 ： 2階にございます。

女の人 ： ああ、そうですか。 (The woman turns around and looks at her son.)

じゃあ、2階に行きましょう。

子供 ： ママは1階にいて。

女の人 ： ここに？

子供 ： うん。

女の人 ： だめよ。いっしょに行きましょう。

子供 ： 一人で行くよ！

[**Unfamiliar words:** 階段 *stairs,* 女性用 *for women,* 男性用 *for men,* 1階にいて *stay (be) on
the first floor,* だめ *no way,* 一人で *alone*]

1. Where is the men's room located? _____

2. Where is the ladies' room located? _____

3. Which floor are they in now? _____

3. Situational Response

In the following situations, what would you say in Japanese?

1. You are walking around in a town trying to find the subway station. You know that there is one
   nearby, but you just cannot find it. You want to ask someone on the street where it is.

2. You are at the bookstore. You would like to spend more time, but you don't know what time the store closes. You want to ask the store clerk what time their business hours (営 業 時間) end.

えいぎょうじかん

_____

3. You came to see professor Tanaka (田中先生), but he is not in his office. You want to ask his secretary where he is.

_____

Listening Comprehension

Locating Places

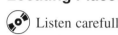 Listen carefully to the narrative about the location of various places, then find the following places on the map provided. Give your answers in numbers.

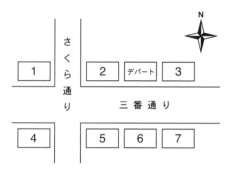

1. 本や: _____

2. ぎんこう: _____

3. びょういん: _____

Reading Comprehension

Locating Places

Let's read the following passage carefully and identify the location of the places listed below using the map in the previous exercise.

　　山田ビジネスはさくら通りと三番通りの交差点にあります。三番通りの北です。さくら通りの東です。ABC英語学校も三番通りにあります。駐車場の前です。デパートも三番通りにあります。山田ビジネスと駐車場の間にあります。

1. 山田ビジネス *Yamada Business*: _____
2. ABC英語学校 *ABC English School*: _____

Writing

Giving Directions

Pretend that your Japanese school, ICA ジャパン, is located at #1 on the map on the previous page, write a short note to your friend in Japanese, showing him the location of your school, so he can come to visit you.

_____

_____

_____

_____

New Vocabulary Reference List

NOUN

あいだ（間）*the position between (two items)*
うえ（上）*top part, above*
うしろ（後）*behind*
えき（駅）*railway station*
かようび（火曜日）*Tuesday*
き（木）*tree*
きた（北）*north*
きんようび（金曜日）*Friday*
げつようび（月曜日）*Monday*
こうさてん（交差点）*intersection*
さくら（桜）*cherry tree, cherry blossom*
じしょ（辞書）*dictionary*
した（下）*bottom part, below, under*
しゃしん（写真）*photograph*
すいようび（水曜日）*Wednesday*
そば *vicinity, near (cf. ちかく)*
たんす（箪笥）*clothes chest*
ちか（地下）*basement*
ちかく（近く）*vicinity, near*
ちゅうしゃじょう（駐車場）*parking lot, parking garage*
でんき（電気）*electric light, electricity*
とおり（通り）*street*
となり（隣）*next door, next position*
どようび（土曜日）*Saturday*
なか（中）*inside, middle*
にし（西）*west*
にちようび（日曜日）*Sunday*
ひがし（東）*east*

ひきだし（引き出し）*drawer*
ひだり（左）*left*
へや（部屋）*room*
ほんばこ（本箱）*bookcase*
まえ（前）*front, front position, before*
みぎ（右）*right*
みなみ（南）*south*
もくようび（木曜日）*Thursday*
よこ（横）*side*

VERB (Ru-Verb)

いる *to exist*

VERB (U-Verb)

ある *to exist* (*slightly irregular: the plain negative form of ある is ない)
いらっしゃる *to exist* (honorific) (*slightly irregular: the stem form of いらっしゃる is いらっしゃい)

COUNTER

〜かい（〜階）*...th floor*

PARTICLE

〜まで *up to, until*

OTHERS

もしもし *Hello (on the phone)*
〜どおり（〜通り）*... street* (三番通り *Third Street*)

CHAPTER EIGHT

Expressing What You Have

Objectives:
- to express what you have and what exist
- to learn simple phrases for asking about family and scheduling
- to learn and use number phrases and conjunction ですから

Kanji and Vocabulary

1. Reading and Writing Kanji Characters

A) Let's read each kanji word or phrase aloud several times.

<small>ほん／ぼん／ぽん</small>
〜　本　　　counter for cylindrical objects such as pencils

<small>まい</small>
〜 枚　counter for flat objects such as paper

<small>さつ</small>
〜 冊　counter for bounded items such as books

<small>だい</small>
〜 台　counter for mechanical items such as cars

<small>ひき・びき・ぴき</small>
〜　匹　　　counter for animals such as dogs and cats

<small>にん</small>
〜 人　counter for people

<small>あね</small>
姉　*one's older sister*

<small>ねえ</small>
お姉さん　*someone else's older sister*

<small>いもうと</small>
妹　*one's younger sister*

<small>きょうだい</small>
兄弟　*siblings*

<small>おとうと</small>
弟　*one's younger brother*

<small>べんきょう</small>
勉強する　*to study*

B) In the boxes provided, write each kanji character following the correct stroke order.

枚 マイ counter for flat items	一 十 才 木 朮 朾 枚 枚 　　　　　[8]
• 木 (*tree*) + 攵 (*hand holding stick*) = 枚	*Example:* 1 枚　*one* (for flat items such as paper) <small>いちまい</small>

冊 サツ counter for books	丨 冂 冂 冊 冊 　　　　　[5]
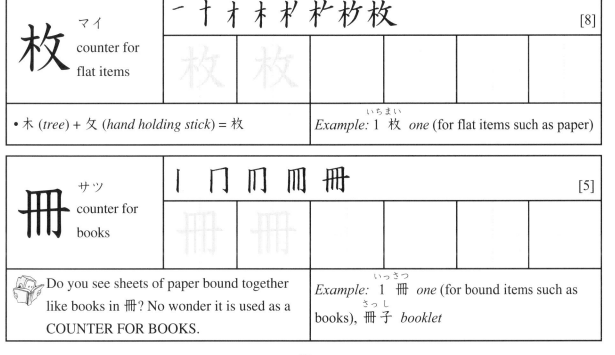 Do you see sheets of paper bound together like books in 冊? No wonder it is used as a COUNTER FOR BOOKS.	*Example:* 1 冊　*one* (for bound items such as books), 冊子 *booklet* <small>いっさつ</small> <small>さっし</small>

台　ダイ・タイ　board, table, base, counter for mechanical items

ㄥ　ム　ㄙ　台　台　[5]

- ム + 口 (mouth) = 台 (table/counter for mechanical items)

resembles a Xerox machine

Example: 1 台 one (for machines), 台風 typhoon
(いちだい) (たいふう)

姉　あね・シ　older sister

く　乄　女　女゛　女ヒ　姉　姉　[8]

- 女 (woman) + 市 (city) = 姉 (older sister)

OLDER SISTERs are "women" who love to shop in the "city"!

Example: 姉 one's older sister, お姉さん someone else's older sister, 姉妹 sisters, 姉妹 都市 sister city
(あね) (ねえ) (しまい) (しまい) (とし)

妹　いもうと・マイ　younger sister

く　乄　女　女゛　女゠　妹　妹　[8]

- 女 (girl/woman) + 未 (not yet) = 妹 (younger sister)

The "girl" who is "not yet" a grown-up is my YOUNGER SISTER.

Example: 妹 one's younger sister, 姉妹 sisters
(いもうと) (しまい)

弟　おとうと・テイ・ダイ　younger brother

丶　丷　丷　凹　弟　弟　[7]

- 丷 + 弓 (bow) + | + ノ = 弟 (younger brother)

Example: 弟 one's own younger brother, 兄弟 siblings
(おとうと) (きょうだい)

Who would mischievously add two ears, a spine and a tail to the character 弓 and turn it into 弟? My YOUNGER BROTHER of course!

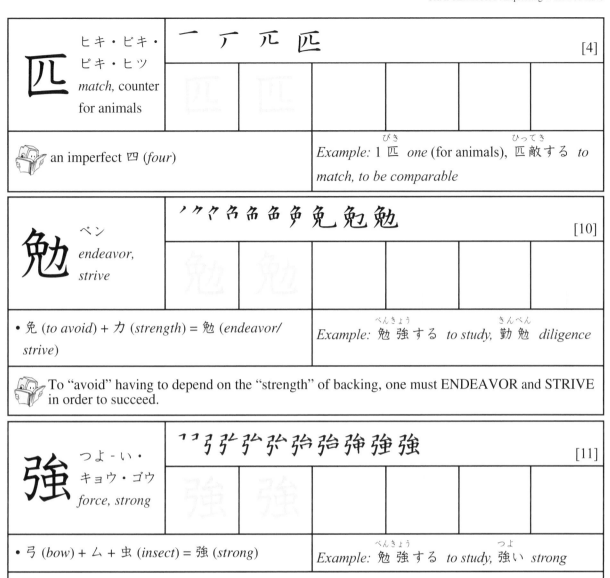

匹	ヒキ・ビキ・ ピキ・ヒツ match, counter for animals	一　丁　兀　匹				[4]

an imperfect 四 (four)

Example: 1 匹 one (for animals), 匹敵する to match, to be comparable

勉	ベン endeavor, strive	ノク々 名 奋 台 免 免 勉 勉				[10]

• 免 (to avoid) + 力 (strength) = 勉 (endeavor/strive)

Example: 勉強する to study, 勤勉 diligence

To "avoid" having to depend on the "strength" of backing, one must ENDEAVOR and STRIVE in order to succeed.

強	つよ-い・ キョウ・ゴウ force, strong	¹ ²³ 弓 弘 弘 弘 弘 弘 強 強 強				[11]

• 弓 (bow) + ム + 虫 (insect) = 強 (strong)

Example: 勉強する to study, 強い strong

a STRONG "insect" wearing a "ム-shaped" helmet and carrying a huge "bow" at the side.

C)　Read the following number phrases aloud.

A counter is pronounced differently when it is used with certain numbers. In general, if it begins with a voiceless consonant such as s, h, f and t, it tends to have a "double-consonant" (small っ) when used with number 1, 6, 8, or 10, and "voicing" when it is with number 3. However, there are many exceptions.

いっぽん	にほん	さんぼん	よんほん	ごほん	ろっぽん / ろくほん	ななほん	はっぽん / はちほん	きゅうほん	じゅっぽん
1 本	2 本	3 本	4 本	5 本	6 本	7 本	8 本	9 本	10 本
いっさつ	にさつ	さんさつ	よんさつ	ごさつ	ろくさつ	ななさつ	はっさつ	きゅうさつ	じゅっさつ
1 冊	2 冊	3 冊	4 冊	5 冊	6 冊	7 冊	8 冊	9 冊	10 冊
いちまい	にまい	さんまい	よんまい	ごまい	ろくまい	ななまい	はちまい	きゅうまい	じゅうまい
1 枚	2 枚	3 枚	4 枚	5 枚	6 枚	7 枚	8 枚	9 枚	10 枚
いちだい	にだい	さんだい	よんだい	ごだい	ろくだい	ななだい	はちだい	きゅうだい	じゅうだい
1 台	2 台	3 台	4 台	5 台	6 台	7 台	8 台	9 台	10 台
ひとり	ふたり	さんにん	よにん	ごにん	ろくにん	ななにん / しちにん	はちにん	きゅうにん	じゅうにん
1 人	2 人	3 人	4 人	5 人	6 人	7 人	8 人	9 人	10 人
いっぴき	にひき	さんびき	よんひき	ごひき	ろっぴき	ななひき / しちひき	はっぴき	きゅうひき	じゅっぴき
1 匹	2 匹	3 匹	4 匹	5 匹	6 匹	7 匹	8 匹	9 匹	10 匹

D) Read the following passage aloud.

　私は兄弟が 4 人います。兄と、姉と、妹と、弟です。父はアメリカ人です。母は日本人です。それから、うちには犬が 3 匹います。それから、ねこが 1 匹います。弟はこうこうせいです。よくテレビを見ます。テレビはぜんぶで 5 台あります。私は大学生です。せんこうはぶん学です。明日はしけんがあります。ですから、今晩はたくさん勉強します。本を 3 冊よむつもりです。

E) Fill in the boxes with appropriate kanji characters.

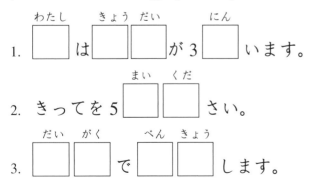

1. ［わたし］は［きょう］［だい］が 3 ［にん］います。

2. きってを 5 ［まい］［くだ］さい。

3. ［だい］［がく］で［べん］［きょう］します。

F) As many as you can, write the kanji characters that include the following as a component.

女 ☐ ☐ ☐ ☐

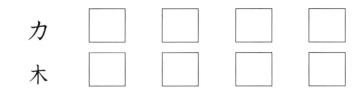

2. Matching Academic Subjects

Draw lines to match.

しゃかい学 • • literature

すう学 • • English

ぶん学 • • sociology

けいざい学 • • mathematics

日本ご • • Japanese

えいご • • economics

3. Using Counters

The quantity or amount of things and people must always be expressed by the number with a counter. Which counter to use depends on the type, shape, function and size of the item you are counting or measuring. For example, two cats is 2 匹 (にひき) in Japanese, where 匹 is the counter for animals.

Following the example given, specify the number of each item using an appropriate counter.

Example: バナナ ： _2 本_

1.
きって

2.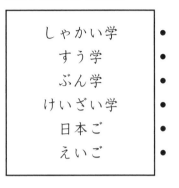
本

3.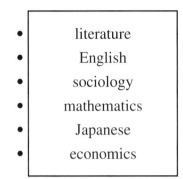
れいぞうこ

4.
りんご

5.
男の人

6.
ねこ

1: _____   4: _____

2: _____   5: _____

3: _____   6: _____

Note: つ is a native counter used for a variety of items such as apples and chairs.

ひとつ	ふたつ	みっつ	よっつ	いつつ	むっつ	ななつ	やっつ	ここのつ	とお
1つ	2つ	3つ	4つ	5つ	6つ	7つ	8つ	9つ	10

Grammar

1. XにはYがある

The existential verbs ある, いる and いらっしゃる express not only the location of things and people (as discussed in Chapter Seven), but also what exists or what one has. For the latter case, the items that exist or you have should not be marked by the topic marker は, but should be marked by the subject marker が.

Following the example, form a sentence using the words provided for each question. Can you see that you are expressing the existence of the items in each sentence?

Example: うち・犬 ⟶ うちには犬がいます。

1. テーブルの下・ねこ ⟶ _____
2. 父のベッドの下・お金 (money) ⟶ _____
3. うちの近く・レストラン ⟶ _____
4. 私のうち・プール ⟶ _____
5. この本やの中・コーヒーショップ ⟶ _____

2. Number Phrases

To specify the quantity of an item referred to in a sentence, place the number phrase right after the item and its particle. For example, うちにはテレビが5台あります means *there are five TVs in (my) house*. You can also use 少し (*a few*) or たくさん (*a lot*) instead of a specific number phrase like 5台.

Following the example, form a grammatical sentence for each question.

Example: うちにはテレビがあります・5台 ⟶ うちにはテレビが5台あります。

1. うちには犬がいます・4匹 ⟶ _____

2. さいふの中にはクレジットカードがあります・3枚

    ⟶ _____

3. 山田さんのうちには車があります・2台 ⟶ _____

4. かばんの中には本があります・2冊 ⟶ _____

5. このクラスには日本人の学生がいます・たくさん

    ⟶ _____

3. ですから

The connective (conjunction) word ですから is always placed at the beginning of a sentence, just like でも and それから. However unlike でも and それから, ですから indicates, in a sentence, the conclusion or consequence of the fact stated in the preceding sentence.

Fill in the blanks with ですから, でも, or それから.

1. うちにはねこがいます。＿＿＿＿＿＿＿＿＿、ねずみがいません。(ねずみ *mice*)

2. 昨日は日本ごのしゅくだいをしました。＿＿＿＿＿＿＿＿＿、すう学を勉強しました。

3. 私は学生です。＿＿＿＿＿＿＿＿＿、あまり勉強しません。

Conversation and Usage

1. Asking about Family (Informal Conversation)

You can ask someone whether he/she has any siblings with 兄弟がいますか.

Listen carefully to the conversation between Yuka and her friend Tetsuya on the CD and answer the questions that follow.

ゆか　　：てつやさんは兄弟がいるの？

てつや　：うんん。ぼくは一人っ子。

ゆか　　：ああ、そう。

てつや　：ゆかさんは。

ゆか　　：私は姉が３人。

てつや　：じゃあ、ぜんぶで女の子が４人？

ゆか　　：ええ。

てつや　：じゃあ、若草物語だ。

ゆか　　：うん。

てつや　：けんかはする？

ゆか　　：ぜんぜんしない。すごく仲がいいんだ。

てつや　：いいね。

[***Unfamiliar words:*** 女の子 *girl*, 若草物語 The Japanese title of *Little Women* by Louisa M. Alcott, すごく *a colloquial form of* とても, 〜と仲がいい *to get along with ... well/to be friendly with ...,* 〜んだ *the informal version of* 〜んです]

1. How many siblings does Tetsuya have? _____

2. How many siblings does Yuka have? _____

3. Does Yuka get along well with her siblings? _____

2. Making a Plan

Jane and Kent are taking Japanese language lessons from Ms. Tanaka once a week. Listen to their conversation and answer the questions that follow.

Jane : あさっての晩は田中先生のレッスンだよね。

Kent : うん。

Jane : しゅくだいは？

Kent : まだ。

Jane : いっしょにしない？

Kent : うん。いいよ。

Jane : 今日の午後はひま？

Kent : うんん。空手のクラスがあるんだ。

Jane : ああ、そう。じゃあ、明日の午後は？

Kent : 合気道のクラス。

Jane : ああ、そう。じゃあ、明日の晩は？

Kent : うん。いいよ。

[**Unfamiliar words:** 合気道 *aikido* (martial arts)]

1. When is the Japanese lesson? _____

2. Is Kent free this afternoon? _____

3. When will they meet to do homework together? _____

3. Situational Response

In the following situations, what would you say in Japanese?

1. You want to ask your friend, Mr. Tanaka (田中さん), how many cars he has in his household (うち).

_____

2. You want to ask your friend, Ms. Yamashita (山下さん), whether she has any siblings.

_____

3. You want to ask your friend, Yoshiko (よしこさん), whether she has an English class tomorrow evening.

_____

Listening Comprehension

Using Onomatopoeia

Japanese has a huge inventory of imitating words (onomatopoeia and mimetic words), each of which consists of the repetition of one (or two) syllable(s) and is usually written in katakana, for example, ワンワン is the onomatopoeia for a dog's bark.

 In this exercise, you will hear phrases that contain imitating words. Choose the appropriate illustration for each of them.

1.  2.   3. 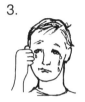 4.  5.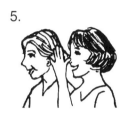

1: _____ 2: _____ 3: _____ 4: _____ 5: _____

Reading Comprehension

Going Through Yoshiko's Schedule

The following is a page from Yoshiko's weekly scheduler. Go through it carefully and answer the questions that follow. You will encounter unfamiliar hand-written kanji characters, but you should be able to answer the questions.

6月	1日 （月曜日）	2日 （火曜日）	3日 （水曜日）	4日 （木曜日）	5日 （金曜日）	6日 （土曜日）	7日 （日曜日）
	銀行に行く	田中さんに電話をする	6 p.m. 英会話 7:45 p.m. からて	3 p.m. 歯医者 7 p.m. リーさんに日本語をおしえる	8 p.m. ようこのうちでカラオケ	4:15 p.m. 川口さんとえいがを見る	3 p.m. ようこと買いもの

1. When will she go shopping with Yoko? _____

2. When will she practice karate? _____

3. To whom will she teach Japanese on 4 June? _____

4. Who will watch a movie with her on 6 June? _____

5. To whom will she need to make a phone call on 2 June? _____

Writing

Scheduling

On the schedule sheet provided below, fill in your schedule for the following week in Japanese.

	＿＿日 （月曜日）	＿＿日 （火曜日）	＿＿日 （水曜日）	＿＿日 （木曜日）	＿＿日 （金曜日）	＿＿日 （土曜日）	＿＿日 （日曜日）
＿月							

New Vocabulary Reference List

NOUN

あお（青）*blue color*

あか（赤）*red color*

あさって（明後日）*the day after tomorrow*

アルバイト／バイト　*part-time job* (the German
　word, *Arbeit*)

いとこ（従兄弟・従姉妹）*cousin*

いろ（色）*color*

きって（切手）*stamp*

きょうだい・ごきょうだい（兄弟・御兄弟）
　siblings

くろ（黒）*black color*

けいざいがく（経済学）*economics*

けしゴム（消しゴム）*eraser*

ごぜんちゅう（午前中）*forenoon (during the
　morning)* (*c.f.* ごぜん *a.m.*)

しけん（試験）*exam, test*（試験をうける *to take
　an exam*）

しごと（仕事）*job*（仕事をする *to work*）

しゃかいがく（社会学）*sociology*

そふ・おじいさん（祖父・おじいさん）
　grandfather

そぼ・おばあさん（祖母・おばあさん）
　grandmother

デート　*date*

ノート　*notebook*

ひとりっこ（一人っ子）*only child*

ふとん（布団）*futon mattress*

ベッド　*bed*

ぼく（僕）*I, me* (the first person pronoun for male)

めんせつ（面接）*interview*

りょうしん・ごりょうしん（両親・御両親）
　parents

れいぞうこ（冷蔵庫）*refrigerator*

ADJECTIVE

うるさい　*noisy*

おもしろい（面白い）*funny, interesting, amusing*

さびしい（寂しい）*lonely*

ADVERB

すこし（少し）*a little, a few, slightly*

たくさん（沢山）*a lot*

CONJUNCTION

ですから　*therefore, so*

COUNTER

〜さつ（〜冊）a counter for bound objects such as
　books and magazines

〜だい（〜台）a counter for mechanical objects

〜つ　a native counter for a variety of objects

〜にん／り（〜人）a counter for people

〜ひき／びき／ぴき（〜匹）a counter for animals

〜ほん／ぼん／ぽん（〜本）a counter for
　cylindrical objects

〜まい（〜枚）a counter for flat objects

CHAPTER NINE

Describing the Property of Things and People

Objectives:

- to describe people and things using a variety of adjectives
- to learn simple phrases for visiting and describing someone's apartment
- to learn and use the i-type and na-type adjectives, the negative forms of adjectives and the degree adverbs あまり and ぜんぜん

Kanji and Vocabulary

1. Reading and Writing Kanji Characters

A) Let's read each kanji word or phrase aloud several times.

おお
大きい *big*
ちい
小さい *small*
あたら
新しい *new*
ふる
古い *old*
あか
明るい *bright*

くら
暗い *dark*
ひろ
広い *spacious*
ちか
近い *near*
にほんご
日本語 *Japanese language*

ぶん
文 *sentence*
さくぶん
作文 *composition*
ぶん
文ぽう *grammar*
ぶんがく
文学 *literature*

B) In the boxes provided, write each kanji character following the correct stroke order.

小	ちい‑さい・こ・お・ショウ *small, little*	亅 小 小 [3]

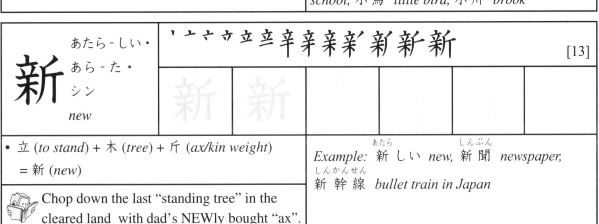

resembles someone who is trying to look SMALL by crouching

Example: 小さい *small*, 小学校 *elementary school*, 小鳥 *little bird*, 小川 *brook*

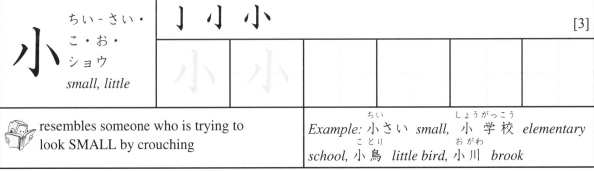

新	あたら‑しい・あら‑た・シン *new*	` ㇒ ㇆ ㇉ 立 立 辛 辛 亲 亲´ 新 新 新 [13]

- 立 (*to stand*) + 木 (*tree*) + 斤 (*ax/kin weight*) = 新 (*new*)

Chop down the last "standing tree" in the cleared land with dad's NEWly bought "ax".

Example: 新しい *new*, 新聞 *newspaper*, 新幹線 *bullet train in Japan*

古 ふる-い・ コ *old*	一 十 十 古 古 [5] 古　古	
• 十 *(ten)* + 口 *(mouth)* = 古 *(old)* 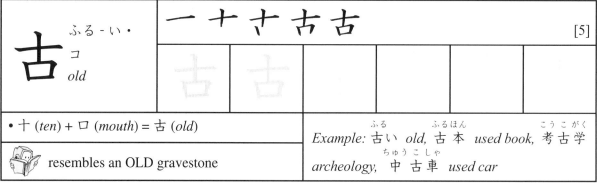 resembles an OLD gravestone	*Example:* 古い *old*, 古本 *used book*, 考古学 *archeology*, 中古車 *used car*	

暗 くら-い・ アン *dark*	丨 冂 日 日 日' 旷 旷 暗 暗 暗 暗 暗 暗 [13] 暗　暗	
• 日 *(sun)* + 音 *(sound)* = 暗 *(dark)*	*Example:* 暗い *dark*, 暗記する *to memorize*	

What would you do if you are lost and it is DARK? Heading toward a "sound" or "light" source of course (taking 日 as "light").

広 ひろ-い・ コウ *wide,* *spacious*	` 亠 广 広 広 [5] 広　広	
• 广 *(linen/building)* + ム = 広 *(wide/spacious)*	Example: 広い *spacious*, 広告 *advertisement*, 広島 *Hiroshima* (place name)	

語 かた-る・ ゴ *speak, word,* *language*	` 亠 亠 言 言 言 言 訂 語 語 語 語 語 [14] 語　語	
• 言 *(say/talk)* + 五 *(five)* + 口 *(mouth)* = 語 *(language)*	*Example:* 日本語 *Japanese language*, 英語 *English*, 言語学 *linguistics*, 語る *to talk*	

 Who can "say" in 5 LANGUAGES at the same time? The monster who has "five mouths", of course. *Note that 語 and 五 have the same pronunciation.

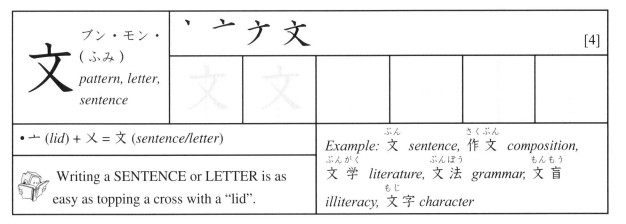

文 ブン・モン・（ふみ）pattern, letter, sentence	` 一 ナ 文					[4]

• 亠 (lid) + 乂 = 文 (sentence/letter)

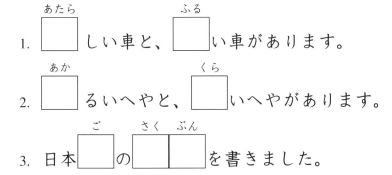 Writing a SENTENCE or LETTER is as easy as topping a cross with a "lid".

Example: 文 *sentence,* 作文 *composition,* 文学 *literature,* 文法 *grammar,* 文盲 *illiteracy,* 文字 *character*

C) The following sentences contain many of the kanji characters you have learned. Can you still remember them? Let's read each sentence aloud.

1. うちには大きい犬が一匹と、小さい犬が二匹います。
2. 新しいプリンターを買いました。
3. このたてものはとても古いです。
4. 私のへやは暗いです。本は明るいへやでよんでください。
5. 大学の近くに広いこうえんがあります。うちからも近いです。
   歩いて5分です。
6. 文ぽうのテストがありました。日本語の文をたくさん書きました。
7. 作文のしゅくだいに2時間かかりました。
8. 文学と、日本語と、えい語と、すう学を勉強します。

D) Fill in the correct kanji characters in the boxes provided.

1. あたら □ しい車と、ふる □ い車があります。

2. あか □ るいへやと、くら □ いへやがあります。

3. 日本 ご □ の さく □ ぶん □ を書きました。

E) Add the correct おくりがな to each kanji character.

Example: 高 ___い___ です。

1. 明 ____ です。　　　3. 広 ____ です。　　　5. 古 ____ です。
2. 暗 ____ です。　　　4. 新 ____ です。　　　6. 安 ____ です。

2. Comparing Buildings

Fill in the blank with an appropriate adjective to describe each building.

1.

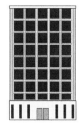

(a) ＿＿＿＿＿＿＿です　　　　(b) ＿＿＿＿＿＿＿です

2.

(a) ＿＿＿＿＿＿＿です　　　　(b) ＿＿＿＿＿＿＿です

3.

(a) ＿＿＿＿＿＿＿です　　　　(b) ＿＿＿＿＿＿＿です

3. Different Aspects of a Language

Fill in the blank with an appropriate word from the list provided.

{かいわ・文ぽう・作文・はつおん}

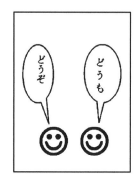

1. ＿＿＿＿＿＿＿　　2. ＿＿＿＿＿＿＿　　3. ＿＿＿＿＿＿＿　　4. ＿＿＿＿＿＿＿

Grammar

1. I-type and Na-type Adjectives

Japanese adjectives are classified into i-type and na-type. When followed by a noun, an i-type adjective has the inflection い, while a na-type adjective has the inflection な, as in 小さい 車 (*small car*) and しずかな車 (*quiet car*). However, when they are followed by です, the inflection い remains, but な is dropped, as in 小さいです and しずかです, respectively.

Form grammatical sentences following the examples.

Example: 小さいです・ホテルです ⟶ 小さいホテルです。

りっぱです・ホテルです ⟶ りっぱなホテルです。

1. 大きいです・犬です ⟶ _____

2. 新しいです・たてものです ⟶ _____

3. りっぱです・大学です ⟶ _____

4. きれいです・レストランです ⟶ _____

5. おもしろいです・ざっしです ⟶ _____

6. きたないです・えきです ⟶ _____

Note: Be careful with the na-type adjectives whose stems end in い. For example, きれいです appears to look like an i-type adjective, but it is actually a na-type adjective. You can identify it easily if it is placed before a noun, as in きれい<u>な</u>人.

2. Negative Forms of Adjectives

The negative form of an i-type adjective is created by adding くありません at the end of its stem. The negative form of a na-type adjective is created by adding じゃありません at the end of its stem. The stem form of an adjective is without the inflection い or な.

Following the example, create a negative answer to each question.

Example: たのしいですか。 ⟶ たのしくありません。

1. むずかしいですか。 ⟶ _____

2. かんたんですか。 ⟶ _____

3. おもしろいですか。 ⟶ _____

4. きれいですか。 ⟶ _____

5. とおいですか。 ⟶ _____

6. しずかですか。 ⟶ _____

7. いいですか。 ⟶ _____

Note:

- いい is irregular and its negative counterpart is よく ありません.
- The variation of じゃありません is ではありません, where は is pronounced as **wa**.

3. Degree Adverbs あまり **and** ぜんぜん

あまり and ぜんぜん must be used with a negative adjective (or verb), whereas とても must be used with an affirmative adjective, regardless of whether the property is favorable or unfavorable.

Following the examples, join the two phrases provided to make a sentence.

Example:　あまり・たのしいです　　➡　　あまりたのしくありません。

　　　　　　とても・たのしいです　　➡　　とても たのしいです。

1.　ぜんぜん・かんたんです　　➡　　＿＿＿＿＿＿＿＿＿＿＿＿＿＿＿＿

2.　あまり・きれいです　　　　➡　　＿＿＿＿＿＿＿＿＿＿＿＿＿＿＿＿

3.　とても・新しいです　　　　➡　　＿＿＿＿＿＿＿＿＿＿＿＿＿＿＿＿

4.　ぜんぜん・べんりです　　　➡　　＿＿＿＿＿＿＿＿＿＿＿＿＿＿＿＿

5.　とても・高いです　　　　　➡　　＿＿＿＿＿＿＿＿＿＿＿＿＿＿＿＿

Conversation and Usage

1. Visiting a Friend's Apartment (Informal Conversation)

おじゃまします is a phrase commonly used when one enters someone else's residence.

Mihoko has gone to Toshiko's apartment for a visit. Listen to their conversation carefully and answer the questions that follow.

みほこ　：こんにちは。

としこ　：ああ、みほちゃん。どうぞ。

みほこ　：どうも。おじゃまします。(Toshiko offers a seat to Mihoko.)

としこ　：どうぞ。ごめんなさい。ちらかってて。

みほこ　：ぜんぜん。きれいよ。私のアパートはもっとちらかってるわよ。

としこ　：そう？

みほこ　：うん。

としこ　：コーヒーがいい？お茶(ちゃ)がいい？

みほこ　：じゃあ、お茶。

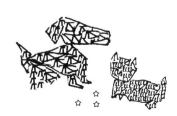

としこ　：はい。(While Toshiko prepares tea, Mihoko looks around the room.)

みほこ　：ああ、このクリスタルきれい！それに、かわいい！

としこ　：ああ、それ？その小さいのはネコ。その大きいのは犬。

みほこ　：スワロフスキーの？

としこ　：うん。

みほこ　：やっぱり。私ももってる。

としこ　：どんなの？

みほこ　：バレリーナのとバイオリンの。

としこ　：ああ、そう。

[**Unfamiliar words:** ごめんなさい *I'm sorry*, ちらかってて (= ちらかっていて) *to be messy and ...*, ちらかってる (= ちらかっている) *to be messy*, もっと *more*, お茶 (*Japanese) tea*, もってる (= もっている) *to have*]

1. What drink will Toshiko serve?　　　　_____
2. What kind of crystals does Toshiko have?　_____
3. What kind of crystals does Mihoko have?　_____

Note:
- わ is the particle to emphasize one's emotions or feelings or soften the tone of a statement by women.
- The noun that occurs after an adjective may be replaced by の if contextually understood.

2. Situational Response

In the following situations, what would you say in Japanese?

1. You are going to visit your friend's (田中さん) company (会社) for the very first time, and you want to know what kind of building it is.

    _____

2. You visited your friend's (川口さん) apartment for the first time. You think it is a pretty nice apartment and you want to find out how much his rent is.

    _____

3. Your friend (マイクさん) is learning French. You want to ask him whether it is difficult pronouncing French words.

    _____

Listening Comprehension

About Yoko's Apartment

Listen carefully to the narrative about Yoko's apartment, then state whether the following sentences are "true" or "false".

1. Yoko's apartment is far from the subway station.   (True • False)

2. Yoko's apartment is spacious.   (True • False)

3. Yoko's apartment is quiet.   (True • False)

Reading Comprehension

At the Library

Let's read the following passage carefully and answer the questions that follow.

私の町の図書館はとてもきれいです。それに、とても明るいです。でも、あまり大きくありません。2階建てですが、地下があります。私は図書館でよく新聞を読みます。

[*Unfamiliar words:* 町 *town*, 2階建て *two-story (building)*]

1. Is this library very big?   _____

2. Is it pretty?   _____

3. What does this person often do at the library?   _____

Writing

Essay Writing

Write about the public library in your town.

_____

_____

_____

_____

_____

_____

New Vocabulary Reference List

NOUN

いえ（家）*house (c.f.* うち *)*
がいこくご（外国語）*foreign language*
かいわ（会話）*conversation*
ききとり（聞き取り）*listening comprehension*
さくぶん（作文）*composition*
たんご（単語）*word, vocabulary*
はつおん（発音）*pronunciation*
ぶん（文）*sentence*
ぶんぽう（文法）*grammar*
やちん（家賃）*rent for houses and apartments*

QUESTION WORD

どう　*how*
どんな　*what kind of*

ADJECTIVE

あかるい（明るい）*bright, cheerful*
あたらしい（新しい）*new*
おおきい（大きい）*big*
きたない（汚い）*dirty*
くらい（暗い）*dark, gloomy*
しずかな（静かな）*quiet*
せまい（狭い）*non-spacious, narrow*
たのしい（楽しい）*fun, entertaining, amusing*
ちいさい（小さい）*small*
ちかい（近い）*near (c.f.* 近く *)*
とおい（遠い）*far*
ひくい（低い）*low, not tall*
ひろい（広い）*spacious, wide*
ふべんな（不便な）*inconvenient*
ふるい（古い）*old (for non-animate items)*
べんりな（便利な）*convenient*
りっぱな（立派な）*splendid, elegant, gorgeous, great*

CONJUNCTION

それに　*furthermore, moreover*
おじゃまします（お邪魔します）*I'll come in. (lit. I am going to disturb you.)*

CHAPTER TEN

Requesting

Objectives:

- to describe movements and actions
- to learn simple phrases for making requests and giving directions
- to learn about te-form verbs and adverbs

Kanji and Vocabulary

1. Reading and Writing Kanji Characters I

A) Let's read each kanji word or phrase aloud several times.

言う *to say*
話す *to speak*
読む *to read*
聞く *to listen*

立つ *to stand up*
出す *to submit, to take out*
入る *to enter*
見せる *to show*

B) In the boxes provided, write each kanji character following the correct stroke order.

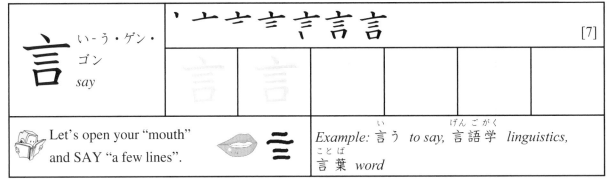

| 言 いーう・ゲン・ゴン *say* | ヽ 亠 亠 言 言 言 言 [7] |
| | |

 Let's open your "mouth" and SAY "a few lines".

Example: 言う *to say*, 言語学 *linguistics*, 言葉 *word*

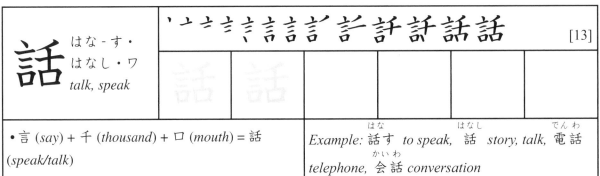

| 話 はなーす・はなし・ワ *talk, speak* | ヽ 亠 亠 言 言 言 言 訐 訐 話 話 [13] |
| | |

• 言 (*say*) + 千 (*thousand*) + 口 (*mouth*) = 話 (*speak/talk*)

Example: 話す *to speak*, 話 *story, talk*, 電話 *telephone*, 会話 *conversation*

 We tend to "say thousands" of words when we open our "mouth" to SPEAK or TALK.

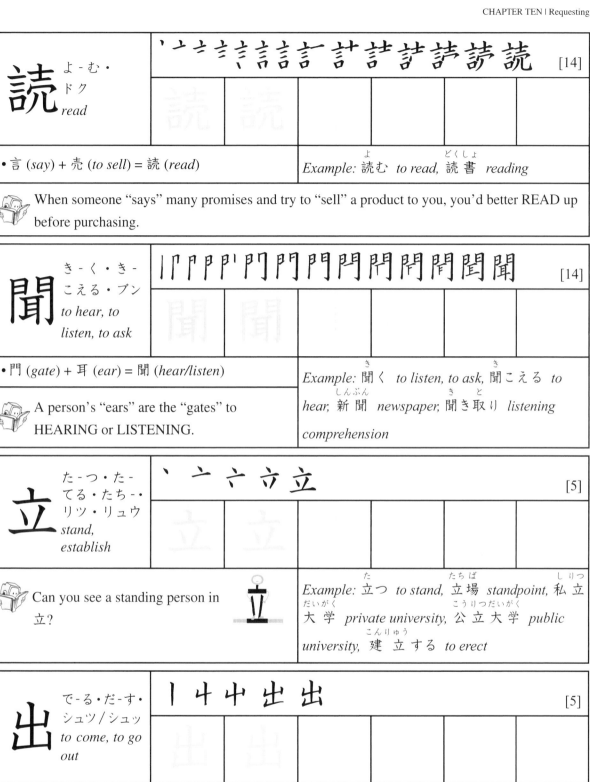

読 よ-む・ドク *read*

ノ 亠 亠 言 言 言 言 計 計 計 誌 誌 読 [14]

• 言 (*say*) + 売 (*to sell*) = 読 (*read*)

Example: 読む *to read,* 読書 *reading*

When someone "says" many promises and try to "sell" a product to you, you'd better READ up before purchasing.

聞 き-く・き-こえる・ブン *to hear, to listen, to ask*

｜ ｒ ｆ ｆ ｆ' 門 門 門 門 門 門 門 聞 聞 [14]

• 門 (*gate*) + 耳 (*ear*) = 聞 (*hear/listen*)

A person's "ears" are the "gates" to HEARING or LISTENING.

Example: 聞く *to listen, to ask,* 聞こえる *to hear;* 新聞 *newspaper,* 聞き取り *listening comprehension*

立 た-つ・た-てる・たち-・リツ・リュウ *stand, establish*

ヽ 亠 六 立 立 [5]

Can you see a standing person in 立?

Example: 立つ *to stand,* 立場 *standpoint,* 私立大学 *private university,* 公立大学 *public university,* 建立する *to erect*

出 で-る・だ-す・シュツ / シュッ *to come, to go out*

｜ 屮 屮 出 出 [5]

My little brother would like to stack two 山 (*mountains*), one on top of the other in the sea, to help the sea animals to COME ashore easily.

Example: 出る *to come out,* 出す *to hand in, to take out,* 出口 *exit,* 出国する *to leave the country,* 出席する *to attend, to be present,* 引き出し *drawer*

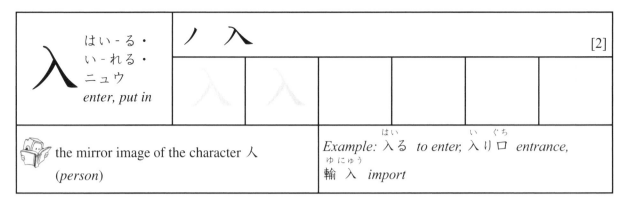

| 入 はい-る・い-れる・ニュウ enter, put in | ノ 入 | | | | | [2] |

the mirror image of the character 人 (person)

Example: 入る to enter, 入り口 entrance, 輸入 import

C) Let's read these sentences aloud. You have already learned all the kanji characters included in these sentences.

1. すみません。もういちど言ってください。
2. よく日本語の本を読みます。それから、日本語のCDを聞きます。
3. 父とはあまり話しません。
4. しゅくだいを出してください。それから、ワークブックを見せてください。
5. どうぞ入ってください。
6. すみません。ちょっと田中さんのよこに立ってください。

D) How many kanji characters can you create by combining the characters below? The first one has been done for you.

{口・千・言・耳・門 gates・売 to sell・五・日}

語 [ ] [ ] [ ] [ ]

2. Reading and Writing Kanji Characters II

A) Let's read each kanji word or phrase aloud several times.

早い early
速い fast
習う to learn
れん習 practice
ふく習 review
道 road

曲がる to make a turn
東 east
西 west
南 south
北 north

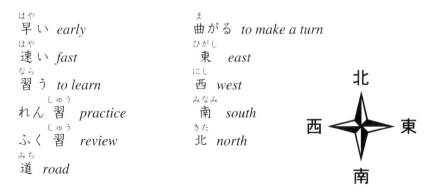

B) In the boxes provided, write each kanji character following the correct stroke order.

早
はや‐い・
ソウ
early, prompt

丶 冂 日 日 旦 早 　[6]

• 日 *(sun)* + 十 *(ten)* = 早 *(early)*

Example: 早い *early*, 早く *early, soon*,
早朝 *early morning*

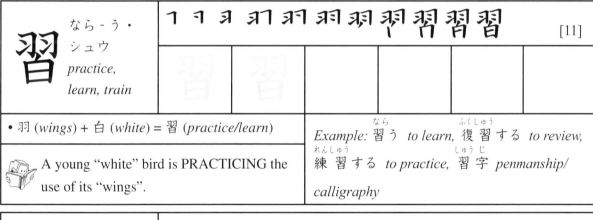 In the Chinese legend of "Chang Er", Hou Yi must have woken up very EARLY for his mission to save the earth by shooting down nine of the "ten suns."

速
はや‐い・
ソク
speedy

一 厂 戸 戸 申 束 束 ̇束 㳡 速 　[10]

• 束 *(bundle)* + 辶 *(movement)* = 速 *(speedy)*

"Bundle" up your long hair when you want to "move" FAST or SPEEDILY.

Example: 速い *speedy*, 速く *fast*, 高速道路 *highway*

習
なら‐う・
シュウ
practice,
learn, train

ㄱ ㄱ ㄱ ヨ 习 羽 羽 羽 羽 習 習 習 　[11]

• 羽 *(wings)* + 白 *(white)* = 習 *(practice/learn)*

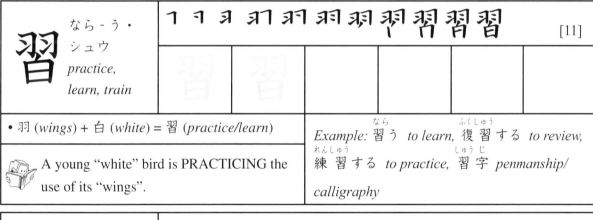 A young "white" bird is PRACTICING the use of its "wings".

Example: 習う *to learn*, 復習する *to review*,
練習する *to practice*, 習字 *penmanship/*
calligraphy

道
みち・ドウ
street, road,
way

丶 丷 丷 ⺍ 产 芒 芦 首 首 首 首 道 道 　[12]

• 首 *(head/chief/main)* + 辶 *(movement)* = 道 *(road/street)*

Example: 道 *street*, 北海道 *Hokkaido*, 鉄道 *railway*, 書道 *calligraphy*

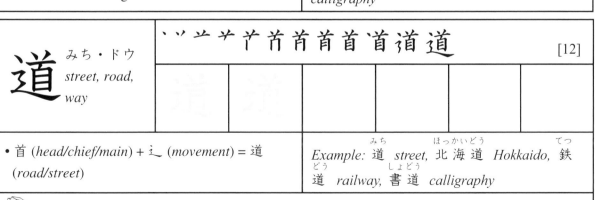 a ROAD formed by the "movement" of many people along a "main" path

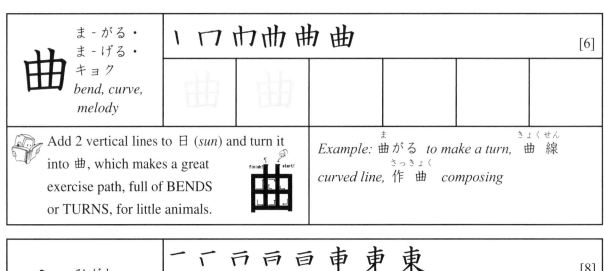

曲 ま‐がる・ま‐げる・キョク
bend, curve, melody

一 冂 冂 曲 曲 曲 [6]

Add 2 vertical lines to 日 (*sun*) and turn it into 曲, which makes a great exercise path, full of BENDS or TURNS, for little animals.

Example: 曲がる (ま) *to make a turn,* 曲線 (きょくせん) *curved line,* 作曲 (さっきょく) *composing*

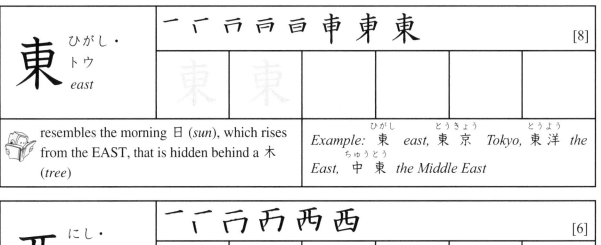

東 ひがし・トウ
east

一 「 「 「 百 百 車 東 東 [8]

resembles the morning 日 (*sun*), which rises from the EAST, that is hidden behind a 木 (*tree*)

Example: 東 *east* (ひがし), 東京 *Tokyo* (とうきょう), 東洋 *the East* (とうよう), 中東 *the Middle East* (ちゅうとう)

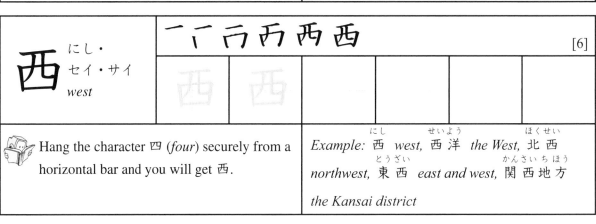

西 にし・セイ・サイ
west

一 「 「 丙 两 西 [6]

Hang the character 四 (*four*) securely from a horizontal bar and you will get 西.

Example: 西 *west* (にし), 西洋 *the West* (せいよう), 北西 *northwest* (ほくせい), 東西 *east and west* (とうざい), 関西地方 *the Kansai district* (かんさいちほう)

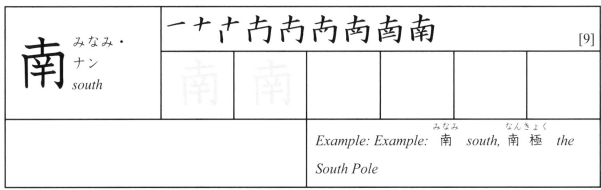

南 みなみ・ナン
south

一 十 十 南 南 南 南 南 [9]

Example: Example: 南 *south* (みなみ), 南極 *the South Pole* (なんきょく)

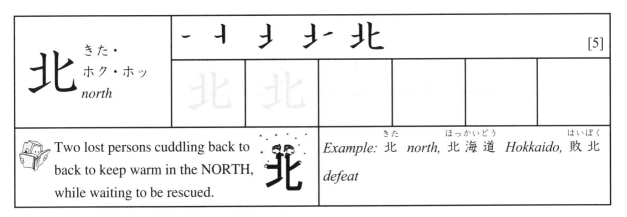

北　きた・ホク・ホッ　north

[5]

Two lost persons cuddling back to back to keep warm in the NORTH, while waiting to be rescued.

Example: 北 *north,* 北海道 *Hokkaido,* 敗北 *defeat*

C) For each of the following, write down the pronunciation of the underlined kanji character in hiragana and translate the sentence.

1. ピアノを習います。　　＿＿＿＿＿＿＿＿＿＿＿＿＿＿＿＿

2. ピアノをれん習します。　＿＿＿＿＿＿＿＿＿＿＿＿＿＿＿＿

3. 日本語をふく習します。　＿＿＿＿＿＿＿＿＿＿＿＿＿＿＿＿

4. 昨日はテレビを見ました。　＿＿＿＿＿＿＿＿＿＿＿＿＿＿＿＿

5. しゅくだいを見せてください。　＿＿＿＿＿＿＿＿＿＿＿＿＿＿

D) Fill in the boxes with appropriate kanji characters.

North

West

East 東

South

1. ☐く 歩く（ある）

2. ☐く 帰る（かえ）

3. Describing Movements

Fill in the blank with an appropriate phrase to describe the movement shown by each illustration.

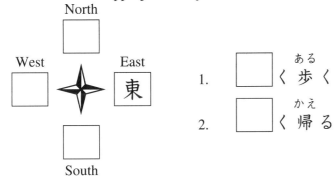

1. この道を ＿＿＿＿＿ 行く（い）。

2. 左（ひだり）に ＿＿＿＿＿＿

3. 3つ目（め）の ＿＿＿＿＿＿ を右（みぎ）に曲がる。

4. 道を ＿＿＿＿＿＿＿

5. はしを ＿＿＿＿＿＿＿

6. レストランを ＿＿＿＿＿＿＿

Note: In Japanese, 目 is added at the end of a number phrase to create an ordinal number, as in 3 つ目 のこうさてん (*the third intersection*) and 3 人目の学生 (*the third student*).

4. Describing Actions

Fill in the blanks with appropriate phrases for the actions illustrated.

1. 　2. 　3. 　4. 　5.

1. *to say one's name* なまえを _____
2. *to speak Japanese* 日本語を _____
3. *to read a book* 本を _____

4. *to stand up* _____
5. *to sit down at the chair* いすに _____

Grammar

1. Te-form Verbs

Japanese verbs, just like English verbs, exist in different forms and one of them is the "te-form". In a sentence, a verb must be in the "te-from" when it is followed by another verb or an auxiliary. For requesting someone to do something, the verb must be followed by an auxiliary ください and so, it must be in the te-form. For example, たべて is the te-form of the verb たべる , and たべてください means *Please eat.*

 Following the example, conjugate each verb to its te-form.

Example: たべる *to eat* ⟶ たべて

1. みる *to look* ⟶ _____
2. ねる *to sleep* ⟶ _____
3. のむ *to drink* ⟶ _____
4. よむ *to read* ⟶ _____
5. しぬ *to die* ⟶ _____
6. あそぶ *to play* ⟶ _____
7. かう *to buy* ⟶ _____
8. つくる *to make* ⟶ _____
9. まつ *to wait* ⟶ _____
10. きく *to listen* ⟶ _____

11. いく *to go*   ⟶   _____

12. およぐ *to swim*   ⟶   _____

13. はなす *to speak*   ⟶   _____

14. する *to do*   ⟶   _____

15. くる *to come*   ⟶   _____

Note: The general rules for converting a verb (from its dictionary form) to its te-form are as follows:

- If a verb ends in る and it is a ru-verb, just replace る with て. (Example: たべる ⟶ たべて)
- If a verb ends in る, and it is an u-verb, replace る with って. (Example: とる ⟶ とって)
- If a verb ends in う or つ, replace it with って. (Examples: かう ⟶ かって and まつ ⟶ まって).
- If a verb ends in む, ぬ, or ぶ, replace it with んで.
  (Examples: のむ ⟶ のんで, しぬ ⟶ しんで, and あそぶ ⟶ あそんで).
- If a verb ends in く or ぐ, replace it with いて or いで.
  (Examples: かく ⟶ かいて, およぐ ⟶ およいで)
- If a verb ends in す, replace it with して. (Example: はなす ⟶ はなして)
- する, くる, and いく are irregular verbs, and their te-forms are して, きて, and いって, respectively.

2. Requesting an Action 1

A request can be expressed using a te-form verb + ください. For example, 書いてください means *Please write (it)*. However, for requesting someone not to do something, the verb in the plain negative form + で + ください is used, as in 書かないでください which means *Please do not write (it)*.

For each of the following, make a request using ください.

Example: じしょをもってくる ⟶ じしょをもってきてください。

1. 日本語で話す   ⟶   _____

2. えい語で話さない   ⟶   _____

3. お金 (money) をかす   ⟶   _____

4. 漢字を書く   ⟶   _____

5. てがみを読まない   ⟶   _____

3. Creating Adverbs

An action can be performed differently, for example one can eat "quickly" or "slowly". These attributes—"quickly" and "slowly"—which describe or express the manner of an action are what we called "adverbs" in English. In Japanese, an adverb is created by adding に at the end of a na-type adjective stem (as in きれいに, *neatly*), or by adding く at the end of an i-type adjective stem (as in 速く *fast*).

Following the examples, create an adverb using the adjective provided.

Example: きれいです ⟶ きれいに   安いです ⟶ 安く

1. まじめです ⟶ _____   4. やさしいです ⟶ _____

2. 早いです ⟶ _____   5. きびしいです ⟶ _____

3. しずかです ⟶ _____

Note: いい is irregular, thus its adverb counterpart is よく.

4. Requesting an Action 2

For asking someone to do something in some manner, use the format: adverb + te-form verb + くださ い, as in きれいに書いてください (*Please write (it) neatly*) and 速く歩いてください (*Please walk fast*). However, for asking someone to behave in a certain manner or to make something in a certain way, して (the te-form of the verb する) should be used, as in しずかにしてください (*Please be quiet*) and へやをきれいにしてください (*Please make your room neat*).

Following the example, complete the sentences.

Example: *to write a bit more neatly*   もう少し __きれいに__ 書いてください。

1. *to come to class a bit earlier*   もう少し _____ クラスに _____ ください。

2. *to eat quietly*   もう少し _____ 食べてください。

3. *to be serious*   まじめ _____ ください。

4. *to turn down the volume of the radio*   ラジオのおとを _____ ください。

5. *to review kanji well*   漢字を _____ ふく習してください。

Conversation and Usage

1. Buying a Digital Camera

Asking for a discount is 安くしてください in Japanese.

 You will hear the conversation between a sales clerk and a customer at a store. Listen carefully and answer the questions that follow.

客　　　：このデジカメはいくらですか。

店員　　：3万5千円です。

客　　　：ちょっと高いわね。もう少し安くしてよ。

店員　　：ああ、それはちょっと。

客　　　：3万円は？

店員　　　　：いやあ。

客　　　　　：じゃあ、いいです。

店員　　　　：じゃあ、このバッグをサービスしましょうか。

客　　　　　：じゃあ、この 三脚 もサービスしてください。

店員　　　　：その 三脚 は 1 万円ですよ。

客　　　　　：ええ。

店員　　　　：じゃあ、デジカメだけで、3 万円。

客　　　　　：それでいいんですよ。

[*Unfamiliar words:* デジカメ *digital camera,* 三 脚 *tripod,* 〜だけ *just ...*]

Note: 〜ましょうか can be used for offering help or service. For example, 私が書きましょうか means *Shall I write it?*

1. How much discount did the customer get?　　_____
2. Did the customer get the tripod for free?　　_____
3. Did the customer get the bag for free?　　_____

2. Giving Directions

Verbs describing movements such as 行く (*to go*), 曲がる (*to turn*), すぎる (*to pass*) and わたる (*to cross*) are often used when one is giving directions. The area covered by these movements is marked by the particle を , and the direction taken by them is marked by the particle に . For example, こうさてん を 右 に 曲がる means *to make a right turn at the intersection.*

You will hear a conversation between a man and a woman in front of the West Entrance (西口) of the JR Shinjuku Railway Station (Ｊ　Ｒ　新 宿 駅). It is 6 p.m. and the woman is asking the man the directions to an Izakaya called Ginger House. Listen carefully and answer the questions that follow.

女 の 人　：すみません。ジンジャーハウスといういざかやをしっていますか。

男 の 人　：ああ、あの西 洋 風のいざかやですか。

女 の 人　：はい。どこにありますか。

男 の 人　：あの 大きい交差点をわたってください。それから、二つ目のかどを 左 に曲が ってください。そうすると、右 にハンバーガーショップがあります。その建 物 の 2 階です。

女 の 人　：ああ、そうですか。どうも。

男の人 ：いいえ。ああ、でも、今日は休みですよ。

女の人 ：えっ。

男の人 ：今日は木曜日ですから。

女の人 ：いいえ、今日は金曜日ですよ。

男の人 ：あっ、そう？じゃあ、休みじゃありません。どうもすみません。

[**Unfamiliar words:** 〜をしっていますか *Do you know ~?*, 西洋風 *Western style*, 休み *closed*]

Note:

- Both それから and そうすると mean *and then*, but the former is used for connecting two consecutive actions, but the latter is used for connecting one action and the resulting state.
- A という B means *B named A*, for example, ECCという学校をしっていますか means *Do you know the school called ECC?*

1. Where is Ginger House located? Choose from A-H in the map.

   _____

2. On which day of the week is Ginger House closed?

   _____

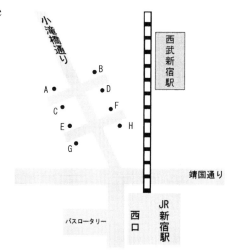

3. Situational Response

In the following situations, what would you say in Japanese?

1. You have just realized that you have forgotten to bring a pen, and you want to ask the lady next to you to loan you her pen politely.

   _____

   Note: To make your request politely, use くださいませんか instead of ください as in 書いてくださいませんか *Could you please write (it)?*.

2. Your friend is using your computer, and you want to warn him not to break it. (こわす *to break*)

   _____

3. Your next-door neighbor is making a lot of noise and you couldn't study. You want to ask him to be quiet.

   _____

4. You are about to enter your teacher's office.

_____

5. You are about to leave your teacher's office.

_____

6. Based on the map below, give the directions to the bookstore from ☺☺ .

本や

銀行

_____

_____

_____

_____

_____

_____

_____

_____

Listening Comprehension

Physical Response

 Listen to the CD and do the actions as you are requested.

Reading Comprehension

Reading a Memo

The following is a memo to Yoko from her mother. Let's read it out loud and then answer the questions (in English) that follow. You may need to use a dictionary.

ようこ
　今日は仕事で早く帰れません。お父さんの晩御飯を作ってください。れいぞうこの中に魚があります。それを焼いてください。それから、豆腐の味噌汁を作ってください。8時ごろ帰ります。

　　　　　　　　　　　　　　　　　　　　母より

Note: 早く帰れません means *(I) cannot come home early.*

1. Why does Yoko have to cook tonight? _____
2. Does Yoko need to buy fish? _____
3. Who will come home at 8 p.m.? _____

Writing

Writing a Memo

Pretend that you are going away for a week on a vacation, and your friend will be moving into your apartment in that week to take care of your pet. Write a memo to your friend on what he/she can or cannot do when staying in your apartment.

New Vocabulary Reference List

NOUN

おと（音）sound, volume

かど（角）corner

つきあたり（突き当たり）the end (of a street)

ねだん（値段）price

はし（橋）bridge

みち（道）street, road

ADJECTIVE

きびしい（厳しい）strict

はやい（早い）early

はやい（速い）fast, speedy

まじめな（真面目な）serious

やさしい（優しい）kind, nice

ADVERB

まっすぐ straight

もうすこし（もう少し）a little more

VERB (Ru-verb)

あつめる（集める）to collect

すぎる（過ぎる）to pass

みせる（見せる）to show

VERB (U-verb)

いう（言う）to say（こたえを言う to say the answer）

かす（貸す）to loan, to lend

きく（聞く）to listen, to inquire, to ask（おんがくをきく to listen to the music, 先生にきく to ask the teacher）

すわる（座る）to sit（いすにすわる to sit at the chair）

だす（出す）to hand in, to take out（しゅくだいを出す to hand in one's homework）

たつ（立つ）to stand up

なくす to lose（さいふをなくす to lose one's purse）

ならう（習う）to learn

はいる（入る）to enter（へやに入る to enter the room）

はなす（話す）to tell, to talk（ともだちと話す to talk with one's friend）

まがる（曲がる）to make a turn（こうさてんを右に曲がる to make a right turn at the intersection）

もっていく（持って行く）to take/bring (something) (there)

わたる（渡る）to cross, to cross over

IRREGULAR VERB

おねがいする（お願いする）to ask a favor of someone

ふくしゅうする（復習する）to review

もってくる（持って来る）to bring (something) (here)

れんしゅうする（練習する）to practice

CONJUNCTION

そうすると then, if (you do) so

OTHERS

（～て）ください Please do ....

～という～ ... called ...

しつれいします（失礼します）I'll come in./I'll leave. (Lit. I will be rude.)

CHAPTER ELEVEN

Expressing the Characteristics of People and Things

Objectives:
- to learn the words and phrases for describing the people and things around us
- to use ～は～が～です for describing people and things

Kanji and Vocabulary

1. Reading and Writing Kanji Characters I

A) Let's read each kanji word or phrase aloud several times.

くち
口　　*mouth*

みみ
耳　　*ear*

て
手　　*hand*

なが
長い　　*long*

おお
多い　　*many, much, a lot*

め
目　　*eye*

あし
足　　*leg, foot*

せ
背　　*height of human and animals*

みじか
短い　　*short*

すく
少ない　　*scarce, little, few*

B) In the boxes provided, write each kanji character following the correct stroke order.

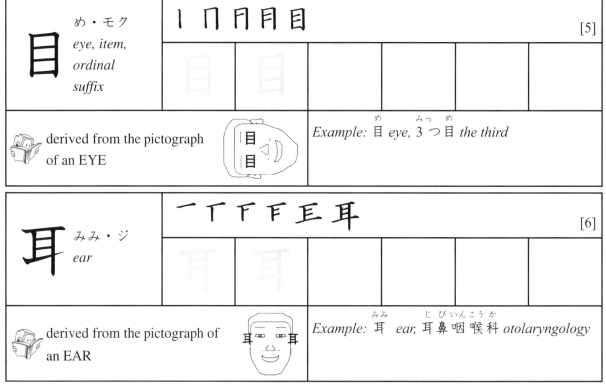

| 目 | め・モク *eye, item, ordinal suffix* | 丨 冂 冃 月 目 | | | | [5] |

derived from the pictograph of an EYE

Example: 目 *eye*, 3 つ目 *the third*

| 耳 | みみ・ジ *ear* | 一 丁 干 干 丰 耳 | | | | [6] |

derived from the pictograph of an EAR

Example: 耳 *ear*, 耳鼻咽喉科 *otolaryngology*

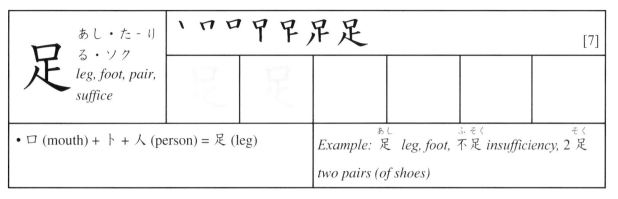

足 あし・た-りる・ソク
leg, foot, pair, suffice

丶 口 口 尸 尸 尸 足 足 [7]

- 口 (mouth) + ト + 人 (person) = 足 (leg)

Example: 足 あし *leg, foot,* 不足 ふそく *insufficiency,* 2 足 そく *two pairs (of shoes)*

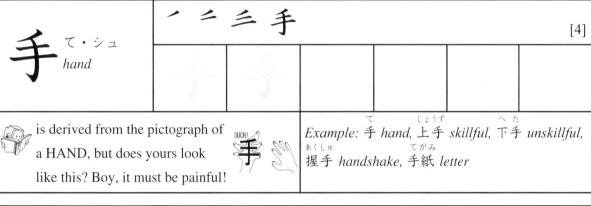

手 て・シュ
hand

丶 二 三 手 [4]

is derived from the pictograph of a HAND, but does yours look like this? Boy, it must be painful!

Example: 手 て *hand,* 上手 じょうず *skillful,* 下手 へた *unskillful,* 握手 あくしゅ *handshake,* 手紙 てがみ *letter*

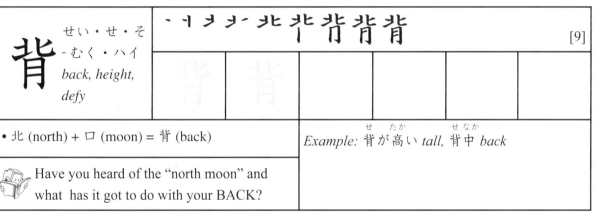

背 せい・せ・そ-むく・ハイ
back, height, defy

丶 丿 爿 爿 丬 北 北 背 背 背 [9]

- 北 (north) + 口 (moon) = 背 (back)

Have you heard of the "north moon" and what has it got to do with your BACK?

Example: 背が高い せたか *tall,* 背中 せなか *back*

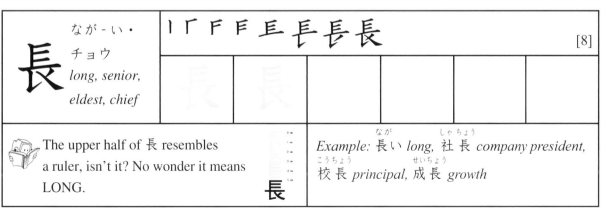

長 なが-い・チョウ
long, senior, eldest, chief

丨 厂 戶 𠄌 巨 長 長 長 [8]

The upper half of 長 resembles a ruler, isn't it? No wonder it means LONG.

Example: 長い なが *long,* 社長 しゃちょう *company president,* 校長 こうちょう *principal,* 成長 せいちょう *growth*

短 みじか-い・タン short	ノ ト ヒ チ 失 矢 矢 知 知 知 短 短					[12]
	短	短				

• 矢 (arrow) + 豆 (bean) = 短 (short)	Example: 短い short, 短刀 dagger

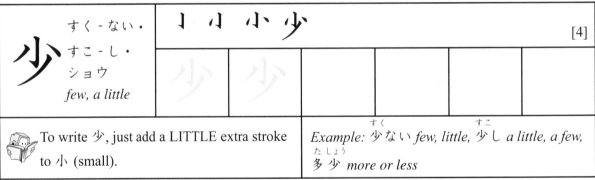 It must be a very SHORT "arrow", otherwise how can it make a perfect match with a "bean"?

多 おお-い・タ many, much	ノ ク タ タ 多 多					[12]
	多	多				

• タ (evening) + タ (evening) = 多 (much/many)	Example: 多い many, much, 多数決 majority
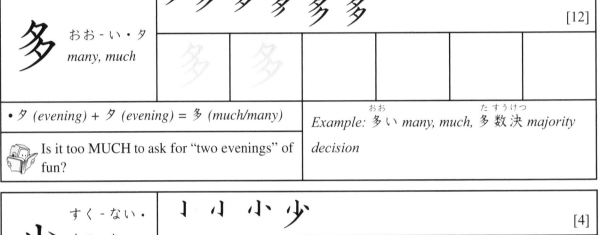 Is it too MUCH to ask for "two evenings" of fun?	decision

少 すく-ない・すこ-し・ショウ few, a little	丨 小 小 少					[4]
	少	少				

To write 少, just add a LITTLE extra stroke to 小 (small).	Example: 少ない few, little, 少し a little, a few, 多少 more or less

C) Let's read the following sentences aloud. Do you know what they mean?

1. 母はかみが長いです。でも、姉はかみが短いです。

2. 父は背が高いです。でも、兄は背がひくいです。

3. 日本語のクラスはしゅくだいが多いです。少したいへんです。
　　でも、しけんは少ないです。

D) Fill in the specified parts of the body in kanji.

1. ☐　　3. ☐　　5. ☐

2. ☐　　4. ☐

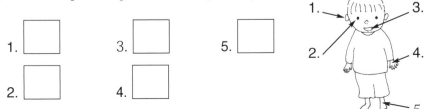

2. Reading and Writing Kanji Characters II

A) Let's read each kanji word or phrase aloud several times.

<ruby>国<rt>くに</rt></ruby> *country*

かん<ruby>国<rt>こく</rt></ruby> *South Korea*

<ruby>食<rt>た</rt></ruby>べもの *food*

<ruby>好<rt>す</rt></ruby>き *to like*

<ruby>上手<rt>じょうず</rt></ruby> *skillful*

<ruby>名前<rt>なまえ</rt></ruby> *name*

<ruby>教<rt>おし</rt></ruby>える *to teach*

<ruby>休<rt>やす</rt></ruby>む *to take a rest*

<ruby>会社<rt>かいしゃ</rt></ruby> *company*

<ruby>会社<rt>かいしゃ</rt></ruby>いん *company employee*

<ruby>中国<rt>ちゅうごく</rt></ruby> *China*

<ruby>来月<rt>らいげつ</rt></ruby> *next month*

<ruby>読書<rt>どくしょ</rt></ruby> *reading*

<ruby>大好<rt>だいす</rt></ruby>き *to like (something) a lot*

<ruby>下手<rt>へた</rt></ruby> *unskillful*

<ruby>運転<rt>うんてん</rt></ruby> *to drive*

お<ruby>金<rt>かね</rt></ruby> *money*

<ruby>社長<rt>しゃちょう</rt></ruby> *company president*

<ruby>社会学<rt>しゃかいがく</rt></ruby> *sociology*

<ruby>働<rt>はたら</rt></ruby>く *to work*

B) In the boxes provided, write each kanji character following the correct stroke order.

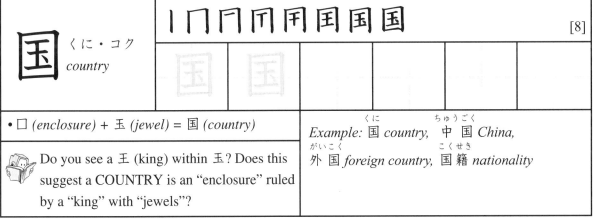

国　くに・コク　*country*

丨 冂 冂 冂 用 国 国 国　[8]

• 囗 (enclosure) + 玉 (jewel) = 国 (country)

Do you see a 王 (king) within 玉? Does this suggest a COUNTRY is an "enclosure" ruled by a "king" with "jewels"?

Example: 国 *country*, 中国 *China*, 外国 *foreign country*, 国籍 *nationality*

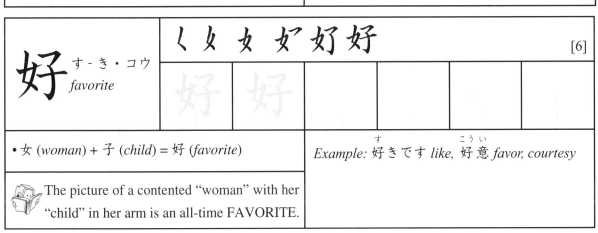

好　す-き・コウ　*favorite*

く 夕 女 女 好 好　[6]

• 女 (woman) + 子 (child) = 好 (favorite)

The picture of a contented "woman" with her "child" in her arm is an all-time FAVORITE.

Example: 好きです *like*, 好意 *favor, courtesy*

名	な・ メイ・ミョウ name, fame, member	ノ ク タ タ 名 名						[6]
		名	名					

• 夕 (evening) + 口 (mouth) = 名 (name)

Example: 名前 name, 有名 famous

前	まえ・ゼン before, front, previous	ゝ ゛ ゛ ゛ 广 前 肖 前 前 前						[9]
		前	前					

• ゝ゛ + 一 (one) + 月 (moon) + (cut) = 前 (before)

Example: 名前 name, 〜の前 in front of ...,
前後 back and forth/before and after

運	みじか-い・ タン carry, fate, luck	ゝ ニ ニ 戸 吊 吊 宣 宣 軍 軍 渾 運						[12]
		運	運					

• 冖 + 車 (car) + 辶 (move/movement) = 運 (carry)

 Do you see a sheltered "car" being "moved" and CARRIED away?

Example: 運転 driving, 運動 exercise, 運ぶ to transport/carry

転	ころ-ぶ・ テン roll, turn	ー ナ 亓 亓 亘 亘 車 車 軒 転 転						[11]
		転	転					

• 車 (car) + 二 + ム = 転 (roll)

Example: 運転 driving, 自転車 bicycle, 回転 revolution

休	やす-む・ キュウ rest	ノ イ 仁 什 休 休						[6]
		休	休					

• イ (person) + 木 (tree) = 休 (rest)

A "person" can get a good REST in the shade of a "tree".

Example: うちで休む to rest at home, クラスを休む to miss the class, 休日 holiday

教 おしえ－る・キョウ teach	一 十 土 耂 耂 考 孝 孝 孝 教 教 教						[11]

• 土 (soil/ground) + ノ + 子 (child) + 夂 (strike) = 教 (teach)

 In some countries, TEACHING of "children" may still involve "caning" them (taking as 土 "countries", ノ and 夂 as "caning").

Example: 教える to teach, 教師 teacher, 教育 education, 教授 professor, 教会 church

---

社 やしろ・シャ・ジャ shrine, company, assembling	` ラ ネ ネ ネ 社 社						[7]

• ネ (altar) + 土 (ground) = 社 (shrine)

 The "ground" and "altar" make up the simplest SHRINE.

Example: 会社 a company, 社長 company president, 社員 company employee, 社会 society, 神社 (Shinto) shrine

---

会 あ－う・カイ・エ meeting, association	ノ 人 人 스 会 会						[6]

• ヘ + 云 (say) = 会 (meeting)

 When people gather under a "roof" and "say" a lot, they are having a MEETING (taking as a ヘ "roof").

Example: 会社 a company, 社会学 sociology, 会う to meet, 会議 conference

---

働 はたら－く・ドウ work	ノ イ イ ケ ケ 佇 佇 佇 俥 俥 俥 働 働						[13]

• イ (person) + 重 (heavy) + 力 (strength) = 働 (work)

 a "heavy person" has great "strength" to do WORK

Example: 働く／労働する to work, 労働力 labor force

C) Let's read the following sentences aloud. Do you know what they mean?

1. 兄は運転が上手です。でも、弟は下手です。

2. 姉は読書が好きです。私も大好きです。

3. 会社で働きます。それか、大学でえい語を教えます。

4. 昨日は社会学のクラスを休みました。

5. 来月社長と中国に行きます。かん国にも行きます。

6. すみません。お名前を書いてください。

3. Naming Favorite Activities

Draw lines to match.

cooking •
reading •
music •
sport •
traveling •

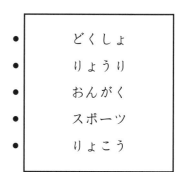
• どくしょ
• りょうり
• おんがく
• スポーツ
• りょこう

4. Naming the Items One Desires

Can you name the following items in Japanese?

1. _____
money

2. _____
time

3. _____
house

4. _____
car

Grammar

1. ～は～が～です for Describing People and Things

One should use ～は～が～です when making a specific description of people and things—～は indicates "who" or "what" is being described, while ～が narrows down the description. For example, ようこさんはきれいです is a general description of Yoko, but ようこさんは目がきれいです is a more specific description of her.

Fill in the blanks to complete the sentences.

1. けんじくんは＿＿＿＿＿＿＿＿＿＿＿です。

2. ひろゆきくんは＿＿＿＿＿＿＿＿＿です。

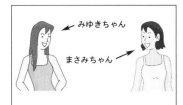

3. みゆきちゃんは＿＿＿＿＿＿＿＿＿です。

4. まさみちゃんは＿＿＿＿＿＿＿＿＿です。

5. よしこちゃんは＿＿＿＿＿＿＿＿＿です。

6. しずかちゃんは＿＿＿＿＿＿＿＿＿です。

2. ～は～が～です **for Describing Places**

Following the example, form a grammatical sentence to describe the place listed in each question, then translate the sentence.

Example: フランス・ちかてつ・べんり ⟶ フランスは　ちかてつが　べんりです。

1. きょうと・たてもの・古い ⟶ ＿＿＿＿＿＿＿＿＿＿＿＿＿＿＿

2. あきはばら・カメラ・安い ⟶ ＿＿＿＿＿＿＿＿＿＿＿＿＿＿＿

3. とうきょう・人や車・多い ⟶ ＿＿＿＿＿＿＿＿＿＿＿＿＿＿＿

4. 中国・新しいたてもの・多い ⟶ ＿＿＿＿＿＿＿＿＿＿＿＿＿＿＿

5. ドイツ・ビール・おいしい ⟶ ＿＿＿＿＿＿＿＿＿＿＿＿＿＿＿

Note: The particle ～や is used to randomly list two or more nouns as examples, as in "A, B, C, and so on." For example, 私はワインや、ビールや、お酒を飲みました means *I drank wine, beer, sake, etc.*

3. ～は～が～です **for Describing Skills and Preferences**

For each of the following, form a grammatical sentence following the example.

Example: 母・テニス・好き ⟶ 母は テニスが 好きです。

1. 姉・読書・好き ⟶ ＿＿＿＿＿＿＿＿＿＿＿＿＿＿＿
あね

2. 兄・じゅうどう・大好き ⟶ ＿＿＿＿＿＿＿＿＿＿＿＿＿＿＿

3. 妹 ・作文・にがて ⟶ ＿＿＿＿＿＿＿＿＿＿＿＿＿＿＿
いもうと　さくぶん

4. 山田さん・テニス・上手　　→　_____

5. 私・りょうり・とくい　　　→　_____

4. Noun-maker の

For using a verb right before が in the 〜は〜が〜です construction, the particle の must be added at the end of the verb, as in 私は食べるのが好きです (*I like eating*).

Make grammatical sentences following the example given.

Example: 姉・食べる・好き　　　→　　　姉は食べるのが好きです。

1. 姉・えいがを見る・好き　　　→　_____

2. 私・うたをうたう・とくい　　→　_____

3. 弟　・本を読む・にがて　　　→　_____
    おとうと　　よむ

4. 兄・ギターをひく・上手　　　→　_____

5. Suffix たい for Desire

The desire for doing some action must be expressed by the suffix たい. It follows a verb in the stem form.

Make grammatical sentences following the example given.

Example: 社長になる　→　　社長になりたいです。

1. きょうしになる　　　→　_____

2. 大学で教える　　　　→　_____

3. びょういんで働く　　→　_____

4. レストランをけいえいする　→　_____

6. れる・られる for Describing Ability and Potential

Verbs in the potential form should be used to express one's ability and potential. These verbs are converted from the dictionary form as follows:

- Replace る at the end of the dictionary form of a ru-verb with られる.
  Example: たべる (*to eat*) ⟶ たべられる (*to be able to eat*)
- Replace u at the end of the dictionary form of an u-verb with e-る.
  Example: かく (*to write*) ⟶ 　かける (*to be able to write*)
- Irregular verbs:
  する (*to do*) ⟶ 　できる (*to be able to do*)
  くる (*to come*) ⟶ 　こられる (*to be able to come*)

Conjugate the verbs. Remember to change the particle を to が when the verb is in its potential form.

Example: カタカナを書く ⟶ カタカナが書ける

1. すしを作る ⟶ _____

2. 中国語を話す ⟶ _____

3. はしで食べる ⟶ _____

4. 日本語を教える ⟶ _____

5. テニスをする ⟶ _____

6. トラックを運転する ⟶ _____

Note: One's potential or ability can also be expressed with the construction ことができる, as in (a) below. Both sentences (a) and (b) are synonymous:

(a) 日本語を話すことができます。　*(I) can speak Japanese.*

(b) 日本語が話せます。　*(I) can speak Japanese.*

Conversation and Usage

1. Talking about What One Would Like To Do in the Future

 Kenji is checking with Heather what she would like to do in the future. Listen to their conversation carefully and answer the questions that follow.

けんじ ： ヘザーさん、将来は何をしたいですか。

ヘザー ： 私は日本で英語を教えたいです。

けんじ ： ああ、そうですか。教えるのは好きですか。

ヘザー ： ええ。文法を教えるのは嫌いですが、会話を教えるのは大好きです。

けんじ ： 日本では英語のネイティブは引っ張りだこですよ。

ヘザー ： ええ。でも、けっこう競争があるんですよ。

けんじ ： そうですか。

ヘザー ： ええ。ですから、アメリカの大学では言語学や、教育や、TESOL のコースを

とりました。

けんじ ： TESOL ってなんですか。

ヘザー ： Teaching English to Speakers of Other Languages　です。

けんじ ： へえ。じゃあ、ヘザーさんは鬼に金棒ですね。

ヘザー ： えっ。鬼に金棒って何ですか。

けんじ ： 強い鬼が金棒を持っているっていう意味です。

ヘザー　：　じゃあ、私は鬼ですか。

けんじ　：　いいえ、ダブル・アドバンテージっていう意味です。

[Unfamiliar words: 引っ張りだこ *a person/item in great demand,* けっこう *quite,* 競争 *competition,* 言語学 *linguistics,* 教育 *education,* 〜って何ですか *What is ...?/What do you mean by ...?,* 鬼 *ogre,* 金棒 *metal rod,* 強い *strong,* 持っている *to be holding,* 〜っていう意味です *It means ...*]

Note:

- The particle は is used for highlighting the items being contrasted.

  Example: 私は犬は好きです。でも、ねこはきらいです。　*I like DOGS. But I hate CATS.*

- The particle が is used to connect two sentences that are in contrast, conflict or contradiction.

  Example: 私は犬は好きですが、ねこはきらいです。*I like DOGS, but I hate CATS.*

1. Where does Heather want to work in the future? _____
2. What kind of courses did Heather take in her college? _____
3. What does 鬼に金棒 mean? _____

2. Do You Cook? (Informal Conversation)

Listen carefully to the conversation between Kenji and Takako, then answer the questions that follow.

けんじ　：　たかこさん。暇なときは何をしますか。

たかこ　：　そうですね。暇なときはいつも料理をします。

けんじ　：　えっ、たかこさんが料理をするんですか。

たかこ　：　はい。

けんじ　：　本当ですか。

たかこ　：　本当ですよ。私は料理がとくいなんです。

けんじ　：　ええ？うそ。

たかこ　：　まあ、しつれいですね。

けんじ　：　何を作るんですか。

たかこ　：　ごはんや、サラダや、ゆでたまごや、ラーメン。

けんじ　：　ああ、やっぱり。

[Unfamiliar words: うそ *lie,* ゆでたまご *boiled egg,* ラーメン *ramen noodles,* やっぱり *as (one) expected*]

1. What does Takako do when she has time? _____
2. List the dishes that Takako cooks as many as you can. _____
3. Why did Kenji say やっぱり at the end of the conversation? _____

3. Situational Response

In the following situations, what would you say in Japanese?

1. Ask your friend (たけし) what he wants the most now.

    _____

2. Ask your friend (けんじ) whether he can swim.

    _____

3. Ask your friend (たかこ) what she wants to do in the future.

    _____

Listening Comprehension

Using Potential Forms

Listen to the CD and circle the one that is read out to you.

1. (make • can make)   3. (read • can read)   5. (use • can use)

2. (write • can write)   4. (sleep • can sleep)

Reading Comprehension

Studying a Bank Account Application Form

The following is the application form (申 込 書) for opening a savings account (普通預金) at a Japanese Bank called さくら銀行. In this form, applicants are required to fill in their full address (おところ), name (おなまえ), sex (男 or 女), date of birth (生年月日) and work place or school (お勤め先・学校). If the name or address is written in kanji, its pronunciation in kana (フリガナ) must be provided. For signature, stamp the personal seal (印鑑) in the box with the character 印 for those who own one, or simply sign in the same box.

Study the form completed by Manabu Takabe and answer the following questions.

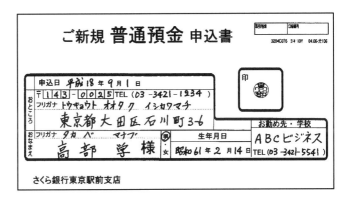

1. When was the date of application? _____

2. When is Manabu's birthday? _____

3. What is Manabu's work phone number? _____

Note: 昭和1年 was 1926, and 平成1年 was 1989.

Writing

Filling out an Application Form

Pretend that you are opening a bank account in Japan. Fill out the following form.

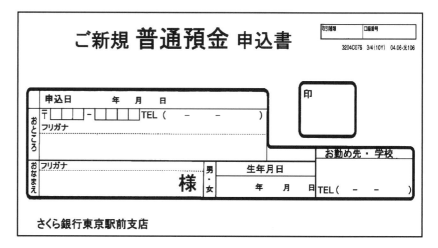

New Vocabulary Reference List

NOUN

あたま（頭）　*head*

いしゃ・おいしゃさん（医者・お医者さん）
　medical doctor

うた（歌）　*song*

おかね（お金）　*money*

おみやげ（お土産）　*souvenir*

おんがく（音楽）　*music*

かいしゃ（会社）　*company*

かいしゃいん（会社員）　*company employee*

かみ（髪）　*hair*

きょうし・せんせい（教師・先生）　*teacher*

くに（国）　*country*

こんど（今度）　*next time, this time*

さけ・おさけ（酒・お酒）　*rice wine, alcoholic beverage in general*

しゃちょう（社長）　*company president*

しょうらい（将来）　*future*

じかん（時間）　*time*

せ・せい（背）　*height of people and animals*

たべもの（食べ物）　*food*

ところ（所）　*place*

どくしょ（読書）　*reading*

べんごし（弁護士）　*lawyer*

ぼうえき（貿易）　*trading*

もの（物）　*thing, item, object*

らいげつ（来月）　*next month*

りょうり（料理）　*cooking*

りょこう（旅行）　*traveling*

PRONOUN

かのじょ（彼女）　*she, her*
かれ（彼）　*he, him*

ADJECTIVE

おいしい（美味しい）　*delicious*
おおい（多い）　*many, a lot*
きらいな（嫌いな）　*to hate*
じょうずな（上手な）　*to be good at*
すきな（好きな）　*to like*
すくない（少ない）　*scarce, little, few*
だいすきな（大好きな）　*to like very much*
とくいな（得意な）　*to be good at*
ながい（長い）　*long*
にがてな（苦手な）　*to be not good at*
にぎやかな（賑やかな）　*bustling, cheerful, lively, crowded*
へたな（下手な）　*to be not good at*
ほしい（欲しい）　*to want*
まずい　*not delicious*
みじかい（短い）　*short*

ADVERB

いちばん（一番）　*the most, the best*
じつは（実は）　*as a matter of fact*
べつに（別に）　*(not) particularly*
もちろん（勿論））　*surely, certainly*

VERB (Ru-verb)

かりる（借りる）　*to borrow*
おしえる（教える）　*to teach*

VERB (U-verb)

あそびにいく（遊びに行く）　*to go to visit (there) for fun*
おどる（踊る）　*to dance*
なる　*to become*
はたらく（働く）　*to work*
やすむ（休む）　*to rest, to take a day off, to be absent from*

IRREGULAR

あそびにくる（遊びに来る）　*to come to visit (here) for fun*
うんてんする（運転する）　*to drive*
けいえいする（経営する）　*to run (a business)*

CONJUNCTION

それか　*or*

PARTICLE

〜か　*or*
〜が　*but*
〜や　*and, so on, etc.*

OTHERS

〜たい　*to want to do something*

CHAPTER TWELVE

Talking about the Past

Objectives:

- to name the four seasons, dates and months in a year
- to learn simple phrases for describing experiences in the past
- to learn about the polite past tense form of adjectives, plain past affirmative form of verbs, and indefinite/negative pronouns

Kanji and Vocabulary

1. Reading and Writing Kanji Characters

A) Let's read each kanji word or phrase aloud several times.

はる 春 *spring*		らいねん 来 年 *next year*	
なつ 夏 *summer*		がっき 学 期 *school term*	
あき 秋 *fall*		にち 〜 日 *... th date*	
ふゆ 冬 *winter*		ねん 〜 年 *... th year*	
なつやす 夏 休 み *summer vacation*		まえ 前 *the previous time, earlier*	
あ 会 う *to meet*		がいこく 外 国 *foreign country*	
かいわ 会 話 *conversation*		ど 〜 度 *... times*	
ことし 今 年 *this year*		こんど 今 度 *next time/this time*	
きょねん 去 年 *last year*			

B) In the boxes provided, write each kanji character following the correct stroke order.

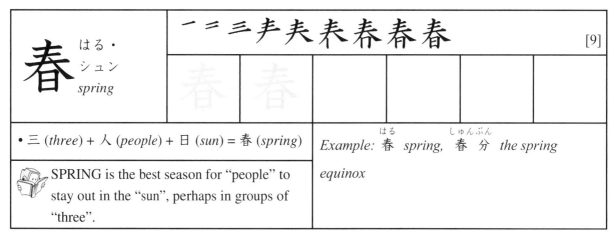

春 はる・ シュン *spring*	一 二 三 声 夫 表 春 春 春 [9]

• 三 (*three*) + 人 (*people*) + 日 (*sun*) = 春 (*spring*)	*Example:* はる 春 *spring,* しゅんぶん 春 分 *the spring equinox*
📖 SPRING is the best season for "people" to stay out in the "sun", perhaps in groups of "three".	

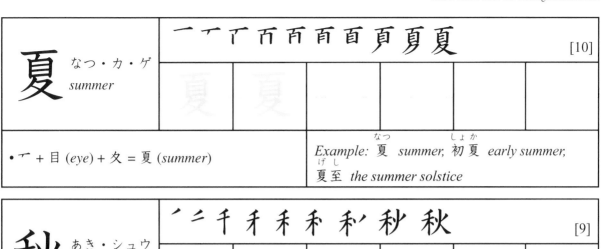

夏 なつ・カ・ゲ *summer*

一 一 ア 严 百 百 百 頁 夏 夏 [10]

• 一 + 目 (eye) + 夊 = 夏 (summer)

Example: 夏 summer, 初夏 early summer, 夏至 the summer solstice

秋 あき・シュウ *fall, autumn*

丿 二 千 禾 禾 禾 秒 秋 秋 [9]

• 禾 (plant) + 火 (fire) = 秋 (autumn)

Example: 秋 autumn, fall, 秋分 autumn equinox

AUTUMN is the best season for making "fire" because there're a lot of "fallen leaves" (taking 禾 as "plants with fallen leaves").

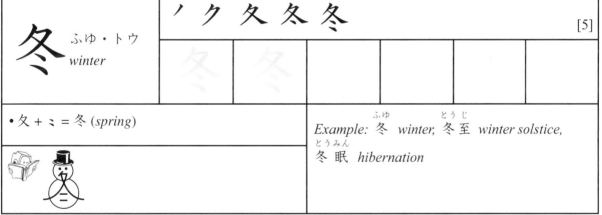

冬 ふゆ・トウ *winter*

丿 ク 夂 冬 冬 [5]

• 夂 + ニ = 冬 (spring)

Example: 冬 winter, 冬至 winter solstice, 冬眠 hibernation

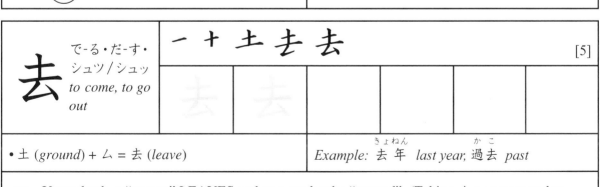

去 で-る・だ-す・シュツ/シュッ *to come, to go out*

一 十 土 去 去 [5]

• 土 (ground) + ム = 去 (leave)

Example: 去年 last year, 過去 past

Upon death, a "person" LEAVES and goes under the "ground" (Taking ム as a nose and to represent a "person").

期 キ・ゴ term, period, expect	一 十 甘 甘 甘 其 其 其 期 期 期 期 [12]				
	期 期				

- 其 (that) + 月 (month) = 期 (term/expect)

The school TERM is EXPECTED to end in "that month."

Example: 今学期 (こんがっき) *current school term,* 期待 (きたい) *expectation*

外 そと・ ガイ・ゲ out, outer, ther, foreign	ノ ク タ 夘 外 [5]				
	外 外				

- 夕 (evening) + ト = 外 (out)

Grandpa loves to go OUT for a stroll with his "walking stick" every "evening" (taking ト as a "walking stick").

Example: 外 (そと) *outside,* 外国 (がいこく) *foreign country,* 外人 (がいじん) *foreigner,* 外科 (げか) *surgery*

度 ド・タク・ たび degree, frequency, times	' 亠 广 庁 庐 庐 庐 庐 度 [9]				
	度 度				

- 广 (linen/building) + 廿 (twenty) + 又 (again/hand) = 度 (degree)

Example: 一度 (いちど) *once,* 今度 (こんど) *this time/next time,* この度 (たび) *this time,* 温度 (おんど) *temperature*

C) Write the pronunciation of the underlined phrase in each sentence, then translate its meaning.

Example: (a) スミスさんに<u>会い</u>ます。　　　　　あいます *(meet)*

(b) 日本語の<u>会話</u>はむずかしくありません。　かいわ *(conversation)*

1. (a) 日本には<u>3度</u>行きました。　　　　　_____

   (b) <u>今度</u>テニスをしましょう。　　　　　_____

2. (a) <u>今年</u>から日本語を勉強するつもりです。　_____

   (b) 私は<u>3年生</u>です。　　　　　　　　　　_____

   (c) <u>来年</u>日本に行くつもりです。　　　　　_____

   (d) <u>去年</u>フランスに行きました。　　　　　_____

3. (a) <u>前</u>の車は小さかったです。　　　　　_____

   (b) えきの<u>前</u>にゆうびんきょくがあります。_____

   (c) すみません。<u>名前</u>を書いてください。　_____

D) Fill in the boxes with appropriate kanji characters.

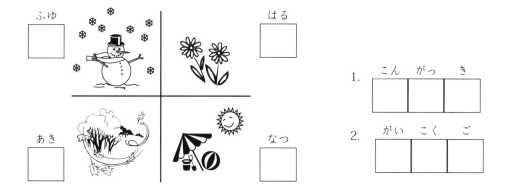

1. こん　がっ　き

2. がい　こく　ご

2. Describing a Restaurant

Fill in the blanks with appropriate words from the box.

あのレストランはとても＿＿＿＿＿＿＿＿です。スパゲッティーがとても＿＿＿＿＿＿＿＿です。

レストランの中はとてもきれいです。それに、＿＿＿＿＿＿＿＿です。ウエーターはとても

＿＿＿＿＿＿＿＿です。でも、ねだんはちょっと＿＿＿＿＿＿＿＿です。

ゆうめい　　しずか　　うるさい　　しんせつ	
いじわる　　おいしい　　高（たか）い　　安（やす）い	

3. Naming the Dates in a Month

Complete the following table. Then read out the dates aloud several times.

月曜日	火曜日	水曜日	木曜日	金曜日	土曜日	日曜日
		1日 ついたち	(　　　　) ふつか	3日 みっか	4日 よっか	5日 いつか
6日 むいか	7日 なのか	8日 ようか	9日 ここのか	10日 とおか	11日 じゅういち にち	12日 じゅうに にち
13日 じゅうさん にち	14日 (　　　　)	15日 じゅうご にち	16日 じゅうろく にち	17日 じゅうしち にち	18日 じゅうはち にち	19日 じゅうく にち
(　　　　) はつか	21日 にじゅういち にち	22日 にじゅうに にち	23日 にじゅうさ んにち	24日 (　　　　)	25日 にじゅうご にち	26日 にじゅうろ くにち
27日 (　　　　)	28日 にじゅうは ちにち	29日 (　　　　)	30日 さんじゅう にち	31日 さんじゅう いちにち		

4. Naming the Months in a Year

Fill in the blanks appropriately, then read out the months in a year several times until fluent.

いちがつ 1 月 January	にがつ 2 月 February	(　　　　　) 3 月 March	しがつ (　　)月 April	ごがつ 5 月 May	ろくがつ 6 月 June
しちがつ (　　)月 July	はちがつ 8 月 August	くがつ (　　)月 September	じゅうがつ 10 月 October	(　　　　　) 11 月 November	じゅうにがつ 12 月 December

5. Reading Dates

Write the pronunciation of each date in hiragana.

1. 1 月 10 日　_____
2. 2 月 4 日　_____
3. 4 月 1 日　_____
4. 1998 年 9 月 3 日 _____
5. 2005 年 12 月 18 日 _____

Grammar

1. Polite Past Tense

The following table summarizes the polite form of verbs and adjectives. Note how different are the past tense forms from their present counterparts.

The Polite Form of Verbs and Adjectives		
	Affirmative	**Negative**
Verb　*present* 　　　*past*	食べます 食べました	食べません 食べませんでした
Noun　*present* + copula　*past*	学生です 学生でした	学生じゃありません (学生じゃないです) 学生じゃありませんでした (学生じゃなかったです)
Na-type　*present* adjective　*past*	便利です 便利でした	便利じゃありません (便利じゃないです) 便利じゃありませんでした (便利じゃなかったです)
I-type　*present* adjective　*past*	高いです 高かったです	高くありません (高くないです) 高くありませんでした (高くなかったです)
Irregular　*present* adjective　*past*	いいです よかったです	よくありません (よくないです) よくありませんでした (よくなかったです)

＊じゃ in the negative forms in the above table can be では .

Following the example, convert the given phrases to their past counterparts.

Example: 会います ⟶ 会いました

1. 好きです ⟶ _____
2. はずかしいです ⟶ _____
3. かんたんなテストです ⟶ _____
4. しんせつじゃありません ⟶ _____
5. 高くありません ⟶ _____
6. いいです ⟶ _____

2. Indefinite/Negative Pronouns

Japanese indefinite pronouns are composed of a question word and か, as in 何か (*something/anything*). Japanese negative pronouns are composed of a question word and も, as in 何も (*nothing*), but must be used with a negative verb. Importantly, も is placed after the grammatical particle, as in どこにも行きませんでした (*I went nowhere*), but if the grammatical particle is either が or を, it must be deleted, as in だれも来ませんでした (*No one came*).

Fill in the blanks appropriately.

1. 昨日は _____ 行きましたか。

   Did you go anywhere yesterday?

   — いいえ、_____ 行きませんでした。

   — *No, I did not go anywhere.*

2. 昨日は _____ しましたか。

   Did you do anything?

   — いいえ、_____ しませんでした。

   — *No, I didn't do anything.*

3. 昨日は _____ 話しましたか。

   Did you talk with anyone yesterday?

   — いいえ、_____ 。

   — *No, I didn't talk with anyone.*

4. 昨日は _____ 来ましたか。

   Did anyone come yesterday?

   — いいえ、_____ 。

   — *No, no one came yesterday.*

3. Plain Past Affirmative Form of Verbs

It is easy to create the plain past affirmative form of a verb if you know its te-form. Just change the final syllable て or で of the te-form to た or だ, respectively. For example, the te-forms of たべる (*eat*) and のむ (*drink*) are たべて and のんで, thus their plain past affirmative forms are たべた and のんだ, respectively.

Conjugate the verbs following the example.

Example: たべる ⟶ たべた

1. きく ⟶ _____
2. よむ ⟶ _____
3. およぐ ⟶ _____
4. あう ⟶ _____
5. とる ⟶ _____

6. はなす ⟶ _____
7. あそぶ ⟶ _____
8. ねる ⟶ _____
9. する ⟶ _____
10. くる ⟶ _____

4. Expressing Experiences

For expressing your experiences, use the verb in the plain past affirmative form plus ～ことがある, rather than just the verb in the past tense form. For example, 富士山を見たことがあります or 富士山を見たことがありません expresses what experience you have or you do not have and it doesn't matter "when". An experience is what you have. That's why you say あります in the present tense. On the other hand, 富士山を見ました or 富士山を見ませんでした just states what you did or you did not do at some specific time in the past, and the question of "when" is crucial.

Following the example, form a question to ask someone whether he/she has performed the given activity.

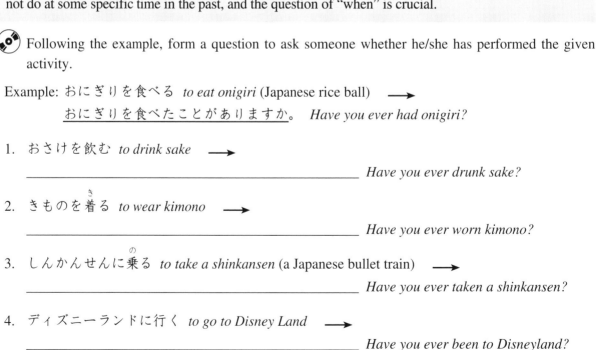

Example: おにぎりを食べる *to eat onigiri* (Japanese rice ball) ⟶
おにぎりを食べたことがありますか。 *Have you ever had onigiri?*

1. おさけを飲む *to drink sake* ⟶
_____ *Have you ever drunk sake?*

2. きものを着る *to wear kimono* ⟶
_____ *Have you ever worn kimono?*

3. しんかんせんに乗る *to take a shinkansen* (a Japanese bullet train) ⟶
_____ *Have you ever taken a shinkansen?*

4. ディズニーランドに行く *to go to Disney Land* ⟶
_____ *Have you ever been to Disneyland?*

Conversation and Usage

1. Asking about Past Summer Vacation

Takeshi is chatting with his college friend, Yoko. He is asking her whether she had gone anywhere in the past summer vacation. Listen carefully to their conversation and then answer the questions that follow.

たけし ： 夏休みにはどこかに行きましたか。

ようこ ： はい。ニュージーランドに行きました。

たけし ： 一人で行ったんですか。

ようこ ： いいえ、えみこさんと二人で行きました。

たけし ： ああ、そうですか。何をしたんですか。

ようこ ： スキーをしました。

たけし ： えっ？夏にスキーをしたんですか。

ようこ ： 日本は夏ですが、ニュージーランドは冬ですよ。

たけし ： ああ、そうですね。

ようこ ： たけしさんは夏休みにどこかに行きましたか？

たけし ： いいえ、今年の夏休みはどこにも行きませんでした。でも、去年の夏休みは四国の香川県に行きました。友達に会ったんです。

ようこ ： ああ、そうですか。あそこは讃岐うどんで有名ですよね。

たけし ： ええ。たくさん食べました。とてもおいしかったです。

ようこ ： ああ、よかったですね。

たけし ： ようこさんは四国に行ったことがありますか？

ようこ ： いいえ、まだありません。

[**Unfamiliar words:** 四国 *one of the four biggest islands in Japan,* 香川県 *Kagawa Prefecture,* 讃岐うどん *Sanuki white noodles*]

Note:

• The particle 〜で marks the condition or circumstance that underlies a given event or activity, showing how it is done, for example, 三人で行きました means *I went there in a group of three*. It also marks the reason, as in 私はかぜでクラスを休みました (*I missed the class due to cold*).

• Absolute time expressions such as *Monday, May 17th, 3 p.m., summer,* and *2005,* are marked by the particle に, as in 月曜日にクラスに行きます (*I will go to class on Monday*). By contrast, relative time expressions such as *yesterday* and *next time* are not marked by the particle に , as in あしたクラスに行きます (*I will go to class tomorrow*).

- The verb 会う needs the particle に or と rather than を for the person to be met as in ようこさんに会いました (*I met Yoko*) and ようこさんと会いました (*I met with Yoko*).

1. With whom did Yoko go to New Zealand? _____

2. What did Yoko do in New Zealand? _____

3. Did Takeshi go anywhere during this summer vacation? _____

2. Situational Response

In the following situations, what would you say in Japanese?

1. Your friend (メイリンさん) went to the department store yesterday. You want to ask her whether she bought anything.

    _____

2. Your friend (ようこさん) said that she ate sushi at the new restaurant. You want to ask her whether their sushi was delicious.

    _____

3. You want to ask your friend (マイクさん) when his birthday is.

    _____

4. You want to ask your friend (サムさん) whether he had ever tried sake.

    _____

Listening Comprehension

Dictation

Listen carefully to the dates, months and years as they are read out to you. In the spaces provided, write them down in Arabic numerals and kanji.

Example: 2005 年 3 月 13 日

1. _____ 3. _____
2. _____ 4. _____

Reading Comprehension

Reciting a Poem

The facing page is a poem about four girls, 春子 (はるこ), 夏子 (なつこ), 秋子 (あきこ) and 冬子 (ふゆこ), and four seasons, 春 (はる) (*spring*), 夏 (なつ) (*summer*), 秋 (あき) (*fall*) and 冬 (ふゆ) (*winter*). It is written vertically. Let's read it aloud, then match the items in box A with those in box B.

春夏秋冬

春子ちゃんは春が好きです。

春にシロツメクサの花で
ネックレスを作ります。

夏子ちゃんは夏が好きです。

夏に砂浜で砂のお城を作ります。

秋子ちゃんは秋が好きです。

秋に枯葉でしおりを作ります。

冬子ちゃんは冬が好きです。

冬に雪で雪だるまを作ります。

私は、春も、夏も、秋も、冬も、

ぜんぶ大好きです。

Box A	Box B
シロツメクサの花	sandy beach
砂浜	castle
砂	fallen leaves
お城	white clover flower
枯葉	sand
しおり	snowman
雪	bookmark
雪だるま	snow

Writing

Essay Writing

Write about your last summer vacation.

New Vocabulary Reference List

NOUN

あき（秋）*autumn, fall*

うそ（嘘）*lie*（うそをつく *to lie*）

かぞく（家族）*family member*

がいこく（外国）*foreign country*

がっき（学期）*(academic) term*

きょねん（去年）*last year*

けんか（喧嘩）*fight, quarrel*（弟とけんかをする *to have a fight with one's younger brother*）

ことし（今年）*this year*

じょうだん（冗談）*joke*

たんじょうび（誕生日）*birthday*

とりあい（取り合い）*fight over taking something*

なつ（夏）*summer*

なつやすみ（夏休み）*summer vacation*

はる（春）*spring*

ふゆ（冬）*winter*

まえ（前）*the previous time, the front position*

らいねん（来年）*next year*

QUESTION WORD

いつ　*when*

ADJECTIVE

いじわるな（意地悪な）*mean, nasty*

おそい（遅い）*late, slow*

しんせつな（親切な）*kind, thoughtful*

つまらない　*boring*

はずかしい（恥ずかしい）*embarrassing, shameful*

ゆうめいな（有名な）*famous*

わるい（悪い）*bad*

VERB (Ru-verb)

おきる（起きる）*to wake up and get up*

VERB (U-verb)

あう（会う）*to meet*

おとす（落とす）*to drop, to lose*

PARTICLE

〜へ　*(e) to, toward, *Exceptional pronunciation*

COUNTER

〜ど（〜度）*... times*

〜にち（〜日）*...th date*

〜ねん（〜年）*... years, ... th year*

OTHERS

このあいだ（この間）*the other day*

〜ごろ（〜頃）*approximately* (6時ごろ *about 6 o'clock*)

たとえば（例えば）*for example*

〜とか　*... etc.*

CHAPTER THIRTEEN

Relating States and Events

Objectives:
- To name various academic subjects and routine activities
- To learn simple phrases for talking about jobs
- To use verbs and adjectives in their te-forms for relating states and events

Kanji and Vocabulary

1. Reading and Writing Kanji Characters

A) Let's read each kanji word or phrase aloud several times.

言語学 *linguistics*
楽しい *enjoyable, fun*
楽です *easy* (in terms of workload)
漢字 *kanji*
難しい *difficult*
洗う *to wash*

洗たく *laundry*
乗る *to ride/get on/take*
買いもの *shopping*
薬 *medicine*
〜点 *... points*

B) In the boxes provided, write each kanji character following the correct stroke order.

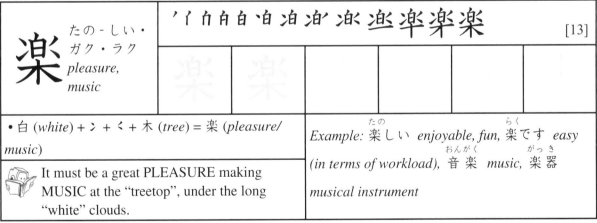

| 楽 | たの‐しい・ガク・ラク pleasure, music | ′ 冂 冖 白 白 冃 泊 治 泊 泊 楽 楽 楽 [13] |

• 白 (*white*) + ⺍ + く + 木 (*tree*) = 楽 (*pleasure/music*)

📖 It must be a great PLEASURE making MUSIC at the "treetop", under the long "white" clouds.

Example: 楽しい *enjoyable, fun,* 楽です *easy (in terms of workload),* 音楽 *music,* 楽器 *musical instrument*

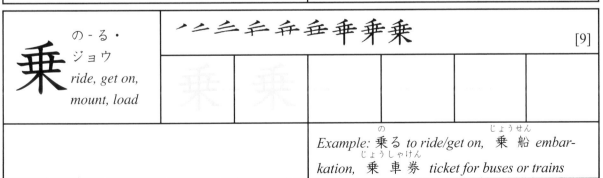

| 乗 | の‐る・ジョウ ride, get on, mount, load | ′ 二 三 千 壬 垂 垂 乖 乗 [9] |

Example: 乗る *to ride/get on,* 乗船 *embarkation,* 乗車券 *ticket for buses or trains*

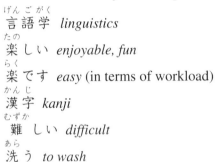

漢 カン Han China, man ｀ ｀ ｺ ｺ ｺ ｺ ｺ ｺ ｺ ｺ ｺ 漢 漢 [13]

漢 漢

- ｺ (water) + 艹 (plants) + 口 (mouth) + 夫 (husband/man) = 漢 (Han China/man)

Example: 漢字(かんじ) Chinese characters

 During war times in CHINA, MAN "survives" by having only "plants" and "water" (taking 口 as "survive").

字 ジ letter, character, symbol ｀ ｀ 宀 宁 字 字 [6]

字 字

- 宀 (roof) + 子 (child) = 字 (characters/script)

Example: 漢字(かんじ) Chinese characters, 数字(すうじ) digit, number, 赤字(あかじ) deficit, 文字(もじ) letter/character/script

 It is more comfortable and fun for "children" to practice writing CHARACTERS under one "roof".

難 むずか-しい・ナン difficult 一 十 卄 艹 芐 苦 苫 莒 堇 菫 剿 剿 難 難 難 難 難 [18]

難 難

- 艹(grass) + 口 (mouth) + 夫 (husband/man) = 菫 (scarecrow);菫 (scarecrow) + 隹 (bird) = 難(difficult)

Example: 難(むずか)しい difficult, 困難(こんなん) difficulty, 難民(なんみん) refugee, 難題(なんだい) difficult problem

 It is DIFFICULT to build a "scarecrow" that scares all kind of "birds" away.

洗 あら-う・セン wash ｀ ｀ ｺ ｺ ｺ 汁 泮 浩 洗 [9]

洗 洗

- ｺ (water) + 先 (ahead) = 洗 (wash)

Example: 洗(あら)う to wash, 洗濯(せんたく) laundry

 Perhaps you should WASH the dirty socks "ahead" with clean "water" before putting them in the washing machine.

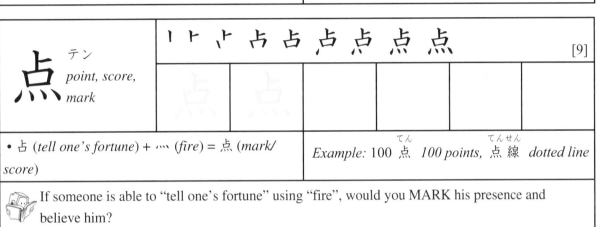

薬
くすり・
ヤク
medicine, drug

一 十 艹 艹 ヴ 芍 芍 莳 莳 莳 菏 菏 菏 薬 薬 薬 [16]

薬 薬

• 艹 (grass) + 楽 (pleasure/joy) = 薬 (medicine)

Most traditional MEDICINE are made of "plants", and they bring "joy" when people are cured after taking them.

Example: 薬 (くすり) medicine, 薬局 (やっきょく) pharmacy,
頭痛薬 (ずつうやく) medicine for headache

点
テン
point, score,
mark

丨 卜 卜 占 占 占 点 点 点 [9]

点 点

• 占 (tell one's fortune) + 灬 (fire) = 点 (mark/score)

Example: 100 点 (てん) 100 points, 点線 (てんせん) dotted line

If someone is able to "tell one's fortune" using "fire", would you MARK his presence and believe him?

C) Write the pronunciation of the underlined phrase in each sentence, then translate its meaning.

1. (a) 言語学を勉強します。　＿＿＿＿＿＿＿＿＿＿＿＿
   (b) 名前を言ってください。　＿＿＿＿＿＿＿＿＿＿＿＿
2. (a) 手を洗います。　＿＿＿＿＿＿＿＿＿＿＿＿
   (b) 洗たくをします。　＿＿＿＿＿＿＿＿＿＿＿＿
   (c) 先生と学生　＿＿＿＿＿＿＿＿＿＿＿＿
3. (a) クラスは楽しいです。　＿＿＿＿＿＿＿＿＿＿＿＿
   (b) このしごとは楽です。　＿＿＿＿＿＿＿＿＿＿＿＿
   (c) 薬をのみます。　＿＿＿＿＿＿＿＿＿＿＿＿

D) Fill in the boxes with appropriate kanji characters.

1. かん じ　は むずか しいです。

2. 車に の ります。

3. 30 てん をとりました。

4. か いものをします。

2. Naming Academic Subjects

Draw lines to match.

れきし　　　●	●　English
言語学　　　●	●　Japanese
文学　　　　●	●　history
すう学　　　●	●　literature
えい語　　　●	●　mathematics
日本語　　　●	●　economics
けいざい学　●	●　linguistics
しゃかい学　●	●　physics
ぶつり　　　●	●　sociology

3. Listing Daily Routines

What are they doing? Fill in the blanks.

1. ＿＿＿＿＿＿＿ を洗う

2. はを ＿＿＿＿＿＿＿

3. シャワーを ＿＿＿＿＿＿＿

4. ＿＿＿＿＿＿＿をする

5. ＿＿＿＿＿＿＿をする

6. ＿＿＿＿＿＿＿をする

Grammar

1. Consequences and Results

それで is a conjunction that means *as a result*.

Complete the following sentences using the verbs and adjectives provided in the box. Conjugate the verbs and adjectives appropriately.

> つかれる・やめる・いそがしい・いたい・おくれる

1. きゅうりょうが安かったです。それで、会社を ＿＿＿＿＿＿＿＿＿＿。

2. 昨日はしごとが三つありました。それで、とても ＿＿＿＿＿＿＿＿＿＿。

3. ＿＿＿＿＿＿＿＿＿＿。それで、早くねました。

4. あたまが _____。それで、薬をのみました。

5. ねぼうしました。それで、クラスに _____。

2. Listing Actions and Properties

For listing two or more verbs and adjectives in a sentence, you need to convert them to their te-forms except for the last verb or adjective in the sentence. (Remember that the particle と can only list nouns but not verbs and adjectives.)

- To form the te-form of a na-type adjective, add で to its stem (for example: まじめな ⟶ まじめで).
- To form the te-form of an i-type adjective, add くて to its stem (for example: 高い ⟶ 高くて).
- To form the te-form of a verb, refer to Chapter Ten.

Depending on the context, sentences with te-form verbs and adjectives yield the interpretation "and then," "furthermore," or "as a result."

Following the example, combine the two sentences in each set to form a grammatical sentence.

Example: 昨日はテニスをしました。それから、えいがを見ました。

⟶ 昨日はテニスをして、えいがを見ました。

1. よく勉強しました。それで、100点をとりました。

⟶ _____

2. ぼくの車は新しいです。それに、大きいです。

⟶ _____

3. 5時間歩きました。それで、つかれました。

⟶ _____

4. 安かったです。それに、よかったです。

⟶ _____

5. そうじをします。それから、昼ごはんを食べます。それから、テニスをします。

⟶ _____

3. Expressing the Purpose of Coming and Going

For expressing the purpose of coming and going, create a purpose phrase by combining the verb in the stem form and the particle に . For example、としょかんに本をかえしに行きました means *I went to the library to return the books.*

Following the example, combine the two phrases to specify the purpose of coming and going.

Example: 本やに行く・じしょを買う (*to buy a dictionary*)

⟶ 本やにじしょを買いに行きました。

1. マイクさんのうちに行く・あそぶ (*to play/to have a good time*)

　　⟶ _____

2. 日本に来る・日本語を勉強する

　　⟶ _____

3. うちに帰る・さいふをとる

　　⟶ _____

4. ほっかいどうに行く・ゆきまつり (*snow festival*) を見る

　　⟶ _____

Conversation and Usage

1. Talking about a New Job

Toshihiko has recently started working for a new company. His friend Takako is asking him how his new job is. Listen carefully to their conversation on the CD, and state whether the following statements are "true" or "false".

たかこ　：　新しい仕事はどうですか。

としひこ：　上司がやさしくて、仕事が簡単で、とても楽しいです。

たかこ　：　ああ、そうですか。よかったですね。

としひこ：ええ。でも、うちから会社まで時間がかかるんです。

たかこ　：　車ですか。

としひこ：いいえ。バスに30分乗って、電車に1時間乗ります。それから、会社まで30分
　　　　　歩きます。

たかこ　：　えっ。30分歩くんですか。

としひこ：ええ。大変です。

たかこ　：　でも、歩くのは健康にいいですよ。がんばってください。

[***Unfamiliar words:*** 上司 *boss, superior,* 健康 *health*]

1. Toshihiko's new boss is kind. 　　　　　　　　　(True • False)
2. Toshihiko commutes by car. 　　　　　　　　　(True • False)
3. Toshihiko spends 90 minutes to commute one way. 　(True • False)

Note:

• The verb 乗る means *to ride, to get on* or *to take*. It is used with any form of transportation such as car, train, bicycle, boat and plane. The latter is marked by the particle に , as in 車に乗る .

• Properties such as "beneficial", "harmful", "suitable", "necessary" and "useful" can be understood only if we specify for what or for whom they hold. The latter is marked by the particle に , as in ビタミンＣは健康^{けんこう}にいいです (*Vitamin C is good for health*).

2. Offering Help

When you notice that something is wrong with someone, you can ask him/her どうしたんですか which means *What is the matter with you?* or *What happened?*.

 It is Friday and Toshihiko is asking his colleague, Takeshi to go for a drink after work. Listen to their conversation carefully and then answer the questions that follow.

としひこ: 今日^{きょう}、飲^のみに行きませんか。

たけし　：ああ。でも、

としひこ: どうしたんですか。

たけし　：今日は仕事^{しごと}がたくさんあるんです。たぶん残業^{ざんぎょう}です。

としひこ: 今日は金曜日^{きんようび}ですよ。

たけし　：ええ。でも、

としひこ: じゃあ、手伝^{てつだ}いましょうか。

たけし　：いいんですか。

としひこ: ええ、まあ。

たけし　：ああ、助^{たす}かります。じゃあ、これと、これと、これをお願^{ねが}いします。

[**Unfamiliar words:** たぶん *probably*, 残業^{ざんぎょう} *overtime work*, 手伝^{てつだ}う *to help*, 助^{たす}かる *helpful (lit. to be helped)*]

1. What did Toshihiko suggest to Takeshi? _____
2. Will Toshihiko help Takeshi with his job today? _____

3. Situational Response

In the following situations, what would you say in Japanese?

1. Your friend has just told you that he is going to Mr. Tanaka's house. You want to ask him why.

   _____

2. You want to tell your mother that you have brushed your teeth and washed your face.

   _____

3. Your friend said that he doesn't like apples (りんご). You want to tell him that apples are good for health (けんこう).

   _____

Listening Comprehension

How Toshihiko Spent His Sunday

You will hear a narrative about how Toshihiko spent his Sunday. Listen carefully and then answer the following questions in English.

1. Where did he read the novel? _____

2. How much did he spend for playing a pachinko game? _____

3. What did he eat for supper? _____

Reading Comprehension

Osechi Dishes

Let's read the following passage and answer the questions that follow. You may need to use a dictionary.

　日本人は正月に御節料理を食べます。御節料理では、色や、形や、語呂合わせで、無病息災や、子孫繁栄を願います。例えば御節料理には次のような食べ物があります。

- 黒豆 (*black soybean*): まめに働くのを願う。「豆」と、「まめに」は語呂合わせ。
- 数の子 (*herring roe*): 子孫繁栄を願う。数の子はたくさんの卵のかたまり。
- 昆布 (*kelp*):「昆布」と、「喜ぶ」は語呂合わせ。
- えび (*shrimp*): 長寿を願う。えびは腰が曲がっている。
- 紅白かまぼこ (*red-white steamed fish paste*): 赤と白はめでたい色。

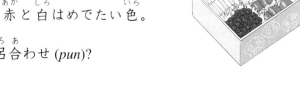

1. Which two foods listed above are used for 語呂合わせ (*pun*)?

   _____

2. Which food listed above wishes for 子孫繁栄 (*prosperity of family descendant*)?

   _____

3. Which food listed above is used because of its 色 (*color*)?

   _____

Writing

Designing a Japanese New Year s Card

Below is a sample of the Japanese New Year's Card called 年賀状 (ねんがじょう), written by 田中太郎 (たなかたろう) (Taro Tanaka). あけましておめでとうございます means *A happy New Year!* 本年(ほんねん)もよろしくお願(ねが)いします roughly means *We look forward to your continuous friendship (and/or support) in this year.* Following the sample, design your own Japanese New Year's Card in the space provided.

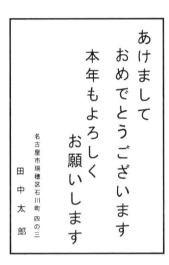

あけまして
おめでとうございます
本年もよろしく
お願いします

名古屋市瑞穂区石川町四の三

田中太郎

New Vocabulary Reference List

NOUN

かいもの（買い物）*shopping*（買い物をする *to go shopping*)

かお（顔）*face*

きゅうりょう（給料）*salary, wages, pay*

くすり（薬）*medicine*（薬をのむ *to take medicine*)

げんごがく（言語学）*linguistics*

しゅうしょく（就職）*employment*

せんたく（洗濯）*laundry*（洗濯をする *to do the laundry*)

そうじ（掃除）*cleaning*（掃除をする *to do the cleaning*)

は（歯）*tooth*（歯をみがく *to brush one's teeth*)

はらじゅく（原宿）*Harajuku* (place name)

ぶつり（物理）*physics*

れきし（歴史）*history*

ADJECTIVE

いそがしい（忙しい）*busy*

いたい（痛い）*painful*（あたまが痛い *to have a headache*)

らくな（楽な）*easy (less labor intensive)*

ADVERB

もう　*already*

VERB (Ru-verb)

おくれる（遅れる）*to be late*（クラスに遅れる *to be late for class*)

きる（着る）*to wear, to put on (one's clothes)*

つかれる（疲れる）*to get tired*

やめる（辞める）*to quit, to resign*

VERB (U-verb)

あらう（洗う）*to wash*

がんばる（頑張る）*to try one's best*

とる（取る）*to take*（日本語を取る *to take a Japanese course*)

のる（乗る）*to ride, to get on, to take (a form of transportation)*（バスに乗る *to take/get on a bus*)

みがく（磨く）*to polish*

IRREGULAR

ねぼうする（寝坊する）*to oversleep*

CONJUNCTION

それで　*as a result*

COUNTER

〜てん（〜点）*... points*

OTHERS

かぜをひく（風邪を引く）*to catch a cold*

シャワーをあびる（シャワーを浴びる）*to take a shower*

CHAPTER FOURTEEN

Talking about Now

Objectives:

- to name various occupations, clothing and accessories
- to express various emotions
- to describe on-going activities and current states of people and things

Kanji and Vocabulary

1. Reading and Writing Kanji Characters

A) Let's read each kanji word or phrase aloud several times.

お茶 *tea*

学長 *school president*

校長 *school principal*

学校 *school*

小学校 *elementary school*

中学校 *junior high school*

高校 *high school*

英語 *English*

石田 *Ishida (family name)*

林 *woods, Hayashi (family name)*

子供 *child*

化学 *chemistry*

遊ぶ *to play*

住む *to live*

着る *to wear*

B) In the boxes provided, write each kanji character following the correct stroke order.

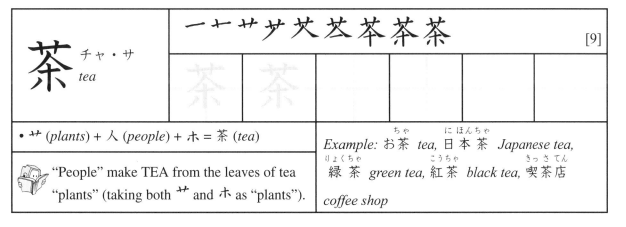

茶 チャ・サ *tea*

一 十 廾 サ 艾 艾 茎 苓 茶 茶 [9]

- サ (*plants*) + 人 (*people*) + 朩 = 茶 (*tea*)

"People" make TEA from the leaves of tea "plants" (taking both サ and 朩 as "plants").

Example: お茶 *tea*, 日本茶 *Japanese tea*, 緑茶 *green tea*, 紅茶 *black tea*, 喫茶店 *coffee shop*

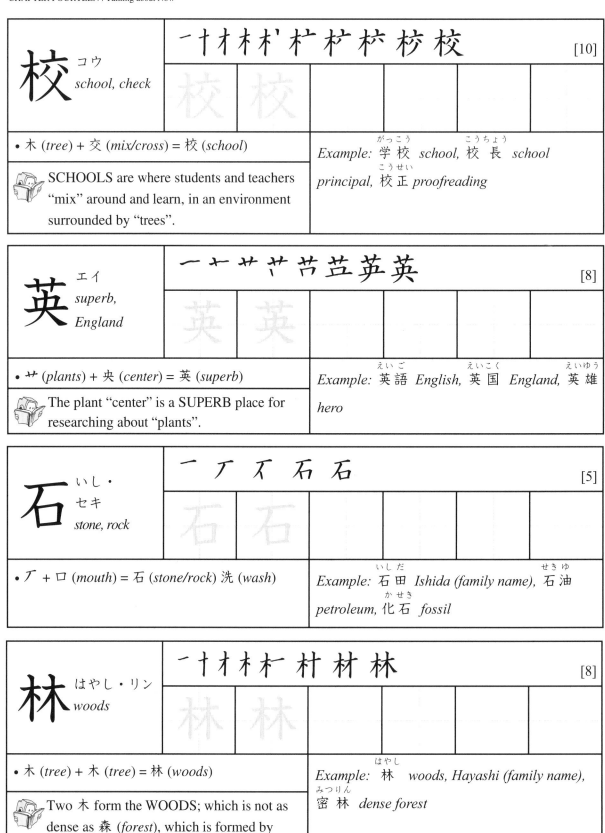

校 コウ
school, check

一 十 才 木 杧 朾 朾 栌 栌 校　[10]

• 木 (tree) + 交 (mix/cross) = 校 (school)

SCHOOLS are where students and teachers "mix" around and learn, in an environment surrounded by "trees".

Example: 学校 school, 校長 school principal, 校正 proofreading
(がっこう, こうちょう, こうせい)

英 エイ
superb, England

一 十 艹 艹 芇 苬 苬 英　[8]

• 艹 (plants) + 央 (center) = 英 (superb)

The plant "center" is a SUPERB place for researching about "plants".

Example: 英語 English, 英国 England, 英雄 hero
(えいご, えいこく, えいゆう)

石 いし・セキ
stone, rock

一 ア 石 石 石　[5]

• ア + 口 (mouth) = 石 (stone/rock) 洗 (wash)

Example: 石田 Ishida (family name), 石油 petroleum, 化石 fossil
(いしだ, せきゆ, かせき)

林 はやし・リン
woods

一 十 才 木 村 村 材 林　[8]

• 木 (tree) + 木 (tree) = 林 (woods)

Two 木 form the WOODS; which is not as dense as 森 (forest), which is formed by three 木.

Example: 林 woods, Hayashi (family name), 密林 dense forest
(はやし, みつりん)

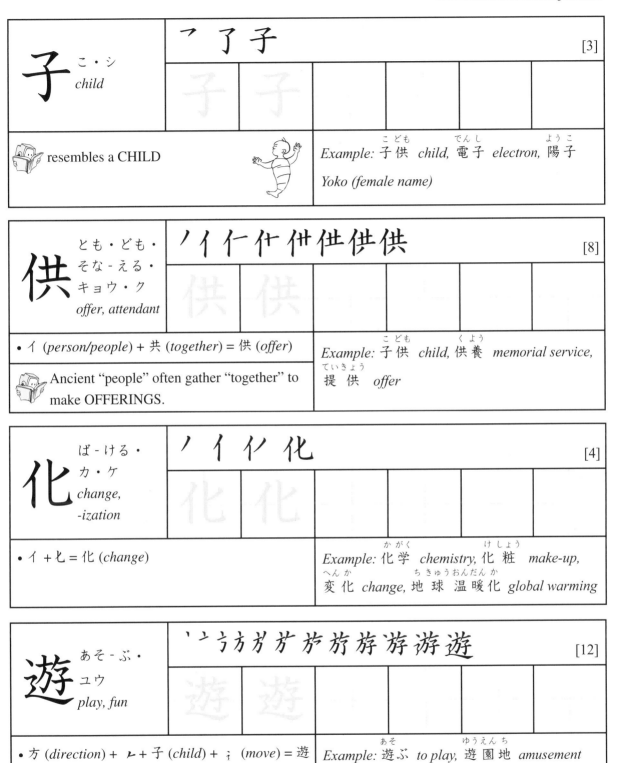

子　こ・シ
child

フ了子　[3]

resembles a CHILD

Example: 子供 child, 電子 electron, 陽子 Yoko (female name)

供　とも・ども・そな-える・キョウ・ク
offer, attendant

ノイイ什什供供供　[8]

• イ (person/people) + 共 (together) = 供 (offer)

Ancient "people" often gather "together" to make OFFERINGS.

Example: 子供 child, 供養 memorial service, 提供 offer

化　ば-ける・カ・ケ
change, -ization

ノイイ化　[4]

• イ + ヒ = 化 (change)

Example: 化学 chemistry, 化粧 make-up, 変化 change, 地球 温暖化 global warming

遊　あそ-ぶ・ユウ
play, fun

方方方方方旅游游遊遊　[12]

• 方 (direction) + レ + 子 (child) + 辶 (move) = 遊 (play/fun)

Example: 遊ぶ to play, 遊園地 amusement park

"Children" have great FUN wearing funny "caps" and "moving" in the same "direction" as they PLAY (taking レ as a "cap").

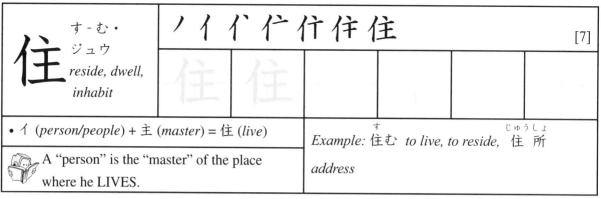

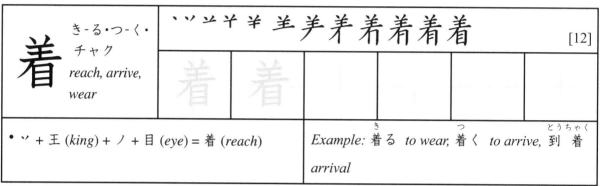

C) Let's read the following passage aloud.

石田先生は小学校の先生です。林先生は中学校の先生です。山田先生は高校の化学の先生です。川口先生は大学の先生です。田中先生は英語学校の先生です。私は大学生です。文学と、言語学と、社会学を勉強しています。

D) Fill in the boxes with appropriate kanji characters.

1. <u>こ</u><u>ども</u> が <u>あそ</u>んでいます。

2. 日本に <u>す</u>みたいです。

3. きものを <u>き</u>ました。

4. お <u>ちゃ</u>を飲みます。

E) Add the おくりがな to each kanji character.

Example: 食 <u>べる</u> to eat

1. 使 _____ to use

2. 作 _____ to make

3. 休 _____ to rest

4. 住 _____ to live

5. 働 _____ to work

2. What's Your Occupation?

Write down each occupation in Japanese.

1. _____
   doctor

2. _____
   nurse

3. _____
   teacher

4. _____
   lawyer

3. Expressing Emotions

Draw lines to match.

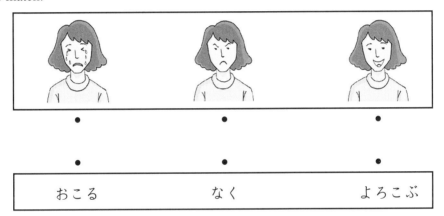

| おこる | なく | よろこぶ |

4. Identifying the Types of Clothing and Accessories

Draw lines to match.

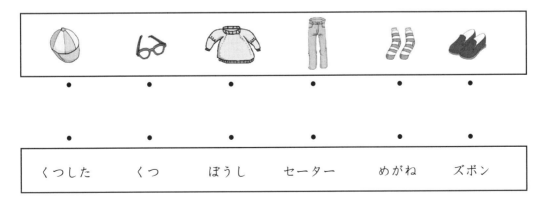

| くつした | くつ | ぼうし | セーター | めがね | ズボン |

5. The Verbs "to Wear"

Fill in the blanks with appropriate Japanese verbs which mean "to wear" or "to put on".

   Example: くつを __はく__

1. イヤリングを ＿＿＿＿＿＿＿＿＿＿

2. めがねを ＿＿＿＿＿＿＿＿＿＿

3. スカートを ＿＿＿＿＿＿＿＿＿＿

4. Ｔシャツを ＿＿＿＿＿＿＿＿＿＿

5. ぼうしを ＿＿＿＿＿＿＿＿＿＿

Grammar

1. 〜ている (Progressive, Habitual and Resulting State)

いる means to exist. It is a verb, but it denotes a state (existing) rather than an action.

いる can also function as an auxiliary verb, used after another verb in the te-form. As an auxiliary verb, it also expresses a state, which is a progressive, habitual, or resulting state. For example, おさけを飲んでいます has the following possible meanings, which are disambiguated by the context:

1. Progressive state (state where an action is on-going):

   ブラウンさんは今おさけを飲んでいます。 Mr. Brown is drinking now (at this moment).

2. Habitual state (state where an action takes place regularly):

   ブラウンさんは毎晩おさけを飲んでいます。 Mr. Brown is drinking every night (regularly).

3. Resulting state (state the results from some action in the past):

   A: ブラウンさんはちょっとへんですよ。 Mr. Brown is a little strange.

   B: ええ。ブラウンさんはおさけを飲んでいますね。 Yes. Mr. Brown is drunk, isn't he?

Specify the state (progressive, habitual, or resulting) of the underlined part in each of the following expresses.

1. A: もしもし、山田さんはいらっしゃいますか。
   B: いいえ、今、大学でテニスをしています。 ＿＿＿＿＿＿＿＿＿＿

2. A: もしもし、社長さんはいらっしゃいますか。
   B: いいえ、今ボストンに行っています。 ＿＿＿＿＿＿＿＿＿＿

3. A: お姉さんは学生さんですか。
   B: はい、姉はサンフランシスコの大学に行っています。 ＿＿＿＿＿＿＿＿＿＿

4. A: たけしさんとはともだちですか。
   B: はい、いつもいっしょに晩ごはんを食べています。 ＿＿＿＿＿＿＿＿＿＿

5. A: よし子さんは？
   B: まだ、来ていませんよ。 ＿＿＿＿＿＿＿＿＿＿

2. Progressive State

State in Japanese what the person is doing in each picture.

1. _____ 2. _____ 3. _____ 4. _____

3. Habitual State

Fill in the blanks with appropriate verbs in the correct conjugated forms.

うちは父と、母と、兄と、弟と、私の5人家族です。父は病院で医者を
_____。母は高校で英語を _____。兄はコンピューターの会
社で _____。弟は小学校に _____。今、5年生です。
私は今、大学生です。社会学を _____。

[**Unfamiliar words:** 5人家族 *five-member family*]

Note: Both 私はいしゃです and 私はいしゃをしています mean *I am a doctor.*

4. Expressing Experiences

The particle ばかり can express extremity. For example, 兄はいつもピザばかり食べています or 兄
はいつもピザを食べてばかりいます means the person's pizza-eating habit is too extreme. Note that
を or が must be deleted if followed by ばかり, just like when followed by は or も .

 Form a grammatical sentence following the example.

Example: タバコをすう ⟶ タバコをすってばかりいます。

1. ねる ⟶ _____
2. しゃべる ⟶ _____
3. なまける ⟶ _____
4. 遊ぶ ⟶ _____
5. パチンコをする ⟶ _____

Note: The difference between 兄はピザばかり食べています and 兄はピザを食べてばかりいます
is very subtle: the former means *my brother eats nothing but pizza*; the latter means *my brother
does nothing but eat pizza.* But native speakers of Japanese often use them interchangeably.

5. Resulting State

Complete each sentence using the appropriate item from the list provided and making the necessary changes, then translate the sentence.

はじまる・とうきょうに行く・あく・こむ・うちに帰る・けっこんする

Example:　妹 (いもうと) はうちに帰っています。

Translation: *My sister has returned home.*

1. ぎんこうは _____ 。

   Translation: _____

2. クラスは _____ 。

   Translation: _____

3. このバスは _____ 。

   Translation: _____

4. 兄は _____ 。

   Translation: _____

5. 父は _____ 。

   Translation: _____

6. Particles

Fill in the blanks with appropriate particles.

1. たけしさんの本 ____ かりました。
2. ブラウンさんは日本 ____ 住んでいます。
3. 母は今うち(いま) ____ います。
4. 母は今うち ____ 晩(ばん) ごはんを作(つく)っています。
5. 父は今とうきょう ____ 行っています。
6. びょういん ____ 働いています。

7. Relative Clauses

Relative clauses in Japanese are always placed right before the noun they modify. The verbs and adjectives in a relative clause must be in the plain form.

Reorder the items in the parentheses to make a grammatical sentence.

1. 石田さんのむすこさんは {あの・めがね・人・かけている・を} です。

   _____

2. 私の兄は {たばこ・あそこ・を・で・人・すっている} です。

   _____

3. よう子さんは {人・しゃべる・よく} ですよ。

_____

4. {立っている・女の人・あそこに} は私のともだちです。

_____

5. {食べた・昨日・すし} はとてもおいしかったです。

_____

Conversation and Usage

1. Visiting a Colleague at Her Apartment

In an informal conversation, い in ～ている is often omitted. For example, 食べている becomes 食べてる, and 食べていた becomes 食べてた.

Tomiko is visiting her colleague, Kazuko's apartment for the first time after work. Listen to their conversation, then state whether the statements that follow are true or false.

かずこ　：どうぞ。入ってください。

とみこ　：おじゃまします。

かずこ　：きたなくて、すみません。私は掃除が苦手なんです。

とみこ　：私もです。日曜日には掃除しますが、月曜日にはまたメチャメチャです。

かずこ　：えっ、本当？うそでしょう？とみこさんはきれい好きでしょう？

とみこ　：まさか。

かずこ　：だって、オフィスのとみこさんの机や引き出しはいつもきれいじゃないですか。

とみこ　：ええ、オフィスでは掃除ばかりしているんです。

かずこ　：仕事は？

とみこ　：仕事はいつもサボっています。

かずこ　：やっぱり。

とみこ　：部長に言わないでくださいよ！

かずこ　：言いませんよ。私もいつもサボってるから。

とみこ　：え？本当？

かずこ　：ええ。昨日は半日オフィスのパソコンでゲームをしてたのよ。

とみこ　：わあ。部長に言いますよ。

かずこ　：駄目よ！

とみこ　：冗談、冗談。

[***Unfamiliar words:*** また *again,* メチャメチャ *mess,* 本当(ほんとう) *true,* きれい好き *person who likes neatness,* まさか *No kidding!,* だって *but, because* (a conjunction that shows a sentence that provides the evidence, reason, additional information, or explanation for the preceding sentence), サボる *to skip one's duties,* やっぱり *I thought so,* 部長(ぶちょう) *division head, manager,* 半日(はんにち) *half day,* パソコン *personal computer,* 駄目(だめ) *not good,* 冗談(じょうだん) *joke (I'm kidding)*]

1. Tomiko usually cleans on Mondays. (True • False)
2. Kazuko likes cleaning. (True • False)
3. Kazuko is a diligent office worker. (True • False)

2. Situational Response

In the following situations, what would you say in Japanese?

1. You want to ask your friend (石田さん) where his father and mother live.

   _____

2. You want to ask your friend (林さん) what her father does for a living.

   _____

3. Someone called and asked for your father, but your father is in Osaka on a business trip.

   _____

Listening Comprehension

Identifying a Group of Office Workers

Listen carefully to the narrative on the CD about a group of office workers. Identify each of them by filling in the blanks with letters A to G.

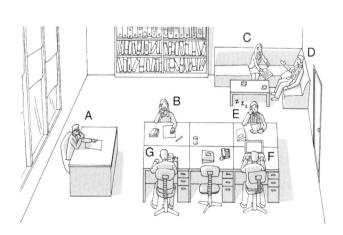

1. 部長 (division head, manager)

   _____

2. 川口さん

   _____

3. 山田さん

   _____

4. 林さん

   _____

5. 石田さん

   _____

6. 田中さん

   _____

Reading Comprehension

Checking the Q&A Section of a Magazine

The following is a Q&A (questions and answers) section of a magazine. Read it carefully and then state whether the statements that follow are true or false.

【653】ねてばかりいて、罪悪感を感じます。

Q: 私は42歳の主婦です。前は料理や洗濯や掃除が好きでした。でも、5ヶ月前から、何もしたくありません。ねてばかりいます。子供は男の子が2人います。8歳と、5歳です。夫は会社員で、朝6時にうちを出ます。ですから、8歳の息子が弟に朝ごはんを作っています。部屋の中はいつもメチャメチャです。内科に行きましたが、何も悪いところはありませんでした。私は母ですが、料理も洗濯も掃除もしないで、ねてばかりいて、罪悪感を感じています。どうしたらいいでしょうか。

A: あなたはうつ病だと思います。早く精神科医のところに行ってください。薬で治療をしてください。必ず治ります。焦らないでください。また、罪悪感を感じないでください。

[*Unfamiliar words:* 罪悪感 *a sense of guilt,* 感じる *to feel,* 主婦 *housewife,* 内科 *internal medicine,* 悪い *bad,* うつ病 *depression,* 〜と思います *I think that ...,* 精神科医 *a psychiatrist,* 治療 *medical treatment,* 必ず *surely,* 治る *be cured,* 焦る *to be impatient*]

1. This woman makes breakfast for her family every day.　　　　(True • False)
2. This woman is having difficulty in getting to sleep.　　　　(True • False)
3. The counselor does not think she should take a medicine.　　　(True • False)

Writing

Essay writing

Write about your family, discussing what they do for a living and the kind of activities they participate, or enjoy on weekends, etc.

New Vocabulary Reference List

NOUN

おちゃ（茶）*(Japanese) tea*

かがく（化学）*chemistry*

がくちょう・がくちょうさん（学長・学長さん）
school president

かんごし・かんごしさん（看護師・看護師さん）
nurse

くつした（靴下）*socks*

けいさつかん（警察官）*police officer*

こうじょう（工場）*factory*

こうちょう・こうちょうせんせい（校長・校長
先生）*school principal*

しょうがっこう（小学校）*elementary school*

しょくぎょう・ごしょくぎょう（職業・御職業）
occupation

ズボン　*pants, trousers*

せんもんがっこう（専門学校）*special
(vocational) school*

タバコ（煙草）*tobacco, cigarette*（タバコをすう
to smoke）

ちゅうがっこう（中学校）*junior high school*

パチンコ　*Japanese pinball game*

まんが（漫画・マンガ）*comic book*

むすこ・むすこさん（息子・息子さん）*son*

むすめ・むすめさん／おじょうさん（娘・娘さ
ん／お嬢さん）*daughter*

めがね（眼鏡）*eyeglasses*

よる（夜）*night*

ADJECTIVE

かっこいい　*good looking* (usually for young men
and boys)

へんな（変な）*strange, weird, unusual*

ADVERB

まだ　*(not) yet*

VERB (U-verb) Irregular verb

あく（開く）*to open*（ドアが開く　*The door
opens.*）

あそぶ（遊ぶ）*to enjoy oneself, to play*

おこる（怒る）*to get angry*

おりる（降りる）*to get off, to come down*（バスを
降りる *to get off the bus*）

かける　*to wear/put on (eyeglasses)*

かぶる　*to wear/put on* (items such as hats and caps)
（ぼうしをかぶる　*to put on a hat*）

けっこんする（結婚する）*to get married*（日本
人と結婚する　*to get married to a Japanese*）

こむ（混む）*to become crowded*（混んでいる　*to be
crowded*）

しゃべる　*to chat*

しる（知る）*to get to know*（知っている　*to know*）

すう（吸う）*to inhale*（タバコをすう　*to smoke*）

すく　*to become not crowded*（すいている　*to be
not crowded*）

すむ（住む）*to live*（日本に住む *to live in Japan*）

ちがう（違う）*to be wrong, to be different*

なく（泣く）*to cry*

なまける（怠ける）*to be lazy*

はく　*to wear* (items such as pants and shoes)（ズボ
ンをはく　*to wear pants*）

はじまる（始まる）*to begin*

よろこぶ（喜ぶ）*to become pleased*

わらう（笑う）*to laugh, to smile*

OTHERS

～くん（～君）*a friendly respectful title for boys
and young men, or a formal respectful title for
one's subordinates*

おなかがすいている　*hungry*

Answers and Translations

Chapter One

Hiragana and Vocabulary

2. Reading and Writing Basic Hiragana I

C) 1. いえ   3. えき   5. きく
     2. か   4. こい

3. Reading and Writing Basic Hiragana II

C) 1. さけ   3. すし   5. つくえ
     2. かさ   4. たこ

4. Reading and Writing Basic Hiragana III

C) 1. なす   3. はな   5. ふね
     2. ねこ   4. ほし

5. Reading and Writing Basic Hiragana IV

C) 1: め   2: くち   3: みみ   4: はな

6. Reading and Writing Basic Hiragana V

C) 1. わに   3. とら   5. れんこん
     2. りす   4. わたあめ

7. Recognizing Voiced and Plosive Sounds

B) 1. (a) だいがく   5. (a) ががく
     2. (c) たいかく   6. (a) はんば
     3. (a) ぎり   7. (b) はんぱ
     4. (b) かがく

8. Recognizing Double Consonants and Long Vowels

     1. きっぷ   3. くき   5. おっと
     2. くうき   4. おと

9. Recognizing Palatalized Sounds

B) 1. (c) ひゃく   3. (c) かいじょう
     2. (b) りょう   4. (a) こんにゃく
C) 1: とうきょう   3: きょうと
     2: おおさか   4: なりた

10. Counting One to Ten

B) 1: いち   4: よん   7: なな   10: じゅう
     2: に   5: ご   8: はち
     3: さん   6: ろく   9: きゅう

11. Naming Japanese Dishes

うなぎ，すきやき，すし，さしみ，てんぷら

Conversation and Usage

1. Introducing Yourself

John   : はじめまして。スミスです。よろしく。
Yoko   : はじめまして。やまだです。
           こちらこそよろしく。

<Translation>
John   : How do you do? I'm Mr. Smith. Pleased to meet you.
Yoko   : How do you do? I'm Ms. Yamada. Pleased to meet you, too.

2. Greeting

ようこ   : ああ、せんせい。おはようございます。
せんせい: ああ、やまださん。おはよう。

ようこ   : (Smiles) じゃあ、しつれいします。
           さようなら。
せんせい: はい。さようなら。

<Translation>
Yoko   : Oh, Professor (lit. teacher)! Good morning!
Teacher   : Oh, Ms. Yamada! Good morning!
Yoko   : (Smiles.) Well, I'll get going. Goodbye.
Teacher   : Okay. Goodbye

3. Small Talk

ようこ   : ああ、マイクさん。
マイク   : ああ、ようこさん。
ようこ   : おげんきですか。
マイク   : ええ、げんきです。ようこさんは？
ようこ   : ええ、おかげさまで。

<Translation>
Yoko   : Oh, Mike!
Mike   : Oh, Yoko!
Yoko   : How are you?
Mike   : (Yes,) I'm fine. How about you, Yoko?
Yoko   : (Yes,) I'm fine, thank you.

4. Getting Attention

たけし   : あのう、ちょっとすみません。
Woman   : はい。
たけし   : (Shows the purse to her.)
Woman   : あ、わたしのです。
たけし   : どうぞ。
Woman   : どうもありがとうございます。
たけし   : いいえ。

<Translation>
Takeshi   : Ummm, excuse me.
Woman   : Yes?
Takeshi   : (Shows the purse to her.)
Woman   : Oh, (that's) mine.
Takeshi   : Here you are.
Woman   : Oh, thank you so much!
Takeshi   : Not at all.

Listening Comprehension

1. Naming Some Places of Japan

1. とうきょう   3. かがわ   5. とっとり
2. よこはま   4. ゆうらくちょう

2. Making Daily Conversation

1. はじめまして。(your name) です。こちらこそよろしく。
2. おはようございます。
3. はい、げんきです。or はい、おかげさまで。
4. いいえ。   5. さようなら。

CD recording:

1. はじめまして。たなかです。よろしく。
2. おはようございます。
3. おげんきですか。
4. どうもありがとうございます。   5. さようなら。

Chapter Two

Kanji and Vocabulary

1. Reading and Writing Kanji Characters I

C) 1. わたしはにほんじんです。

2. あのひともにほんじんです。

3. A: あれは なん ですか。

B: いぬです

4. A: それはなんですか。

B: これはほんです。

2. Reading and Writing Kanji Characters II

C) 1. これは車です。

2. 川口さんは日本人です。

3. 山田さんは先生です。

4. 私は学生です。

D) 日本 , 学生 , 先生

3. Naming the Things Around You

1. かばん　　2. くつ　　3. とけい　　4. いぬ

5. えんぴつ　6. ぼうし　7. ねこ

4. Naming Some Buildings Around You

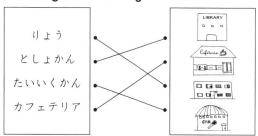

Grammar

1. X は Y です

1. 山田さんは日本人ですか。— はい、私は日本人です。

2. スミスさんはアメリカ人ですか。— はい、私は
アメリカ人です。

3. チェンさんはかんこく人ですか。— いいえ、私は
かんこく人じゃありません。

2. Demonstrative Pronouns

1. (あの・あれ) は犬です。

2. (あの・あれ) 犬はポチです。

3. BMW は (あの・あれ) です。

4. — はい、(これ・それ) はわえいじてんです。

5. — はい、(あれ・これ) はとしょかんです。

3. Question Words

A) 1. しゅみは何 (なん) ですか。

2. これは何 (なん) ですか。

3. あの人はだれですか。

4. あの先生はどなたですか。

5. 川口さんはどちらからですか。

B) 1. あれは何ですか

2. あの人はだれですか

3. あの先生はどなたですか

4. としょかんはどれですか

5. 山田さんはどちらからですか

Conversation and Usage

1. Meeting Someone for the First Time

1. Shanghai　　2. Shanghai

<Translation>

Yamada : Mr. Smith, who is this person?

Smith : This is Mr. Chen.

Chen : Hi! (How do you do?) I'm Mr. Chen. Pleased to meet you.

Yamada : Hi! (How do you do?) I'm Ms. Yamada. Pleased to meet you, too. Mr. Chen, where are you from?

Chen : I'm from Shanghai.

Yamada : Oh. Then, do you know Mr. Lee?

Chen : No.

Yamada : Oh. Mr. Lee is also from Shanghai!

Chen : Oh, really.

2. Asking about Hobby (しゅみ)

1. chanoyu　　2. tennis

<Translation>

Yamada : Mr. Chen, what is your hobby?

Chen : It's chanoyu (tea ceremony).

Yamada : What? Really?

Chen : Yes.

Yamada : Is it difficult?

Chen : No, it is more or less easy.

Yamada : Really?

Chen : Yes. What is your hobby, Ms. Yamada?

Yamada : Tennis.

Chen : Oh, really.

3. Situational Response

1. (a) 川口さんはどちらからですか。

(b) 川口さんのしゅみは何ですか。

(c) せんこうは何ですか。

2. あのたてものは何ですか。

Listening Comprehension

1. Learning Some Japanese names

1. はやし　2. たかだ　3. いいじま　4. はっとり

2. Learning about People

1. 山田さんは日本人です。

2. 私はちゅうごく人じゃありません。

3. 川口さんはおおさかからです。

3. Talking about Yourself

1. はい、日本人です。 or いいえ、日本人じゃありません。

2. はい、大学生です。 or いいえ、大学生じゃありません。

3. はい、むずかしいです。 or いいえ、かんたんです。

CD recording:

1. 日本人ですか。　2. 大学生ですか。

3. 日本ごはむずかしいですか。

Reading Comprehension

Chapter Three

Kanji and Vocabulary

1. Reading and Writing Kanji Characters

C) 1. <u>やまだ</u>さんの<u>おとう</u>さんと<u>おかあ</u>さんはすう<u>が</u>
<u>く</u>の<u>せんせい</u>です。

  2. <u>かわぐち</u>さんの<u>おにい</u>さんは<u>だいがくいん</u>の<u>が</u>
<u>く</u>せいです。

  3. <u>ちち</u>と<u>はは</u>にほんじんです。

  4. これはあの<u>おとこ</u>の<u>ひと</u>の<u>くるま</u>です。それは
あの<u>おんな</u>の<u>ひと</u>のです。

  5. <u>わたし</u>の<u>あに</u>は<u>だいがく</u>の<u>ぶんがく</u>の<u>がくせい</u>
です。

D) 1. あの<u>男</u>の<u>人</u>は<u>私</u>の<u>父</u>です。

  2. あの<u>女</u>の<u>人</u>は<u>私</u>の<u>母</u>です。

A) 3. <u>兄</u>は<u>大学生</u>です。

2. Naming and Describing Things and People

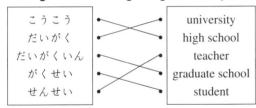

| こうこう
だいがく
だいがくいん
がくせい
せんせい | | university
high school
teacher
graduate school
student |

B) 1. かぎ   3. けいたいでんわ
  2. かさ   4. さいふ

C) 1. 私の<u>兄</u>

  2. ともだちの<u>おねえさん</u>

  3. 私の<u>ちち</u>

  4. ともだちの<u>いもうとさん</u>

  5. ともだちの<u>おとうとさん</u>

D) 1. B: ああ、<u>お母さん</u>ですか。

  2. B: ああ、<u>お父さん</u>ですか。

  3. B: ああ、<u>お兄さん</u>ですか。

  4. B: ああ、<u>おねえさん</u>ですか。

E) 1. B: はい、私の<u>兄</u>です。

  2. B: はい、私の<u>母</u>です。

  3. B: はい、私の<u>父</u>です。

  4. B: はい、私の<u>あね</u>です。

Grammar

1. Noun 1 の Noun 2

1. 日本人の学生   4. 兄のともだちの車
2. こどもの日本ご   5. 大学の日本ごの先生
3. 兄の車

2. A は B です

1. スミスさん<u>は</u>日本ご<u>の</u>学生です。
   Mr. Smith is a student of Japanese.
2. 山田さん<u>は</u>大学いん<u>の</u>学生です。
  Ms. Yamada is a graduate student.
3. 兄<u>の</u>ともだち<u>の</u>お兄さん<u>は</u>先生です。
  My older brother's friend's older brother is a teacher.
4. <u>私</u>の<u>おとうと</u>の<u>ともだち</u>は日本ご<u>の</u>学生です。
  My younger brother's friend is a student of Japanese.
5. これ<u>は</u>いもうと<u>の</u>すう学の本です。
  This is my younger sister's math book.

3. Dropping the Noun after の

1. これは私のかぎです。それは山田さんの (かぎ) です。
2. あれはすう学の本です。あれは日本ごの (本) です。
3. 私の兄の車はこれです。私の父の (車) はあれです。

Conversation and Usage

1. Describing People

1. sales division
2. the assistant of the division head in the sales department

<Translation>

Brown	:	Who is that man over there?
Yamamoto	:	(He) is Mr. Honda. (He) is the assistant of the head of the sales division.
Brown	:	Oh.
Yamamoto	:	He is a very nice person. I will introduce you to him later.
Brown	:	Oh, please! Thank you. Then, who is that woman (over there)?
Yamamoto	:	(She) is my younger sister.
Brown	:	Oh, (she) is your younger sister. She's pretty, isn't she?
Yamamoto	:	No.
Brown	:	Please introduce me to her later, okay?

2. Situational Response

1. あの女の人はだれですか。
2. 兄はおおさかの大学のすう学の学生です。

Listening Comprehension

1. Ms. Yamada's father's
2. Ms. Yamada's friend's older brother's
3. Ms. Yamada's older brother's friend's

CD recording:

あの車は山田さんのお父さんのです。あのトラックは
山田さんのお兄さんのともだちのです。あのバンは山
田さんのともだちのお兄さんのです。

Reading Comprehension

1. (a) hobby   (b) one's wife   (c) teacher
2. tennis   3. graduate student, studying literature

<Translation>
I'm Kevin Brown. I'm a company employee. I was born in North Carolina. My hobby is tennis. My wife is Japanese. She is a graduate student. Her specialty is literature. My wife's father is a high school math teacher. My wife's mother is a high school English teacher.

Chapter Four

Katakana

1. Reading and Writing Basic Katakana I

B) 1. き：<u>キ</u>　2. う：<u>ウ</u>　3. ご：<u>ゴ</u>　4. お：<u>オ</u>

2. Reading and Writing Basic Katakana II

B) 1. つ：<u>ツ</u>　2. そ：<u>ソ</u>　3. た：<u>タ</u>　4. ぐ：<u>グ</u>

3. Reading and Writing Basic Katakana III

B)

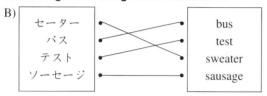

4. Reading and Writing Basic Katakana IV

B) 1. メニュー：*menu*　　3. サッカー：*soccer*
　2. ネクタイ：*necktie*　　4. スカート：*skirt*

5. Reading and Writing Basic Katakana V

B)

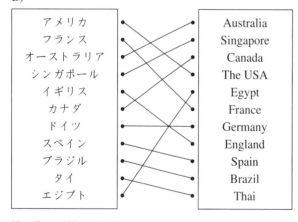

Kanji and Vocabulary

1. Reading and Writing Kanji Characters I

C) 一・二・三・四・五・六・七・八・九・十

2. Reading and Writing Kanji Characters II

C) 1. <u>今</u>、<u>何時</u>ですか。　　3. まあまあ<u>安</u>いです。
　2. ちょっと<u>高</u>いです。　　4. 私は<u>四月生</u>まれです。

3. Pronouncing Number Phrases

1. ななにいち（の）よんにはちいち　2. さんねんせい
3. にねんせい　4. さんまんえん
5. ごまんきゅうせんろっぴゃくえん　6. ごまんえん

4. Telling the Time

1. はちじさんじゅうろっぷん
2. しちじじゅうななふん

3. じゅうじよんじゅうごふん
4. くじにふん

Grammar

1. Listing Nouns Using と

1. りんごとバナナを下さい。
2. ノートと、えんぴつと、けしゴムを下さい。
3. 30円のきってと、50円のきってを下さい。

Conversation and Usage

1. Asking about Time

1. 2:35　　　　　　2. 20 minutes

<Translation>
Woman　：Excuse me. What time is it now?
Man　　：It's 2:15.
Woman　：Oh, thank you.
Man　　：No problem.
Woman　：Ummm, what time does the next bus for Sakura-machi (arrive)?
Man　　：Sorry. I don't know.
Woman　：Oh. Then, how about the bus for Ishikawa-machi?
Man　　：2:35.
Woman　：Oh, I see

2. Asking for Prices

1. a brush and an ink slab　　2. 2 6,975 yen

<Translation>
Takeshi　　：Excuse me. How much is this calligraphy brush?
Store clerk：That's 2,000 yen.
Takeshi　　：Oh, really. Then, I'll take this brush and that ink slab.
Store clerk：Sure. It will be 6,975 yen including the consumption tax.
Takeshi　　：(*Lit*) Please take it from 10,000 yen.
Store clerk：Sure. Your change is 3,025 yen, right? Here you are.
Takeshi　　：Thank you.
Store clerk：Thank you very much.

3. Situational Response

1. すみません。今、何時ですか。
2. 山田さんのでんわばんごうは何ですか。
3. スミスさんのでんわばんごうはわかりますか。

Listening Comprehension

1. Taking Down the Telephone Numbers

1. 011-552-6155　3. 06-6747-0467
2. 03-5437-1892　4. 092-741-0107

CD recording:

さっぽろのたかはしさんのでんわばんごうは 011-552-6155 です。とうきょうのもりさんのでんわばんごうは 03-5437-1892 です。おおさかのたかはしさんのでんわばんごうは 06-6747-0467 です。ふくおかのたかださんのでんわばんごうは 092-741-0107 です。

2. Matching the Age and Grade Level

15 さい		こうこう 1 年生
17 さい		こうこう 2 年生
18 さい		こうこう 3 年生
19 さい		大学 1 年生
21 さい		大学 2 年生
22 さい		大学 3 年生
23 さい		大学 4 年生
24 さい		
28 さい		
30 さい		大学いんの 1 年生
31 さい		大学いんの 2 年生
32 さい		

CD recording:

みゆきさんは 19 さいです。大学 1 年生です。たけしさんは 21 さいです。大学 3 年生です。さちこちゃんは 17 さいです。こうこう 2 年生です。ひろこさんは 28 さいです。大学いんの 1 年生です。

Reading Comprehension

Checking Out a Car-renting Advertisement

1. Hawaii   2. 4,800 yen   3. 34,900 yen

Chapter Five

Kanji and Vocabulary

1. Reading and Writing Kanji Characters

C) 1. <u>たなか</u>さんと<u>かわぐち</u>さんは<u>だいがく</u>の<u>にほん</u>ごのクラスのアシスタントです。
2. <u>やすだ</u>さんと<u>やまだ</u>さんは<u>きょう</u><u>うち</u>に<u>き</u>ます。
3. スミスさんは<u>く</u>るつもりですか。<u>こ</u>ないつもりですか。
4. <u>あした</u>は<u>やま</u>に<u>い</u>きます。<u>うみ</u>には<u>い</u>きません。

D) 1. <u>明日</u>、日本に<u>帰</u>ります。
2. <u>今日</u>、<u>田中</u>さんは<u>来</u>ません。

E) 今日 , 明日 , 日本

2. Naming Fun Places

1. どうぶつえん   4. えいがかん   7. うみ
2. やま   5. ほんや
3. こうえん   6. いざかや

3. Naming Common Institutions

1. ゆうびんきょく   2. びょういん   3. ぎんこう

Grammar

1. ～ます

1. <u>か</u>きます   5. <u>ま</u>ちます   9. <u>と</u>びます
2. <u>およ</u>ぎます   6. <u>ね</u>ます   10. <u>はな</u>します
3. <u>し</u>にます   7. <u>と</u>ります   11. <u>し</u>ます
4. <u>か</u>います   8. <u>み</u>ます   12. <u>き</u>ます

2. ～ません

1. —いいえ、<u>いき</u>ません。   4. —いいえ、<u>き</u>ません。
2. —いいえ、<u>かえり</u>ません。 5. —いいえ、<u>いき</u>ません。
3. —いいえ、<u>いき</u>ません。

3. ～ない

A) 1. <u>か</u>かない   6. <u>また</u>ない   11. <u>はなさ</u>ない
2. <u>のま</u>ない   7. <u>ね</u>ない   12. <u>し</u>ない
3. <u>およが</u>ない   8. <u>とら</u>ない   13. <u>こ</u>ない
4. <u>しな</u>ない   9. <u>み</u>ない
5. <u>かわ</u>ない   10. <u>とば</u>ない

B) 1. 来る・<u>来</u>ない・来ます・来ません
2. 行く・<u>行か</u>ない・行きます・<u>行きません</u>
3. うたう・<u>うたわ</u>ない・<u>うたいます</u>・うたいません
4. わかる・<u>わから</u>ない・<u>わかります</u>・<u>わかりません</u>

4. あまり／ぜんぜん／よく

1. レストランにはあまり行きません。
2. いざかやにはぜんぜん行きません。
3. カラオケにはよく行きます。
4. 本やにはあまり行きません。

Conversation and Usage

1. Making Plans for Tonight

1. No.   2. Kurofune.
3. No. Because the participation fee for the party for the tennis club is too expensive for her.

<Translation>

Yukiko   : Will you go to work (part-time job) tonight?
Akiko   : Nope.
Yukiko   : Oh, really?
Akiko   : Yep.
Yukiko   : Then, will you come to the party for the tennis club tonight?
Akiko   : Where?
Yukiko   : Kurofune.
Akiko   : Is it okay (for me to come)?
Yukiko   : Surely.
Akiko   : What time?
Yukiko   : Seven.
Akiko   : Oh, okay.
Yukiko   : Oh, the participation fee for the party is 3,000 yen.
Akiko   : What? Expensive!
Yukiko   : Really? But you can eat sushi as much as you want.
Akiko   : Yes. But I'm not coming (lit. going). Sorry.

2. Situational Response

1. 今日はクラスに行きますか。
2. いざかやにはよく行きますか。
3. 今晩レストランに行きませんか。
4. 行きましょう。

Listening Comprehension

About the Places to Go

1. True   2. False   3. False

CD recording:

私はよく本やに行きます。でも、としょかんにはあまり行きません。しゅうまつはよくこうえんに行きます。えいがかんにはあまり行きません。デパートにもあまり行きません。

Reading Comprehension

1. Reading a Timetable

1. 2 hours and 36 minutes　　2. 4 hours

3. こだま 561 that departs Tokyo at 6:23 a.m.

2. Planning for Tomorrow and The Day After Tomorrow

1. To the job, library and supermarket

2. To the department store

<Translation>

I will go to work (part-time job) tomorrow. Then, I'll go to the library. Then, I will go to the supermarket. The day after tomorrow, I don't have to go to work. I will not go to the library, either. But I will go to the department store.

Chapter Six

Kanji and Vocabulary

1. Reading and Writing Kanji Characters I

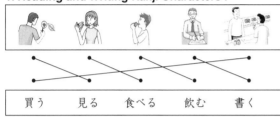

買う　　見る　　食べる　　飲む　　書く

2. Reading and Writing Kanji Characters II

C) 1. わたしはあるいてだいがくにいきます。じゅっぷんぐらいです。たなかさんはくるまでだいがくにいきます。いちじかんぐらいかかります。やまださんはじてんしゃと、でんしゃでいきます。いちじかんにじゅっぷんぐらいかかります。

2. けさはあさごはんをたべませんでした。ひるごはんはサラダをたべました。こんばんはたくさんたべるつもりです。こんばんのばんごはんはてんぷらです。わたしがつくります。ビールものみます。きのうのばんもビールをのみました。

3. きのうはくつをかいました。それから、えいがをみました。

4. かんじをたくさんかきました。ペンをつかいました。

D) 1. でん車と車で四時間です。

2. 昨日すしを作りました。

3. 昼ごはんを食べます。

E) 1. 間・晩・昼・朝・明・昨　2. 明・朝　3. 作・使

F) 1. 書く　　3. 使う　　5. 行く　　7. 飲む

2. 買う　　4. 作る　　6. 歩く　　8. 見る

3. Naming Different Forms of Transportation

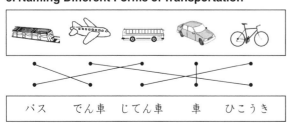

バス　　でん車　　じてん車　　車　　ひこうき

4. Learn about Pastime Activities

1. 兄はよくざっしを読みます。

2. ひまな時、てがみを書きます。

3. 私はしゅうまつえいがを見ます。

4. カラオケ・ボックスでうたをうたいます。

Grammar

1. Present/Past

1. B: いいえ、飲みませんでした。

2. B: いいえ、しません。

3. B: いいえ、買いませんでした。

4. B: いいえ、見ません。

5. B: いいえ、使いませんでした。

2. Particle で

1. ゆきこさんはアメリカに来ます。

2. ゆきこさんはアメリカでべんきょうします。

3. 父はよくレストランに行きます。

4. 父はよくレストランで食べます。

5. スミスさんはうちに帰りました。

6. ペンでてがみを書きます。

7. フォークとナイフでステーキを食べます。

8. 日本のアニメは日本ごで見ます。

3. Particle が / を and Transitive/Intransitive Verbs

<Example answers>

1. てがみを , まんねんひつで

2. 車を , 私のじてん車を

3. 母のベッドで

4. ねこが , 山田さんが , ここに

5. 大学に , としょかんに

6. としょかんで , 日本ごを

4. Particles

1. 車を買いました。

2. 兄が車を買いました。

3. 車を兄が買いました。

4. じてん車で大学に行きました。

5. てですしを食べました。

6. 日本で日本ごを勉強しました。

7. 兄がここに来ました。

Conversation and Usage

1. Sharing Personal Information

1. False　　　　2. False　　　　3. True

<Translation>

Kenji　：　How about going to see a movie together on Saturday, that's tomorrow?

Shizuka　：　Ummm, a bit...

Kenji　：　Are you busy tomorrow?

Shizuka　：　I will go to Matsuzakaya tomorrow. I will see wedding gowns.

Kenji　：　What?

Shizuka　：　I am going to get married in June.

Kenji　：　What? Is that true?

Shizuka　：　Yes.

Kenji　：　Who is your fiancé?

Shizuka : My fiancé is someone who works at the same company.
Kenji : What?
Shizuka : Mr. Yamashita.
Kenji : What? Yamashita, my assistant?
Shizuka : Yes.
Kenji : Is that true?
Shizuka : Yes.
Kenji : Oh, I see. Congratulations...
Shizuka : Thank you.
Kenji : How about the ceremony?
Shizuka : We plan to have the ceremony in Hawaii.
Kenji : Oh.

2. Ordering at the Fast Food Restaurant

1. one   2. two   3. one coke and two orange juices

<Translation>

Store clerk : Welcome! (May I have) your order, (please)?
Customer : One cheese burger, two teriyaki burgers, one coke, and two orange juices, please.
Store clerk : Certainly. One cheese burger, two teriyaki burgers, one coke, and one orange juice, correct?
Customer : No. Two orange juices.
Store clerk : Oh, sorry.

3. Situational Response

1. 田中さんはがっこうに何で行きますか。
2. 山田さんはひまなとき、たいてい何をしますか。
3. トムさんはどこで日本ごをべんきょうしましたか。

Listening Comprehension

Commuting to College

1. Ikebukuro   2. Shinjuku   3. 35 minutes

CD recording:

私は大学生です。大学にはでん車で行きます。山手線（やまのてせん）です。まず、うちから山手線（やまのてせん）の池袋（いけぶくろ）のえきまで歩きます。15分ぐらいです。それから、山手線（やまのてせん）で池袋（いけぶくろ）から新宿（しんじゅく）まで行きます。10分ぐらいです。それから、大学まで歩いて10分です。

Reading Comprehension

Reading a Menu

1. 280 yen   2. 180 yen   3. 250 yen   4. 80 yen

Chapter Seven

Kanji and Vocabulary

1. Reading and Writing Kanji Characters I

C)

2. Reading and Writing Kanji Characters II

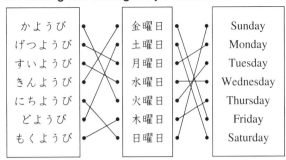

かようび	金曜日	Sunday
げつようび	土曜日	Monday
すいようび	月曜日	Tuesday
きんようび	水曜日	Wednesday
にちようび	火曜日	Thursday
どようび	木曜日	Friday
もくようび	日曜日	Saturday

D) わたしのうちはこうえんと、としょかんのあいだにあります。かわのちかくです。さくらのきがたくさんあります。しがつはとてもきれいです。うちからだいがくまででんしゃでいちじかんかかります。くるまではいちじかんよんじゅうごふんかかります。だいがくにはかようびともくようびにいきます。きょうはすいようびですから、だいがくにいきません。あしたはすうがくのクラスです。こんばんはすうがくのしゅくだいをするつもりです。

3. Naming Common Buildings

1. ゆうびんきょく   4. ぎんこう
2. ほんや   5. びょういん
3. ちゅうしゃじょう

4. Naming Directions

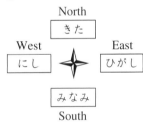

North
きた
West   East
にし   ひがし
みなみ
South

5. Naming the Things in a Room

1: ベッド   3: つくえ   5: たんす
2: まど   4: しゃしん   6: いす

Grammar

1. ある・いる・いらっしゃる。

1. じしょはここにあります。
2. さくらの木はあそこにあります。
3. 私の犬はそこにいます。
4. 母はうちにいます。
5. 山田さんのお母さんはあそこにいらっしゃいます。

2. Relative Location

1: ボールはつくえの下にあります。
2: ボールはつくえのまえにあります。
3: ボールはつくえの右にあります。
4: ボールはつくえのうしろにあります。
5: ボールはつくえの左にあります。
6: ボールはつくえのそばにあります。
7: ボールはつくえのひきだしの中にあります。
8: ボールはつくえといすの間にあります。

3. Particles に and で

1. うちのねこはテーブルの下 で 食べます。
2. ねこはテーブルの下 に います。
3. テレビのリモコンはソファーの上 に あります。
4. 昨日は車でディズニーランド に 行きました。
5. かぎはドアのまえのマットの下 に あります。
6. 兄は今大学 に います。
7. 私は大学のとしょかん で しんぶんをよみます。

4. Location of People and Things

1. 山田さんはぎんこうにいます。
2. 車はちゅうしゃじょうにあります。
3. しゃしんはつくえの上にあります。
4. レストランはえきのみなみにあります

Conversation and Usage

1. Calling the Store

1. Tuesday   2. Thursday   3. All Note PCs

<Translation>

Store clerk : Thank you for your continuous patronage. This is Computer Japan.

Customer : Ummm, when does the next week's sale on NOTE PC start?

Store clerk : It's from Tuesday.

Customer : Oh, it is not from Monday.

Store clerk : Right. It is from Tuesday to Thursday.

Customer : We get 10% off from all the NOTE PCs, right?

Store clerk : Yes.

Customer : Including Sony's and NEC's, too, right?

Store clerk : I'm so sorry, but we don't have any stock for Sony's and NEC's.

Customer : Oh, I see. Thank you.

Store clerk : Yes. We look forward to have more business with you.

2. Looking for the Toilet

1. 2nd floor   2. 3rd floor   3. 1st floor

<Translation>

Woman : Ummm, excuse me.

Store clerk : Yes.

Woman : Where is the toilet?

Store clerk : There is a lady's room near the stairs on the third floor.

Woman : How about the men's room?

Store clerk : It is on the second floor.

Woman : Oh, really. (The woman turns around and looks at her son.) Then, let's go to the second floor.

Child : Mom, you stay on the first floor.

Woman : Here?

Child : Yep.

Woman : No way. Let's go there together.

Child : I will go there by myself!

3. Situational Response

1. すみません。ちかてつのえきはどこにありますか。

2. すみません。えいぎょうじかんは何時までですか。

3. すみません。田中先生は今どちらにいらっしゃいますか。

Listening Comprehension

Locating Places

1. 本や： 6   2. ぎんこう： 5   3. びょういん： 4

CD recording:

デパートは三ばんどおりにあります。本やはデパートのまえにあります。ぎんこうは本やの右にあります。びょういんはさくらどおりと三ばんどおりのこうさてんにあります。さくらどおりのにしです。三ばんどおりのみなみです。

Reading Comprehension

Locating Places

1. 山田ビジネス： 2   2. ABC 英語学校： 7

<Translation>

Yamada Business is located at the intersection between Sakura Street and Third Street. It is in the north of Third Street and is in the east of Sakura Street. ABC English School is also on Third Street. It is in front of the parking lot. The department store is also on Third Street. It is between Yamada Business and the parking lot.

Chapter Eight

Kanji and Vocabulary

1. Reading and Writing Kanji Characters

D) わたしはきょうだいがよにんいます。あにと、あねと、いもうとと、おとうとです。ちちはアメリカじんです。ははにほんじんです。それから、うちにはいぬがさんびきいます。それから、ねこがいっぴきいます。おとうとはこうこうせいです。よくテレビをみます。テレビはぜんぶでごだいあります。わたしはだいがくせいです。せんこうはぶんがくです。あしたはしけんがあります。ですから、こんばんはたくさんべんきょうします。ほんをさんさつよむつもりです。

E) 1. 私は兄弟が 3 人います。
    2. きってを 5 枚下さい。
    3. 大学で勉強します。

F)

女	姉	妹	安
力	男	勉	
木	本	林	枚

2. Matching Academic Subjects

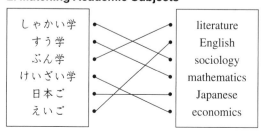

3. Using Counters

1: 4 枚   3: 1 台   5: 2 人

2: 2 冊   4: 3 つ   6: 5 匹

Grammar

1. X には Y がある

1. テーブルの下にはねこがいます。

2. 父のベッドの下にはおかねがあります。

3. うちの近くにはレストランがあります。

4. 私のうちにはプールがあります。

5. この本やの中にはコーヒーショップがあります。

2. Number Phrases

1. うちには犬が 4 匹います。

2. さいふの中にはクレジットカードが 3 枚あります。

3. 山田さんのうちには車が 2 台あります。

4. かばんの中には本が 2 冊あります。

5. このクラスには日本人の学生がたくさんいます。

3. ですから

1. うちにはねこがいます。ですから、ねずみがいません。

2. 昨日は日本ごのしゅくだいをしました。それから、すう学を勉強しました。

3. 私は学生です。でも、あまり勉強しません。

Conversation and Usage

1. Asking about Family

1. None   2. Three   3. Yes

<Translation>

Yuka : Tetsuya, do you have any siblings?

Tetsuya : Nope. I'm an only child.

Yuka : Oh, I see.

Tetsuya : How about you, Yuka?

Yuka : I have three older sisters.

Tetsuya : Wow, then, there are four girls all together?

Yuka : Yep.

Tetsuya : Then, it's like in the novel "Little Women".

Yuka : Yep.

Tetsuya : Do you fight?

Yuka : Not at all. We are very close to each other.

Tetsuya : That's nice.

2. Making a Plan

1. The evening of the day after tomorrow

2. No. He has a karate class.

3. Tomorrow evening

<Translation>

Jane : We have Ms. Tanaka's lesson the day after tomorrow, in the evening, right?

Kent : Right.

Jane : (Did you do your) homework?

Kent : Not yet.

Jane : Why don't we do it together?

Kent : Yes, fine.

Jane : Are you free this afternoon?

Kent : Nope. I have a karate class.

Jane : Oh, really. Then, how about tomorrow afternoon?

Kent : (I have) an aikido class.

Jane : Oh, really. Then, tomorrow evening?

Kent : Okay. Fine.

3. Situational Response

1. 田中さんのうちには車が何台ありますか。

2. 山下さんは兄弟がいますか。

3. 明日の晩はえいごのクラスがありますか。

Listening Comprehension

Using Onomatopoeia

1: 5   2: 4   3: 3   4: 2   5: 1

CD recording:

1. コソコソ話します。   4. ギャアギャアなきます。

2. グーグーねます   5. ゲラゲラわらいます

3. シクシクなきます。

Reading Comprehension

1. Going Through Yoshiko's Schedule

1. On Sunday, June 7th, at 3 p.m.

2. On Wednesday, June 3rd, at 7:45 p.m.

3. Mr. Lee   4. Mr. Kawaguchi   5. Mr. (Ms.) Tanaka

Chapter Nine

Kanji and Vocabulary

1. Reading and Writing Kanji Characters

C) 1. うちには<u>おおきい</u><u>いぬ</u>が<u>いっぴき</u>と、<u>ちいさい</u><u>いぬ</u>が<u>にひき</u>います。

2. <u>あたらしい</u>プリンターを<u>かい</u>ました。

3. この<u>たてもの</u>はとても<u>ふるい</u>です。

4. <u>わたし</u>の<u>へや</u>は<u>くらい</u>です。<u>ほん</u>は<u>あかるい</u>へやで<u>よんで</u><u>ください</u>。

5. <u>だいがく</u>の<u>ちかく</u>に<u>ひろい</u><u>こうえん</u>があります。うちからも<u>ちかい</u>です。<u>あるいて</u><u>ごふん</u>です。

6. <u>ぶんぽう</u>のテストがありました。<u>にほんごのぶん</u>をたくさん<u>かき</u>ました。

7. <u>さくぶん</u>の<u>しゅくだい</u>に<u>にじかん</u>かかりました。

8. <u>ぶんがく</u>と、<u>にほんご</u>と、<u>えいご</u>と、<u>すうがく</u>を<u>べんきょう</u>します。

D) 1. <u>新</u>しい車と、<u>古</u>い車があります。

2. <u>明</u>るいへやと、<u>暗</u>いへやがあります。

3. 日本<u>語</u>の<u>作文</u>を書きました。

E) 1. <u>明</u>るいです。   4. <u>新</u>しいです。

2. <u>暗</u>いです。   5. <u>古</u>いです。

3. <u>広</u>いです。   6. <u>安</u>いです。

2. Comparing Buildings

1. (a) <u>たかい</u>です   (b) <u>ひくい</u>です

2. (a) <u>おおきい</u>です   (b) <u>ちいさい</u>です

3. (a) <u>あたらしい</u>です   (b) <u>ふるい</u>です

3. Different Aspects of a Language

1. 文ぽう   2. かいわ   3. はつおん   4. 作文

Grammar

1. I-type and Na-type Adjectives

1. 大きい犬です。

2. 新しいたてものです。

3. りっぱな大学です。

4. きれいなレストランです。

5. おもしろいざっしです。

6. きたないえきです。

2. Negative Forms of Adjectives

1. むずかしくありません。

2. かんたんじゃありません。

3. おもしろくありません。

4. きれいじゃありません。

5. とおくありません。

6. しずかじゃありません。

7. よくありません。

3. Degree Adverbs あまり and ぜんぜん

1. ぜんぜんかんたんじゃありません。

2. あまりきれいじゃありません。

3. とても新しいです。

4. ぜんぜんべんりじゃありません。

5. とても高いです。

Conversation and Usage

1. Visiting a Friend's Apartment

1. Tea   2. A dog and a cat

3. A ballerina and a violin

<Translation>

Mihoko : Hi!

Toshiko : Oh, Miho. Come in!

Mihoko : Thanks. (Toshiko offers a seat to Mihoko.)

Toshiko : Please (sit down). Sorry. My place is messy.

Mihoko : Not at all! It's neat and tidy. My apartment is messier than yours.

Toshiko : Really?

Mihoko : Yeah.

Toshiko : Which do you like, coffee or tea?

Mihoko : Then, tea, please.

Toshiko : Okay. (While Toshiko prepares tea, Mihoko looks around the room.)

Mihoko : Oh, these crystals are beautiful! And, they are cute!

Toshiko : Oh, those. That small one is a cat. That big one is a dog.

Mihoko : Are they Swarovski's?

Toshiko : Yeah.

Mihoko : I thought so. I have some of them, too.

Toshiko : What kind?

Mihoko : Ballerina's and violin's.

Toshiko : Oh, really.

2. Situational Response

1. 田中さんの会社はどんなたてものですか。

2. やちんはいくらですか。

3. フランス語のはつおんはむずかしいですか。

Listening Comprehension

1. About Yoko's Apartment

1. False   2. True   3. False

CD recording:

ようこさんのアパートはちかてつのえきからとおくありません。とてもべんりです。とてもきれいなアパートです。それに、広いです。でも、しずかじゃありません。

Reading Comprehension

At the Library

1. No   2. Yes   3. To read newspaper

<Translation>

The library in my town is very pretty. And it is very bright. But it is not very big. It is a two-story building, but has a basement. I often read newspaper at the library.

Chapter Ten

Kanji and Vocabulary

1. Reading and Writing Kanji Characters I

C) 1. すみません。もういちどいってください。

2. よくにほんごのほんをよみます。それから、にほんごの CD をききます。

3. ちちとはあまりはなしません。

4. しゅくだいをだしてください。それから、ワークブックをみせてください。

5. どうぞはいってください。

6. すみません。ちょっとたなかさんのよこにたってください。

D) 語 | 読 | 話 | 聞 | 間

2. Reading and Writing Kanji Characters II

C) 1. ピアノをならいます。 *I take a piano lesson. (Lit. I learn piano.)*

2. ピアノをれんしゅうします。 *I practice piano.*

3. 日本語をふくしゅうします。 *I review Japanese language.*

4. 昨日はテレビをみました。*I watched TV yesterday.*

5. しゅくだいをみせてください。 *Please show me your homework.*

D)

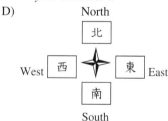

1. 速く歩く   2. 早く帰る

3. Describing Movements

1. この道をまっすぐ行く。

2. 左にまがる (曲がる)

3. 3 つ目のこうさてんを右に曲がる

4. 道をわたる

5. はしをわたる

6. レストランをすぎる

4. Describing Actions

1. いう（言う）   3. よむ（読む）   5. すわる
2. はなす（話す）   4. たつ（立つ）

Grammar

1. Te-form Verbs

1. みて   6. あそんで   11. いって
2. ねて   7. かって   12. およいで
3. のんで   8. つくって   13. はなして
4. よんで   9. まって   14. して
5. しんで   10. きいて   15. きて

2. Requesting an Action 1

1. 日本語で話してください。
2. えい語で話さないでください。
3. お金をかしてください。
4. 漢字を書いてください。
5. てがみを読まないでください。

3. Creating Adverbs

1. まじめに   3. しずかに   5. きびしく
2. 早く   4. やさしく

4. Requesting an Action 2

1. もう少し早くクラスに来てください。
2. もう少ししずかに食べてください。
3. まじめにしてください。
4. ラジオのおとを小さくしてください。
5. 漢字をよくふく習してください。

Conversation and Usage

1. Buying a Digital Camera

1. 5,000 yen   2. No   3. No

<Translation>
Customer : How much is this digital camera?
Store clerk : 35,000 yen.
Customer : A bit expensive! Make it a little cheaper.
Store clerk : Oh, that's a bit …
Customer : How about 30,000 yen?
Store clerk : Ummm…
Customer : Then, fine. (No thanks.)
Store clerk : Then, shall I give you this bag for free?
Customer : Then, please give me this tripod for free, too.
Store clerk : That tripod is 10,000 yen, you know?
Customer : Yes.
Store clerk : Okay, then, 30,000 yen just for the digital camera.
Customer : That is good!

2. Giving Directions

1. A   2. Thursdays

<Translation>
Woman : Excuse me. Do you know the Izakaya called Ginger House?
Man : Oh, the Western-style Izakaya?
Woman : Yes. Where is it?
Man : Cross that big intersection. Then, make a left turn at the second corner. There is a hamburger shop on your right. Ginger House is on the second floor of that building.
Woman : Oh, okay. Thank you.
Man : Not at all. Oh, but it is closed today.
Woman : What?
Man : Because today is Thursday.
Woman : No, today is Friday.
Man : Oh, really? Then, it is not closed. Sorry.

3. Situational Response

1. ペンをかしてくださいませんか。
2. （わたしのパソコンを）こわさないでくださいね。
3. しずかにしてください。
4. しつれいします。
5. しつれいします。
6. この道をまっすぐ行ってください。つきあたりを右に曲がってください。それから、2つ目のこうさてんを右に曲がってください。そうすると、左にぎんこうがあります。そのぎんこうをすぎてください。そうすると、本やは左にあります。ぎんこうのとなりです。

Listening Comprehension

Physical Response

CD recording:

1. 立ってください。 *Stand up.*
2. 左を見てください。 *Look to the left.*
3. 右を見てください。 *Look to the right.*
4. 上を見てください。 *Look up.*
5. 名前を言ってください。 *Say your name.*
6. すわってください。 *Sit down.*

Reading Comprehension

Reading a Memo

1. Because her mother cannot come home early due to her work.
2. No.
3. Yoko's mother.

<Translation>
Dear Yoko, I cannot come home early because of my work. Please make super for your father. There is fish in the refrigerator. Please grill it. Then, make miso soup with tofu. I'll come home at around 8 p.m. Thank you.

Chapter Eleven

Kanji and Vocabulary

1. Reading and Writing Kanji Characters I

C) 1. はははかみがながいです。でも、あねはかみがみじかいです。 *My mother has long hair. But my older sister has short hair.*

2. ちちはせがたかいです。でも、あにはせがひくいです。 *My father is tall. But my older brother is short.*

3. <u>にほんご</u>のクラスは<u>しゅくだい</u>が<u>おおい</u>です。<u>すこ</u>したいへんです。でも、<u>しけん</u>は<u>すくない</u>です。 *Japanese class has a lot of homework. It is a bit hard. But it has few exams.*

D) 1. 耳　　2. 目　　3. 口　　4. 手　　5. 足

2. Reading and Writing Kanji Characters II

C) 1. <u>あに</u>は<u>うんてん</u>が<u>じょうず</u>です。でも、<u>おとうと</u>は<u>へた</u>です。 *My older brother is good at driving. But my younger brother is bad at it.*

2. <u>あね</u>は<u>どくしょ</u>がすきです。<u>わたし</u>もだいすきです。 *My older sister likes reading. I like it very much also.*

3. <u>かいしゃ</u>では<u>たらき</u>ます。それか、<u>だいがく</u>で<u>えいご</u>を<u>おしえ</u>ます。 *I will work at a company. Or, I will teach English at a college.*

4. <u>きのう</u>は<u>しゃかいがく</u>のクラスを<u>やすみ</u>ました。 *I missed the sociology class yesterday.*

5. <u>らいげつ</u> <u>しゃちょう</u>と<u>ちゅうごく</u>に<u>い</u>きます。<u>かんこく</u>にも<u>い</u>きます。 *Next month, I will go to China with the president. (We) will go to South Korea, too.*

6. すみません。<u>お</u><u>なまえ</u>を<u>かいて</u>ください。 *Excuse me. Please write your name.*

3. Naming Favorite Activities

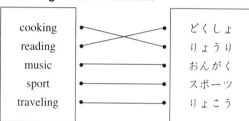

cooking	どくしょ
reading	りょうり
music	おんがく
sport	スポーツ
traveling	りょこう

4. Naming the Items One Desires

1. おかね（お金）
2. じかん（時間）
3. いえ
4. くるま（車）

Grammar

1. 〜は〜が〜です for Describing People and Things

1. けんじくんは背がひくいです。
2. ひろゆきくんは背が高いです。
3. みゆきちゃんはかみが長いです。
4. まさみちゃんはかみが短いです。
5. よしこちゃんは口が大きいです。
6. しずかちゃんは口が小さいです。

2. 〜は〜が〜です for Describing Places

1. きょうとはたてものが古いです。
2. あきはばらはカメラが安いです。
3. とうきょうは人や車が多いです。
4. 中国は新しいたてものが多いです。
5. ドイツはビールがおいしいです。

3. 〜は〜が〜です for Describing Skills and Preferences

1. 姉は読書が好きです。
2. 兄はじゅうどうが大好きです。

3. 妹は作文がにがてです。
4. 山田さんはテニスが上手です。
5. 私はりょうりがとくいです。

4. Noun-maker の

1. 姉はえいがを見るのが好きです。
2. 私はうたをうたうのがとくいです。
3. 弟は本を読むのがにがてです。
4. 兄はギターをひくのが上手です。

5. Suffix たい for Desire

1. きょうしになりたいです。
2. 大学で教えたいです。
3. びょういんで働きたいです。
4. レストランをけいえいしたいです。

6. れる・られる for Describing Ability and Potential

1. すしが作れる
2. 中国語が話せる
3. はしで食べられる
4. 日本語が教えられる
5. テニスができる
6. トラックが運転できる

Conversation and Usage

1. Talking about What One Would Like To Do in the Future

1. Japan
2. Courses such as linguistics, education, TESOL, etc
3. Double advantage

<Translation>

Kenji　: Heather, what do you want to do in the future?

Heather : I want to teach English in Japan.

Kenji　: Oh, really. Do you like teaching?

Heather : Yes. I don't like teaching grammar, but I love teaching conversation.

Kenji　: In Japan, native speakers of English are in great demand!

Heather : Yes. But it is quite competitive.

Kenji　: Really?

Heather : Yes. So, I took linguistics, education, TESOL courses, etc. in my college in the US.

Kenji　: What is TESOL?

Heather : It is Teaching English to Speakers of Other Languages.

Kenji　: Huh. Then, you are "Oni ni kanabo", aren't you?

Heather : What is "Oni ni kanabo"?

Kenji　: It means "a strong ogre is holding a metal rod."

Heather : Then, I'm an ogre?

Kenji　: No. It means "double advantage."

2. Do You Cook?

1. Cooking
2. Cooked rice, salad, boiled egg, and ramen
3. Because the examples of dishes Takako claimed that she often cooks are all extremely easy dishes, which is consistent with Kenji's original belief that Takako is not good at cooking.

<Translation>

Kenji   : Takako. What do you do when you are free?
Takako : Well... I always cook when I'm free.
Kenji   : What? You cook, Takako?
Takako : Yes.
Kenji   : Is that true?
Takako : It is true. I am good at cooking.
Kenji   : What? That's a lie.
Takako : Wow, you are rude.
Kenji   : What do you make?
Takako : Rice, salad, boiled egg, ramen, etc.
Kenji   : Oh, I thought so.

3. Situational Response

1. たけしさんは今何が一番ほしいですか。
2. けんじさんはおよげますか。
3. たかこさんはしょうらい何がしたいですか。

Listening Comprehension

Using Potential Forms

1. can make   3. can read   5. use
2. write   4. can sleep

CD recording:

1. つくれる   3. よめる   5. つかう
2. かく   4. ねられる

Reading Comprehension

Studying a Bank Account Application Form

1. September 1, 2006   3. 03-3421-5541
2. February 14, 1986

Chapter Twelve

Kanji and Vocabulary

1. Reading and Writing Kanji Characters

C) 1. (a) さんど (*three times*)   (b) こんど (*next time*)
   2. (a) ことし (*this year*)
     (b) さんねんせい (*third-year student*)
     (c) らいねん (*next year*)
     (d) きょねん (*last year*)
   3. (a) まえ (*previous*)
     (b) まえ (*front*)
     (c) なまえ (*name*)

D)

     1. 今学期   2. 外国語

2. Describing a Restaurant

あのレストランはとてもゆうめいです。スパゲッティーがとてもおいしいです。レストランの中はとてもきれいです。それに、しずかです。ウエーターはとてもしんせつです。でも、ねだんはちょっと高いです。

3. Naming the Dates in a Month

2 日：ふつか   24 日：にじゅうよっか
14 日：じゅうよっか   27 日：にじゅうしちにち
20 日：はつか   29 日：にじゅうくにち

4. Naming the Months in a Year

さんがつ：3 月   くがつ：9 月
しがつ：4 月   じゅういちがつ：11 月
しちがつ：7 月

5. Reading Dates

1. いちがつとおか
2. にがつよっか
3. しがつついたち
4. せんきゅうひゃくきゅうじゅうはちねんくがつみっか
5. にせんごねんじゅうにがつじゅうはちにち

Grammar

1. Polite Past Tense

1. 好きでした
2. はずかしかったです
3. かんたんなテストでした
4. しんせつじゃありませんでした
5. 高くありませんでした
6. よかったです

2. Indefinite/Negative Pronouns

1. 昨日は<u>どこかに</u> (or <u>どこかへ</u>) 行きましたか。
   – いいえ、<u>どこにも</u> (or <u>どこへも</u>)行きませんでした。
2. 昨日は<u>何か</u>しましたか。
   – いいえ、<u>何も</u>しませんでした。
3. 昨日は<u>だれかと</u>話しましたか。
   – いいえ、<u>だれとも</u>話しませんでした。
4. 昨日は<u>だれか</u>来ましたか。
   – いいえ、<u>だれも</u>来ませんでした。

3. Plain Past Affirmative Form of Verbs

1. きいた   5. とった   9. した
2. よんだ   6. はなした   10. きた
3. およいだ   7. あそんだ
4. あった   8. ねた

4. Expressing Experiences

1. おさけを飲んだことがありますか。
2. きものを着たことがありますか。
3. しんかんせんに乗ったことがありますか。
4. ディズニーランドに行ったことがありますか。

Conversation and Usage

1. Asking about Past Summer Vacation

1. Emiko   2. Ski
3. He went to Kagawa Prefecture in Shikoku.

<Translation>

Takeshi : Did you go anywhere in the summer vacation?
Yoko   : Yes, I went to New Zealand.
Takeshi : Did you go there by yourself?
Yoko   : No, I went there with Emiko, the two of us.
Takeshi : Oh, really. What did you do?
Yoko   : We skied.
Takeshi : What? You skied in summer?
Yoko   : It's summer in Japan, but it's winter in New Zealand!

Takeshi : Oh, you are right.

Yoko : Takeshi, did you go anywhere during the summer vacation?

Takeshi : No, I didn't go anywhere during this year's summer vacation. But during the last year's summer vacation, I went to Kagawa Prefecture in Shikoku. I met up with my friend.

Yoko : Oh, really. That place is famous for Sanuki noodles, right?

Takeshi : Yes. I ate a lot. It was really delicious.

Yoko : Oh, that was nice!

Takeshi : Have you ever been to Shikoku?

Yoko : No, I've never been there yet.

2. Situational Response

1. デパートでは何か買いましたか。
2. すしはおいしかったですか。
3. マイクさんのたんじょうびはいつですか。
4. サムさんはおさけを飲んだことがありますか。

Listening Comprehension

Dictation

1. 1989 年 4 月 1 日
2. 1993 年 7 月 25 日
3. 1994 年 10 月 29 日
4. 2006 年 9 月 3 日

CD recording:

Example: にせんごねんさんがつじゅうさんにち

1. せんきゅうひゃくはちじゅうきゅうねん しがつついたち

2. せんきゅうひゃくきゅうじゅうさんねんしちがつにじゅうごにち

3. せんきゅうひゃくきゅうじゅうよねんじゅうがつにじゅうくにち

4. にせんろくねんくがつみっか

Reading Comprehension

Reciting a Poem

シロツメクサのはな : *white clover flower*

すなはま : *sandy beach* 　　 しおり : *bookmark*

すな : *sand* 　　 ゆき : *snow*

おしろ : *castle* 　　 ゆきだるま : *snowman*

かれは : *fallen leaves*

<Translation>

Spring, Summer, Autumn, and Winter

Haruko likes "haru", spring.

In spring, she makes a necklace with white clover flowers.

Natsuko likes "natsu", summer.

In summer, she makes a sand castle in a sandy beach.

Akiko likes "aki", autumn.

In autumn, she makes bookmarks with fallen leaves.

Fuyuko likes "fuyu", winter.

In winter, she makes a snowman using snow.

I like all of them, spring, summer, autumn, and fall, very much.

Chapter Thirteen

Kanji and Vocabulary

1. Reading and Writing Kanji Characters

C) 1. (a) げんごがくをべんきょうします。
　　　 I study linguistics.
　　 (b) なまえをいってください。
　　　 Please say your name.

2. (a) てをあらいます。 *I wash my hands.*
　 (b) せんたくをします。 *I do (my) laundry.*
　 (c) せんせいとがくせい
　　　 teachers and students

3. (a) クラスはたのしいです。 *The class is fun.*
　 (b) このしごとはらくです。 *This job is easy.*
　 (c) くすりをのみます。 *I take medicine.*

D) 1. 漢字は難しいです。 　 3. 30 点をとりました。
　 2. 車に乗ります。 　 4. 買いものをします。

2. Naming Academic Subjects

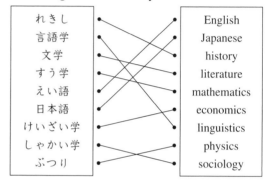

れきし	English
言語学	Japanese
文学	history
すう学	literature
えい語	mathematics
日本語	economics
けいざい学	linguistics
しゃかい学	physics
ぶつり	sociology

3. Listing Daily Routines

1. かおを洗う 　　　 4. そうじをする
2. はをみがく 　　　 5. せんたくをする
3. シャワーをあびる 　 6. かいものをする

Grammar

1. Consequences and Results

1. きゅうりょうが安かったです。それで、会社をやめました。
2. 昨日はしごとが三つありました。それで、とてもいそがしかったです (or つかれました)。
3. つかれました。それで、早くねました。
4. あたまがいたかったです。それで、薬をのみました。
5. ねぼうしました。それで、クラスにおくれました。

2. Listing Actions and Properties

1. よく勉強して、100 点をとりました。
2. ぼくの車は新しくて、大きいです。
3. 5 時間歩いて、つかれました。
4. 安くて、よかったです。
5. そうじをして、昼ごはんを食べて、テニスをします。

3. Expressing the Purpose of Coming and Going

1. マイクさんのうちにあそびに行きました。
2. 日本に日本語を勉強しに来ました。
3. うちにさいふをとりに帰りました。
4. ほっかいどうにゆきまつりを見に行きました。

Conversation and Usage

1. Talking about a New Job

1. True   2. False   3. False

<Translation>

Takako : How is your new job?

Toshihiko : My boss is kind, the job is easy, and it's fun.

Takako : Oh, really. That's great!

Toshihiko : Yes. But it takes time from home to the company.

Takako : (By) car?

Toshihiko : No. I take a bus for 30 minutes, and then take a train for one hour. Then, I walk for 30 minutes to the company.

Takako : Oh, you walk for 30 minutes?

Toshihiko : Yes. It's a lot (of walking).

Takako : But walking is good for health. Good luck and hang on.

2. Offering Help

1. To go for a drink after work.   2. Yes

<Translation>

Toshihiko : Why don't we go for a drink today?

Takeshi : Oh, but …

Toshihiko : What's the matter?

Takeshi : Today, I have a lot of work. I probably have to work overtime.

Toshihiko : Today is Friday.

Takeshi : Yes, but …

Toshihiko : Then, shall I help you?

Takeshi : Is it all right?

Toshihiko : Yes, sort of.

Takeshi : Oh, that's helpful. Then, please do this one, this one, and this one.

3. Situational Response

1. 田中さんのうちに何をしに行くんですか。

2. はをみがいて、かおを洗いました。

3. りんごはけんこうにいいですよ。

Listening Comprehension

How Toshihiko Spent His Sunday

1. Park   2. 2,000 yen   3. Spaghetti

CD recording:

昨日はひまでした。うちで昼までねました。それから、公園に行きました。公園のベンチに座って、村上春樹の小説を読みました。夕方パチンコをしに行きました。10分で 2,000 円使って、うちに帰りました。スパゲッティーを食べて、テレビを見て、ねました。

Reading Comprehension

Osechi Dishes

1. Black soybean and kelp   2. Herring roe

3. Red-white steamed fish paste

<Translation>

Japanese people eat (traditional Japanese dishes called) Osechi dishes during the New Year period. People wish for good health and descendant's prosperity by the color, shape, and pun used in Osechi dishes. The following are some of the examples of Osechi dishes:

- Black soybean: To wish for working "mameni", or diligently. "Mame" (bean) and "mameni" (diligently) are pun.
- Herring roe: To wish for descendent's prosperity. Herring roe exist as a lump of numerous eggs.
- Kelp: "Kombu" (kelp) and "yorokobu" (to be delighted) are pun.
- Shrimp: To wish for longevity. Shrimp has curved back (like aged people's back).
- Red-white steamed fish paste: (The combination of) red and white is a happy color (combination).

Chapter Fourteen

Kanji and Vocabulary

1. Reading and Writing Kanji Characters

C) いしだせんせいは<u>しょうがっこう</u>のせんせいです。はやしせんせいは<u>ちゅうがっこう</u>のせんせいです。やまだせんせいは<u>こうこう</u>の<u>かがく</u>のせんせいです。かわぐちせんせいは<u>だいがく</u>のせんせいです。たなかせんせいは<u>えいご</u>がっこうのせんせいです。わたしは<u>だいがく</u>せいです。<u>ぶんがく</u>と<u>しゃかいがく</u>を<u>べんきょう</u>しています。

D) 1. <u>子供</u>が<u>遊</u>んでいます。
2. 日本に<u>住</u>みたいです。
3. きものを<u>着</u>ました。
4. お<u>茶</u>を<u>飲</u>みます。

E) 1. <u>使</u>う 2. <u>作</u>る 3. <u>休</u>む 4. <u>住</u>む 5. <u>働</u>く

2. What's Your Occupation?

1. いしゃ 2. かんごし 3. きょうし 4. べんごし

3. Expressing Emotions

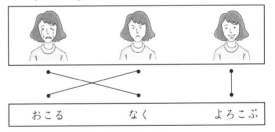

4. Identifying the Types of Clothing and Accessories

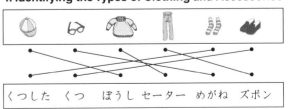

5. The Verbs "to Wear"

1. イヤリングを<u>する</u>   4. Ｔシャツを<u>きる</u>
2. めがねを<u>かける</u>   5. ぼうしを<u>かぶる</u>
3. スカートを<u>はく</u>

Grammar

1. ～ている

1. progressive   3. habitual   5. resulting
2. resulting   4. habitual

2. Progressive State

1. でんわで話しています。   3. ねています。
2. コーラを飲んでいます。   4. 本を読んでいます。

3. Habitual State

うちは父と、母と、兄と、弟と、私の5人家族です。父は病院で医者を<u>して</u>います。母は高校で英語を<u>教え</u>ています。兄はコンピューターの会社で<u>働いて</u>います。弟は小学校に<u>行って</u>います。今、5年生です。私は今、大学生です。社会学を<u>勉強して</u>います。

4. Expressing Experiences

1. ねてばかりいます。
2. しゃべってばかりいます。
3. なまけてばかりいます。
4. 遊んでばかりいます。
5. パチンコをしてばかりいます。

5. Resulting State

1. ぎんこうは<u>あいて</u>います。 *The bank is open.*
2. クラスは<u>はじまって</u>います。 *The class has begun.*
3. このバスは<u>こんで</u>います。 *This bus is crowded.*
4. 兄は<u>けっこんして</u>います。 *My older brother is married.*
5. 父は<u>とうきょうに行って</u>います。 *My father has gone to Tokyo.*

6. Particles

1. たけしさんの本<u>を</u>かりました。
2. ブラウンさんは日本<u>に</u>住んでいます。
3. 母は今うち<u>に</u>います。
4. 母は今うち<u>で</u>晩ごはんを作っています。
5. 父は今とうきょう<u>に</u>行っています。
6. びょういん<u>で</u>働いています。

7. Relative Clauses

1. 石田さんのむすこさんは<u>あのめがねをかけている人</u>です。
2. 私の兄はあそこで<u>たばこをすっている人</u>です。
3. ようこさんは<u>よくしゃべる人</u>ですよ。
4. あそこに<u>立っている女の人</u>は私のともだちです。
5. <u>昨日食べたすし</u>はとてもおいしかったです。

Conversation and Usage

1. Visiting a Colleague at Her Apartment

1. False   2. False   3. False

<Translation>

Kazuko : Please. Come in.
Tomiko : Thanks.
Kazuko : Sorry for the mess. I'm not good at cleaning.
Tomiko : Me, too. I clean on Sundays, but it gets messy again on Mondays.
Kazuko : What? Really? That's a lie, right? Tomiko, you are a neat person, right?
Tomiko : No kidding.
Kazuko : But your desk and drawers at the office, aren't they neat?
Tomiko : Right, at the office, I do nothing but clean.
Kazuko : How about your work?
Tomiko : Not (really) doing.
Kazuko : I thought so.
Tomiko : Don't tell the division head, okay?
Kazuko : I won't. Because I am also not (really) doing my work.
Tomiko : What? Really?
Kazuko : Yes. Yesterday, I was playing a game on my office computer for half a day.
Tomiko : Wow! I will tell the division head about it.
Kazuko : No!
Tomiko : I'm kidding, I'm kidding.

2. Situational Response

1. 石田さんのお父さんとお母さんはどちらに住んでいらっしゃいますか。
2. 林さんのお父さんは何をしていらっしゃいますか。
3. 父は今、大阪に行っています。

Listening Comprehension

Identifying a Group of Office Workers

1. A   2. D   3. B   4. F   5. E   6. G

CD recording:

部長は一人でお茶を飲んでいます。川口さんは女の人と話しています。山田さんは電話で話しています。林さんはEメールを読んでいます。石田さんはねています。田中さんは何か書いています。

Reading Comprehension

Checking the Q&A Section of a Magazine

1. False   2. False   3. False

<Translation>

[653] I do nothing but sleep, and I am feeling guilty

Q: I am 42 years old, and a housewife. Earlier, I liked cooking, laundry, cleaning, etc. But since five months ago, I don't feel like doing anything. I just sleep. I have two sons, eight-year-old and five-year-old. My husband is a company employee, and he leaves home at 6 a.m. in the morning. So, my eight-year-old son fixes breakfast for his little brother. Our rooms are always messy. I went to see an internist, but they didn't find anything wrong with me. I am a mother, but I don't do cooking, laundry, and cleaning, but keep sleeping. I feel guilty. What can I do?

A: I think you are suffering from a depression. Please go to see a psychiatrist. Please treat yourself with medication. You will surely get better. Don't be impatient, and don't feel guilty.